THROUGH THE EYES OF PARENTS, CHILDREN AND A COACH

A Fourteen-Year Participant-Observer Investigation of Youth Soccer

---

Steven Aicinena

University Press of America,® Inc.
Lanham · New York · Oxford

Copyright © 2002 by
University Press of America,® Inc.
4501 Forbes Boulevard
Suite 200
Lanham, Maryland 20706
UPA Acquisitions Department (301) 459-3366

PO Box 317
Oxford
OX2 9RU, UK

British Library Cataloging in Publication Information Available

Library of Congress Cataloging-in-Publication Data

Aicinena, Steven.
Through the eyes of parents, children, and a coach :
a fourteen-year participant-observer investigation of
youth soccer / Steven Aicinena.
p.   cm
Included bibliographical references (p. [241]-246).
1. Soccer for children—Social aspects—Longitudinal studies. I. Title.

GV944.2 .A45 2002
796.334'083—dc21   2002035825 CIP

ISBN 0-7618-2436-7 (paperback : alk. ppr.)

⊖™ The paper used in this publication meets the minimum
requirements of American National Standard for Information
Sciences—Permanence of Paper for Printed Library Materials,
ANSI Z39.48—1984

*This book is dedicated to the children and parents
that I have had the opportunity to work with
in the youth sport setting.*

*It is dedicated to the individuals who choose to
coach sport teams. Most do not understand
what the task requires.*

*It is dedicated to my wife, who has stood behind
me and sacrificed much to enable me to find
professional success and personal
satisfaction.
You are a treasure to me.*

*It is dedicated to my children,
Sandy and Eric.
You have provided me with inspiration
and fulfillment.*

CONTENTS

ACKNOWLEDGMENTS

To the dozens of children and the parents with whom I have had the opportunity to work in the soccer setting, I give my thanks. Specifically, I wish to thank those who were a part of the accounts and descriptions presented within this book. Their names have been replaced in order to protect their anonymity.

INTRODUCTION

As a child, I loved playing sport. It did not matter if it was a pick-up game of football or a little league baseball game. I enjoyed competition and the opportunity to test and compare myself against others. Coaches were absent in the pick-up games and were, to be honest, irrelevant to me in the organized sport setting. Being a bit of a rebel, I often disregarded the instructions of coaches (who wanted to win) in favor of engaging in behaviors that were more exciting and that were, at least to me, a better test. As a participant, I viewed sport as play. There were many athletes who were unlike me. They looked at sport differently. Sport was serious for them, and I understood this at an early age.

It is often stated that I am "different" than most coaches. Such are and have been the words of parents, administrators and athletes. The teams I coached have enjoyed success in spite of (or perhaps because of) my eccentricities. I am currently coaching college volleyball. As in the youth sport setting, I coach because I love it. Sport is still play for me. For others coaching high school, college and even youth sport teams, coaching can be very serious business. I am sure they experience fulfillment, but often it appears that they are not having fun.

Parents also differ in how they view the sport environment. Some really do not seem to care at all if their children are successful. Others drive their children toward some idealized vision of success. Most parents fall somewhere between these extremes.

Conflict in the Sport Setting Arises from Differences in What We Believe

Why do various coaches, parents and athletes look at sport differently? Individuals have different attitudes, opinions and expectations that result from different socialization experiences and how they respond to them.

What we believe guides our responses to incidents that take place in the sport setting. It even affects what we believe the outcomes of sport should be. Conflict arises between individuals as they function within the athletic environment because of the differences that exist between us. The way we view the conflict and how we respond to it has a profound impact upon us in terms of how we behave and interact with others.

This book is intended to provide a framework to assess the source of conflicts that commonly occur in the athletic arena. Simply put, your chosen model of participation will increase or decrease the likelihood of conflict with others in the sport setting. An awareness and understanding of competing sport participation models will assist you in understanding and having tolerance toward others. If you are understanding and tolerant, the sport experience for you and those around you will be enhanced.

The Stories in this Book Will Be Yours

The incidents described within this book are not unusual. In fact, individuals with children in organized sport settings will likely relate to most of them. Those who have coached will have a similar familiarity and understanding of what is presented. If you are simply curious about youth sport, this book may interest you. It will better help you understand the youth sport experience.

What Makes this Book Beneficial?

Though you may have been involved in sport as a participant, as a coach or as a parent, it is unlikely that you were able to gather the impressions, feelings and views of dozens of parents, coaches and athletes. If you have not been a coach or if you have not yet involved your child in sport, you cannot really be aware of the interactions and conflicts that take place between individuals in the sport setting, nor understand the feelings of those involved. Because the study that served as the basis of this book lasted for a period of fourteen years, and because I was involved as a researcher, parent and coach, this book is unique. You will get "inside the heads" of parents, coaches and athletes. You will read about and come to understand the youth sport experience from the point of view of several dozen individuals (parents, athletes and coaches).

This Book Is for Coaches

This book will help aspiring coaches as they contemplate what it would be like to work with others in the sport setting. My desire is that it spurs readers into thinking about how they would handle the problems and issues brought forth within these pages because there is little chance any coach will escape them.

The incidents presented within this book may serve as an introduction to the internal and external conflicts that you will experience as you begin your coaching career. Though the book focuses primarily upon youth soccer, the conflicts and interactions described also take place between parents, players and coaches in a variety of sports and in the college and high school settings as well.

A coach can only do what he or she perceives is the right thing. Your behavior as a coach will be periodically subject to criticism. I hope this book will encourage you to act in a manner that is reflective, thoughtful and purposeful, while realizing that you cannot please everyone.

I have coached for over twenty-eight years. At the end of most chapters, I pose questions and make recommendations for coaches. What I say may be controversial, but it is what I believe. If you disagree, that's fine as long as I assisted you in reflecting upon what the appropriate actions should be. I believe that the human side of athletics has become discounted to a high degree, and my statements often reflect this belief. Athletes are not machines.

This Book Is for Parents

This book was also written for parents who are involved or who are considering involvement with youth sport. I hope that the comments provided in this book assist you in dealing with the conflicts that you may experience. It may also assist you in making sound decisions concerning your child's participation in sport.

A portion of this book also examines high school sport and the transition from competitive youth sport to playing in the high school arena. There are interesting issues for you to consider if you visualize your child someday playing at the high school or college level.

Sociology of Sport

I am not a trained sport sociologist; I was introduced to this sub-discipline of kinesiology/physical education while I worked on my doctorate. The area was one that immediately interested me. I am somewhat familiar with the literature in the area, since I enjoy reading the research and because I teach a sociology of sport course at the graduate and undergraduate level. I include several references, therefore, in order to assist the reader in finding additional research completed in the area of youth sport.

For those who are scholars in the area of sport sociology, I hope this book brings to mind questions that will motivate additional research in the area of youth sport. The qualitative accounts of the experiences of parents, coaches and athletes should be of interest and of value to those interested in the study of youth sport.

The Incidents Described in this Book Are Typical of Those Occurring in the Youth Sport Setting

I want to plainly point out here that what is presented within the covers of this book is happening throughout the country. If something appears unwholesome or unseemly, it is not because it takes place only where the study was conducted. I have served on several boards of directors for youth sport programs and have spoken with many coaches throughout the country. I learned through talking with opposing coaches from other cities and by serving on board hearings concerning complaints, that the issues I present in this book are not uncommon in youth sport.

Chapter Observations: Questions and Comments for Parents and Coaches

I asked several individuals to review the contents of this book before its publication. Many of them were parents and athletes associated with the teams I coached. One reviewer observed that I wore different hats as I completed this project. I was a storyteller, a researcher, a father, a coach and an educator. He believed that the educator was not clearly present in earlier drafts. In chapters 2 through 12, a brief introduction appears at the beginning of the chapter. It is followed by the information collected during the period of the study. To respond to the lack of the educator's presence, I have presented comments for parents and coaches at the end of these chapters. The sections are entitled "Chapter Observations."

The Chapter Observations are based upon the material presented within the chapters and include observations I have made during my coaching activity in other sports and as I coached in high school and college. The comments in Chapter Observations are the things that I would say to parents and coaches if I met them individually. They are my thoughts and should be understood as such.

Why Bother Writing this Book?

Everything presented within this book happened to real people: parents, athletes and coaches. It is an account of our experiences in the youth sport setting. We were the subjects of the research that the book is based upon.

The conflicts and tensions we experienced are being experienced today by a different group of parents, athletes and coaches. How can parents and coaches understand what youth sport is like before getting into it? How can new generations of parents and coaches avoid making the same mistakes as those who have gone before them? It can only be done if those who have gone before share their insights. Such is the purpose of this book.

1

INTRODUCTION, METHOD AND SETTING

In America, organized youth sport enjoys great popularity. A significant percentage of the free time of American children is spent in youth sport activities (Scanlan, 1996). Between 20 and 35 million American youths currently participate in some form of organized youth sport (Ewing and Seefeldt, 1996).[1] Youth sport can be an important part of American family life and often involves a significant investment of time and money for parents. Further, sport serves as an important means of socialization in the community and larger society (Berlage, 1982; Coakley, 1994; Edwards, 1973; Foley, 1990; Gray, 1992; Stevenson & Nixon, 1972). Because of the perceived value of the youth sport experience, millions of parents become involved as coaches and eagerly engage their children in these activities (Eitzen and Sage, 1997; Fact Sheet, 1993).

Sport has truly become an important part of life for millions of American families. Within the social milieu that is youth sport, there are differing views as to the importance of sport, the purpose of sport, desired participant behaviors and expected coaching behaviors.

When individuals participate in youth sport as coaches, athletes and parents, conflicts are likely to occur because of the difference in what the participants view as appropriate goals and behaviors. What conflicts take place within social groups formed around youth sport teams? How do the conflicts change as players mature? What causes the conflict?

Two Models of Sport

Individuals are socialized to believe what sport is and what it should be. People have different sport experiences and consequently they have different goals and expectations for behavior as they come together in the sport context.

It would be a mistake for individuals to believe that all sports are organized around the same set of goals or that the same set of goals or that the same set of behaviors should be expected of all people in all sport settings (Coakley, 2001). According to Coakley, in modern America, the Power and Performance Model of sport is dominant. Within the universe of sports forms, an alternative model, the Pleasure and Participation Model, also exists.

The Power and Performance Model

According to Coakley (2001), the Power and Performance Model of sport contains several distinguishing characteristics. Its major components are presented below. I have altered the characteristics of Coakley's Power and Performance Model with the addition of the italicized material.

- Strength, speed and power are emphasized

- Excellence is demonstrated through success
  o Success is indicated by winning
  o Winning is valued more highly if hard work, dedication, sacrifice, risk and pain are evidenced

- The body is viewed as a machine.
  o *Training and performance should be technologically enhanced and scientific.*
  o *Participants should not be concerned with injury*

- A clear hierarchy of authority structures exists
  o Players should be subordinate to coaches
  o Coaches are in control
  o *It should be clear to observers that coaches are in control*

- Opponents are viewed as enemies

- *Only the best on a team should play.*
  - *If you are unskilled, you will cost the team a game and this is unacceptable.*

The Power and Performance Model of sport is best reflected in professional and major college athletics. Average sports fans (and I venture to state most participants) are inundated with visual and auditory messages through the media teaching them that this form of sport is appropriate and is, indeed, the only form of sport that is legitimate.

Winners are worshiped, at least until they fail to repeat as champions. Losers are ridiculed and viewed with contempt. Losers are those who do not win "the big one." There should be no mistake concerning what the Power and Performance Model of sport is all about: winning and domination.

The joy of participation is not truly a concern to coaches, parents and players who are disciples of the Power and Performance Model. Joy cannot be a concern because winning is the overriding goal. Coaches and athletes should be committed to performance and victory. One must work, pay the price and obtain victory. The quest for victory should be the most important thing in the life of the participant. The unskilled and weak have no place in this version of sport. They interfere with the pursuit of excellence.

Sport is not a source of enjoyment and satisfaction unless victory can be achieved. Someone who feels joy and fulfillment after a loss is considered inadequately committed to victory. Even if victory is obtained, one should not take time to enjoy it. It is immediately time to think about and prepare for a repeat performance. Consider coaches during televised interviews following world championships who immediately address the goal to repeat as champions in the coming year.

The influence of and the adherence to the Power and Performance Model is clearly evidenced in professional and major college sport, but it can also be detected in minor-college, high school, junior high and youth sport settings. A win-at-all-cost philosophy is exhibited by parents, coaches and athletes at all levels of sport: from Little-League, to Podunk high and Wattsa-Matta U.

The Power and Performance Model of sport is associated with and reflective of professionalized sport. The model of sport reflecting these characteristics may be termed the **professionalized model** (Dubois, 1980).

The primary goal of youth sport within the parameters of the professionalized model of sport is the *product*: performance measured in terms of winning. Throughout this book the term professionalized model is used, often interchangeably with the term Power and Performance Model. They are siblings and amount to the same: sport is about winning. Fun is not a goal.

A resident of Overland that emigrated from Guatemala summed up the professionalized model as it exists in youth sport by claiming:

> I think that American society is geared toward winning and it's not just winning, it is winning at all costs. I think Americans believe they have to win, and it doesn't matter how. The development of the kids and the fun they have is not really what is important. The parents have the goal of their children getting scholarships. That destroys the other benefits of playing soccer.

The reader is cautioned not to confuse the term *professionalized model* with the term *professional coach*. A professional coach is simply an individual who is paid for coaching. Some professional coaches may not have a professionalized attitude toward sport participation, though others do. Not all professional coaches are adherents of the Power and Performance Model of sport. I am not.

The Pleasure and Participation Model

The Pleasure and Participation Model of sport dictates that sport should be something that provides participants with a sense of satisfaction and joy, which comes about as a consequence of their participation. There is nothing in the characteristics of this model that indicates a lack of seriousness concerning participation. The parameters within which an individual participates, however, do differ significantly from those associated with the Power and Performance Model of sport. Coakley's (2001) characteristics of the Pleasure and Participation Model, along with my modifications, are presented below:

- Active participation
  - *Participation is the reason for involvement in sport*
  - There is a mind/body/spirit connection

- The participant and the opponent are important
  - ○ The opponent is seen as valued and needed
  - ○ *An opponent is viewed as someone whom participants compete with in order for a test to take place*

- *The participant's control of his or her body and objects in the environment provide satisfaction*
  - ○ *Skilled movement and performance yield satisfaction*
  - ○ *Demonstrating skill and cunning provides satisfaction*
  - ○ *Domination and victory are not requisites of satisfaction*

- Inclusion of all is possible
  - ○ *Weak and unskilled are welcomed and/or tolerated*
  - ○ *Accommodations are acceptable in terms of rules modifications*

- Decisions are shared
  - ○ Cooperation is desired and expected
  - ○ Power is shared
  - ○ There is give and take between coaches and athletes

Winning is not something to be gained at all costs in the Pleasure and Participation Model. The experience of the participants and the opponents are both considered important. In fact, satisfaction can be achieved, even if winning does not occur. The form of sport that reflects the characteristics of the Pleasure and Participation Model is also referred to as the **developmental model** of sport (Dubois, 1980). In the developmental model, the *process* of sport participation is most highly valued.

In my opinion, the Pleasure and Participation Model is best exhibited in informal sport played between friends on playgrounds (Coakley, 2001; Devereux, 1987). Children learn to compete, and they make their own decisions during the process of competition. Rules are negotiated, handicaps are given, and children make their own decisions. **Children can take their participation in these activities quite seriously**, but when the activity is over, it is over.

Organized sport as it is found in youth baseball, youth soccer and other activities does not share all of the characteristics of informal sport. It is a form of sport that is more structured and institutionalized. Formal lessons are learned, and control of the activity is placed in the hands of coaches.

Individuals participating in organized youth sport (parents, coaches and athletes) may have different orientations to sport. They may be partial to the Power and Performance Model, the Pleasure and Participation Model, or lie somewhere in between believing that specific aspects of each Model are appropriate. Some parents, for example, believe that coaches should make all the decisions. Other parents may believe that athletes should have some input, while others may believe that ultimately the athletes should make decisions themselves.

Table 1-1: Selected Characteristics of the Pleasure and Participation and Power and Performance Models of Sport

Model	Emphasis	Excellence	Body	Decisions	Opponents
Pleasure and Participation	Active Participation	Perform to Capabilities	Source of enjoyment	Shared	Needed
Power and Performance	Strength, Speed and Power	Winning	Machine	Coach-Made	Enemies

What Model Best Reflects Your Outlook Toward Sports Participation?

After looking at the characteristics of the Power and Performance and Pleasure and Participation Models of sport, you may feel that some of the characteristics of each are appropriate in the sport setting. On the other hand, various characteristics of each model may seem ridiculous. I believe most individuals can see the value of specific characteristics found within each model, although few individuals would view *all* of the characteristics of either model to be desirable as a guide to behaviors and attitudes in sport. Coakley (2001) stated:

> These two models do not encompass all the ways that sports might be defined or played. In fact, some people play sports that contain elements of both forms and reflect many ideas about what is important in physical activities. p.95

There are times when individuals cannot decide what behaviors and attitudes are appropriate. People sometimes struggle within themselves over

what is appropriate and desirable. Attitudes and behaviors may be inconsistent as a result. For example, if a coach believes that winning is the most
important thing, but she also believes that all children should play, the
coach *will* feel conflicted when placing a poorly skilled player in the game
during a critical moment in the contest. To do so may cost the team the
game! There is a conflict of values at work in such a situation.

There are other times when individuals come into contact with those
who hold an orientation toward sport that is contrary to their own. Conflict
may take place between individuals in such a case. For example, if a parent
believes that all children should play and a coach believes that only the best
should play, there *will* be conflict.

It should also be noted that the desired sporting goals and behaviors
held by an individual might change over time. Change may come about as
a result of experience, education or contemplation.

Children tend to adopt more of the characteristics of the Power and
Performance Model as they mature (Maloney & Petrie, 1972; Petlichkoff,
1992; Shields, Bredemeyer, Gardner & Bostrom, 1995; Webb, 1969). An
adoption of the characteristics of the Power and Performance Model also
has been associated with involvement in organized youth sport (Kleiber &
Roberts, 1981; Maloney & Petrie, 1972). Brower (1979) hypothesized that
this phenomenon is due to the emphasis upon winning in the organized
youth sport setting; however, it is possible that the nature of sport
encourages an emphasis upon winning and dominance (Lipsyte, 1979).

In Appendix I, I have presented a questionnaire that you may use to
assess your beliefs about what behaviors and attitudes are desirable in
youth and amateur athletics. If you complete and score the questionnaire
before continuing with your reading, you will have a good idea as to which
participation model your attitudes and behaviors most closely reflect *at this
time*.

I believe that if you complete the questionnaire before and again after
reading this book that you will find your score has changed. This book will
cause you to think about what youth sport should be like. It will show you
alternative ways of thinking about and responding to situations common in
the youth sport setting. Your attitudes and beliefs may change as a result.

This book was written in order to qualitatively describe and explain the
conflict that parents, children and I experienced while I served not only as
a volunteer head youth soccer coach, but as the parent of a young athlete
over a fourteen-year period.

Method

Gould (1996) stated that qualitative research in the area of youth sport could offer scholars great insight into the youth sport experience and further, that longitudinal studies (lasting a period of years) would be a valuable addition to youth sport literature.

Few studies have been published that offer a description of the experiences of youth sport coaches, participants and their parents in a qualitative manner over an extended period of years. I have, in fact, found none. Long-term studies in youth sport are rare. This book is an effort to partially address the dearth of long-term studies in this area.

In regard to research on coaches, Seefeldt and Gould (1980) stated that, "...we know virtually nothing about the effects of the coaching experiences on the coaches themselves" (p. 124). This book will present information concerning the effect of coaching upon coaches themselves, though the number of coaches included in the study was limited.

This study commenced as some of the children began their participation in organized youth soccer at age four and continued until the athletes reached age seventeen, spanning a period of fourteen years. There is no other published qualitative or quantitative youth sport study that has encompassed such a long period of time.

I served as the head coach of the teams around which the events presented in this book took place (the Strikers and the Force United) and collected data (the recording of comments and observations) as the seasons progressed. This method of study is referred to as participant-observation research. Participant-observation research is prone to the influence of subjectivity (Jorgensen, 1989). This means that what I present within the book is affected by my personal thoughts, feelings and biases. This fact should be kept in mind as you read what is presented.

The guidelines for participant-observation research as described by Friedrichs & Ludtke (1975) and Lofland (1971) were followed as the information used to form the basis of this book was collected. Notes concerning observations, feelings and conversations were taken during the twelve years that I served as the coach of the Strikers and the Force United and for a two-year period after I stopped coaching. Forty-one children played soccer under my supervision during the time I collected data for this book. Over ninety-five individuals are mentioned directly or indirectly and over sixty-five are quoted within.

The names of all cities and individuals mentioned in this book have been changed in an effort to maintain the anonymity of the subjects. Formal interviews with children and adults were only made after explaining to the subjects and their parents (all of the athletes were under age 18) that the information would appear in this book and after verbal permission was given for me to proceed with the interview.

I was able to form life-long friendships with the individuals described and quoted in this book because of the length of my association with them. The duration and intensity of my contact with the individuals associated with the teams resulted in the development of an environment of trust. Consequently, open communication was achieved between the parents, children and me.

Before publication, I shared the contents of this book with several of the individuals whose actions and statements are contained within these pages. I made many revisions in the content in response to the comments and feedback they provided me. However, the reader is cautioned that this book was written by someone who was directly involved in the events that are presented within it. There is no way that the reality as experienced by all has been presented here. It is but a glimpse of reality.

The Setting

The majority of the observations and interviews contained within this book were made in a city supporting a population approaching 92,000. The city is located in the Southwestern United States. The city, I have changed the name to "Overland," is in a region that supports a population of nearly 250,000. Overland is 350 miles from a major city in the southwest, which I will refer to as "Phoenix" in the text. Phoenix, Arizona supports a similar population.

Overland has been known nationally as a high school football town. Traditionally, and at the time of this study, the sport of football has been king based upon media coverage and attendance at high school sporting events. When the high school football teams play an important game, as many as 20,000 fans attend. Overland is considered a "blue collar" town because much of the population works in service-related industries. It has been said that the sport of football has captured the imagination of the city because it reflects the values of hard work, continual striving and total dedication to the cause of winning.

Pen High School, one of the two high schools in the city, has a storied football history. Since 1964, it has participated in eleven state championship games, won six state high school football championships, and was named national champion once. The team is said to have accomplished its success in spite of having under-sized players. The athletes were infused with the attitude that they would never be defeated. They refused to lose.

The coaches in the program have traditionally been tough and demanding individuals who reflected and insisted that the athletes adopt the characteristics of the Power and Performance Model. The children who I coached in this study had fathers who went through this system and who were staunch supporters of the professionalized model of sport.

The local television stations and newspapers dedicate a significant amount of time and space to coverage of high school sporting events. As an outsider, I was shocked at how important high school sport was.

"Midcity" is located twelve miles from Overland. It supports a population approaching 98,000. Football and success are highly valued in Midcity as well, even though the town is considered to be a "white collar" community. Within the past four years, one of the two Midcity public high schools has won three state football championships and one state basketball championship. The other public high school has won a state basketball and baseball championship. The private high schools in Midcity and Overland have celebrated multiple state championships in softball, volleyball and football as well. This year, Midcity will complete a $35 million sports complex that includes an 18,000- seat football stadium to be used by the high schools and a 6,000-seat baseball stadium that will be used by a professional minor league and the high school baseball teams.

In Overland, there are many opportunities for youths to participate in organized athletic competition. The Boys and Girls Club, YMCA, Little League Baseball, Girls Softball Association and the local Soccer Association offered the team sports of soccer, basketball, football, baseball, softball and volleyball. Ice hockey and figure skating were available at the local ice rink. The individual sports of bowling, golf, martial arts, tennis, gymnastics, swimming, track and field, rodeo and many others are available as well.

Coverage is given to youth sport events in the local newspapers and on television stations. The interest in successful and talented athletes seems to know no age limitation. The community loves winners.

Recreational and Competitive Soccer Teams: The Difference in Nature and Cost

The teams forming the social milieu in which this investigation was conducted were affiliated with the Overland Soccer Association (OSA). The OSA fell under the jurisdiction of U.S. Youth Soccer. One thousand six hundred and ninety children played soccer with the local association in the 1999-2000 soccer year.[2]

Ewing and Seefeldt (1996) noted that many factors might preclude children from participating in youth sport programs. These factors may include direct costs, indirect costs, practices and games at an inconvenient time, and/or the diverse interests of youths. In the community, all these factors may have contributed to an individual's ability or willingness to play soccer on a recreational or competitive team. Regardless of factors that may have inhibited soccer's popularity at the youth level, the sport did enjoy a reasonable degree of popularity within the community.

Recreational Soccer Teams

After registration, recreational soccer teams were formed by board members based upon the elementary school attended and/or the section of town the children lived in. A second factor in the formation of teams was the age of the children. In the early years of this study, teams often contained children that may have differed in age by one year. In the middle third of the study, it was rare that children of different ages participated on the same team. Recruiting players from one area of the city to play on a team not within the specified school area was prohibited in recreational soccer.

All children were required to play at least one-half of each match. This requirement was reflective of the developmental orientation of the recreational soccer program. Other modifications in playing rules described later in this book were made in order to achieve the same goals: development and fun. Children could not be expected to enjoy themselves if they did not have an opportunity to play and make contact with the ball. It was often said by those involved in youth soccer that the purpose of the recreational soccer program was to assist in the development of the participants as soccer players (skill) and as people (psycho-social development).

The team referred to in this study as the Strikers was a recreational team and a member of the local soccer association. Recreational soccer was open to children between the ages of four and fourteen. Some parents within the community wanted their children to begin playing soccer *before* the age of four. Betty Burrows, the first president of the association, stated that she "received several calls from parents each year to see if their three year olds could sign up." It seemed that for some it was never too early to begin a child's organized sports experience!

The Strikers' roster included males and females during the first four years of the team's existence but consisted of all males over the final two. The roster was also age-pure for the final two years of the team's existence.

The composition of the roster in terms of age and gender reflected a growth in the popularity of soccer in the community among male and female participants. Age-pure and single-gender teams and leagues were created as a result of an increase in participation in soccer.

The cost associated with recreational soccer was minimal to some families in the community but may have been prohibitive to others. The registration fee in 1989 was $25 for the fall season and $25 for the spring season. The cost included a uniform that would be returned at the end of each season. Shin guards, cleats, and a ball were recommended and these items were available as a package for $40 or less from soccer specialty stores and major department stores. If the team did not travel to tournaments, the total financial investment required to participate in recreational soccer for one year (two seasons) was less than $100.

During the 2001-2002 soccer year, the registration fee for recreational soccer had risen to $40 per season. T-shirt uniforms were provided for children in the under-six age groups and below. In the under-eight age group and above, parents were responsible for purchasing their child's uniform, equipment and supplies. The average cost for participation had risen to approximately $140 per year.

Competitive Soccer Teams

Competitive soccer teams (sometimes referred to as select or club teams) could not be formed until the athletes reached the age of ten according to association guidelines. Competitive soccer was available for children in the community through the soccer association until they reached the age of eighteen.

Playing time was not guaranteed for children participating on competitive teams. The fact that players were not assured playing time was an indication that the governing associations (U.S. Soccer, the state association and the local association) desired to see a greater emphasis on the product (performance) and that they placed a lesser value upon the process (participation) as children matured. This does not seem unreasonable considering that national team players must be developed in the competitive soccer setting. Competitive soccer is the means through which elite players are identified and developed before selection to age-group national teams.

At the ages of ten through thirteen, competitive teams in the community were predominantly age-pure. As attrition occurred with age, teams were often composed of children of various ages in order to make competitive opportunities available for the players.

At age ten, children had the option of continuing to play recreational soccer or joining a competitive team.[3] Children and their parents may have chosen to continue with recreational soccer because competitive soccer required a greater commitment of money and time, or perhaps due to friendships and loyalties to coaches and friends who did not wish to coach or play on a competitive team.

Those joining competitive teams did so because of a perceived higher quality of competition, a desire for greater strides in tactical and technical development, a perceived greater seriousness on the part of the coaches, players and parents, and possibly for "ego enhancement." It is clear that the decision to choose participation in competitive soccer would be a move toward an emphasis upon the product and acceptance of more of the characteristics of the Power and Performance Model associated with the professionalization of youth sport.

When asked what he thought about the players who continued to play recreational soccer, eleven-year old Max Bennett, a competitive team player stated, "They suck." According to David Smelson, a past president of the soccer association, "Those who are serious about playing soccer play club." The comments made by Max and David indicated a level of disdain for those who did not choose to play competitive soccer. The recreational players, in their opinion, could not be serious or committed players. Serious soccer, they believed, took place on the competitive club teams.

Interestingly, there existed a pecking order amongst club teams in the area as well. Players and coaches associated with teams that participated in the state's most prestigious league looked upon the teams that chose not to play in their league (the Phoenix Classic League) as "third or fourth tier" teams in the state's hierarchy of teams. Coaches and players who were either not skilled enough or committed enough to compete in the league were considered inferior.

Stan Barrister stated that his child chose to continue to play recreational soccer at age ten because neither he nor his son were sure if they were willing to make the commitment of time they believed was necessary to play competitive soccer. Participation was for pleasure and making soccer a priority in terms of time and money at that time was not deemed appropriate. Two years later, his son did join a competitive soccer team, "partly because there was no other opportunity to continue to play organized soccer." The recreational team that they were involved with had ceased to exist.

Competitive teams were formed after the youths went through formal tryouts. If the coach believed a player would help the team, he/she was offered a contract. Contracted players could not leave a team to play for another for the entire soccer year.[4] I was told informally by a state soccer association board member that the rule prohibiting regular team transfers was instituted to prevent players from frequently changing from team to team in pursuit of better coaching and higher levels of success during the year. This was not an issue in the local community where few competitive teams existed, but it was a problem in larger metropolitan areas.

There were several competitive clubs that operated in the local community. Clubs consisted of as few as one team and as many as thirteen. Teams were classified based upon the age (soccer year) of the *oldest* player's birthday and were referred to by age group (example: Force 85). The Force 85 was composed of players who were born in the 1985 soccer year. At times, younger players were members of the team.

Individuals formed clubs of their own when disagreements existed between adults over the "way things should be done." For example, Dale Burrows started the Force United because he wanted to run his team without having to answer to a club board of directors with whom he disagreed on several aspects of how their club was run. Overland and Midcity had twelve clubs between them during the course of this study. Clubs supported as many as thirteen teams each. Individual athletes sometimes chose to play for teams in the other city.

The cost associated with competitive soccer could be great. The fees charged for players to participate on the competitive team known as the Force United (Force) amounted to $500 a year. The fee covered state and local player registration fees, uniforms, warm-ups, travel bags and tournament entry fees. In addition to the yearly fee, parents purchased their child's cleats. It was not unusual for competitive players to purchase two or more pair per year, and each pair could run in excess of $120. The parents also paid for shin guards and all travel expenses associated with league play and tournaments. The coaches in the Force club were not paid and that helped keep the cost "reasonable."

The commitment of family financial resources to soccer-related activities was significant for competitive players. Rick Reese, whose son played for the Force, estimated that he spent $3,500 on soccer-related expenses for his son in 1997-98.

Dale Burrows reported that he spent between $10,000 and $12,000 on his oldest son's soccer-related activity in the 1999-2000 soccer year. Participation on his team required extensive travel. Both fathers had two other children who played on competitive teams. When asked why he would spend so much money on soccer activities, Dale stated:

> There are three reasons. First, Chuck is getting experiences that he wouldn't have if we weren't traveling. Second, I hope it will help financially when he goes to college. Maybe he'll get a scholarship. Last, since he was little, he said that when he grows up, he wants to be a coach and a teacher like you. He has never wavered on that. I think that participating in high-level soccer will help him.

The parents were willing to invest a substantial portion of their families' incomes toward soccer-related activities. This indicated the value they placed upon soccer participation.

It should be noted here that the expense associated with competitive soccer was not out of line with other specialized programs. For example, in the immediate area the cost of training in various activities was:

- Piano lessons: $60/month for two lessons a week
- Swimming lessons: $80/month
- Gymnastics lessons: $100/month
- Volleyball practice/participation fee: $48/month

If athletes and their families frequently traveled to competitions, the cost of participation would be in line with that of the competitive soccer teams. Competitive training and special lessons can be expensive, regardless of the chosen activity.

Table 1-2: The Difference in Nature and Cost of Recreational and Competitive Soccer in Overland.

Team Type	Cost	Age	Playing Time	FIFA Rules	Champions
Recreational	$140/yr	4-9	½ Match	Several Modifications	4-7 No 8-9 Yes
Competitive: Includes Travel	$3,500-$12,000/yr	10-18	No Minimum	Few FIFA Rule Changes	Yes

In this study, the experiences of the parents, players and coaches associated with the Strikers and Force are presented. The team referred to as the Strikers was a recreational soccer team. The Force was a competitive youth soccer team.

2

THE COACH

Coaching can be difficult at times. This is true regardless of whether you work with ten-year olds or twenty-year olds. Factors contributing to the difficulties include time, the chosen participation model of the coach, parents and athletes and the sport philosophy of the coach.

I served as the volunteer head coach of the Strikers and later the Force 85 for a period encompassing twelve years. Most youth sport coaches are not paid for their time and efforts. Why would anyone do it? Why did I do it?

How should a coach behave in the youth sport setting? Should a coach's behaviors and attitudes reflect the characteristics of the Power and Performance Model (product emphasis), the Pleasure and Participation Model (process emphasis) or some combination of the two? Parents who have been participants in organized sport carry expectations concerning what a coach should look like, talk like and act like. They, likewise, have primarily a process or product orientation. When coaches do not meet parental expectations for their behavior, conflicts may occur. Conflict may result in change, either within the organization, the parents, the coach, or all three.

Young athletes also have beliefs concerning what sport should be about and what they want or expect from their coaches. Because the goals and expectations of athletes may differ from those of their parents, teammates and their coaches, they will experience and cause conflict within the athletic setting as well.

It is important for the reader to be familiar with my philosophy of sport and my coaching goals. They are presented in this chapter because they had a profound affect upon my behaviors and affected the individuals with whom I associated as I coached. Information is also presented in this chapter about the assistant coaches who worked with the Force.

Why Coach Youth Soccer?

Many individuals coach youth sport teams because their children are involved in an organized sport such as soccer. The work of Weiss and Sisley (1984) supports the contention that parental involvement in coaching is often a result of their child's participation in sport. They found that the attrition of coaches from youth sport often was due to the discontinuation of participation by the coach's child. When their children ceased to participate, they stopped coaching. Seefeldt and Gould (1980) also found that a child's withdrawal from youth sport was an important factor in a coach's decision to discontinue coaching activity.

During the fourteen years of this study, I became aware of only five volunteer head coaches who did not have a child on the team they coached. Three individuals were soccer coaches and two were baseball coaches.

The primary goal of parents may be to have their children play a sport, but someone must coach the team. Since youth sport programs are most often volunteer organizations, there is always a need for coaches. This often places a parent with little training or experience in charge of the organized sport experiences of their child and the children of other well-meaning parents (Gould, 1996; Miller, 1992).

My son Eric stated that he wanted to play soccer when he was four years old. My daughter Sandy was playing at the time, and I believe that is why Eric wanted to play. Why would a four year old want to play organized soccer? We used to dribble and kick balls around the back yard before he started to play, but I was not sure that he really understood what it meant to be on a team. I was an athlete, and I thought that participating in sport would be a good thing for my child, so I encouraged his desire to play.

When my son was registered to play soccer in the fall of 1989, I was asked to coach the team. Martha Finch, the league registrar stated, "There are lots of kids that want to play and too few parents that are willing to coach."[1] I was new in my university teaching position and felt it would be difficult to find the time, but I agreed to coach. I felt that if I coached, it would assure that my son would not be abused by someone who knew little about the sport and who knew less about the development of kids. Through the same process I ended up coaching youth baseball, basketball and softball. It was one way that I could assure that my children participated on a team with a developmental orientation as opposed to a professionalized one.

Will Johnson coached a team that was the rival of the Strikers and the Force. He also was recruited to coach when he signed up his son Brian to play soccer at age four:

> I had coached Pop Warner football and Betty Burrows was aware of that fact, so she asked if I would coach the soccer team. At the time, I didn't know anything about soccer. I was given a one-page introduction to coaching soccer and that was all the preparation I got.

Most coaches in the recreational soccer league were recruited in the same way. In the spring of 2002, one OSA board member, Mitch, coached two teams. He was told, "If you don't coach, these kids will not be able to play." He was hesitant to take on the additional responsibility of a second team, but he stated, "The thought of the kids not getting to play bothered me so much that I decided I would try to arrange it." Mitch asked one of his sons, who had not played soccer in a couple of years, if he would play. Barry agreed to play and Mitch coached the second team. He stated, "If your child is not playing on the team, it is hard to justify coaching the team."

Other youth sports programs in the city recruited coaches during or shortly after the registration period. As a Girls Softball Association board member, I often found myself recruiting coaches so that teams could have leadership, even if that leadership was poor. Coaches had to be recruited or the games could not go on. Experience and knowledge of the sport were desirable, but not requisites for assuming the position of coach.

Even when training was required for the volunteer coaches, most would not show up for it. That put the board in a position of having to look the other way, or releasing the coach. I never became aware of a coach being released after failing to show up for training.

Another reason I was willing to coach youth sport teams was that I received satisfaction from working with kids. I enjoy teaching kids.

Coaching provides me with an opportunity to teach skills, but it also provides me with an opportunity to affect young people's lives. I am an idealist of sorts. I always wanted to make the world a little better place and that is why I teach and coach: it provides me with a means to teach sport skills and life skills.

I hold a developmental orientation toward sport and try to engage in behaviors that reflect the Pleasure and Participation Model. I believe athletes should enjoy themselves, test themselves, make decisions and live with the consequences. They should demonstrate concern for themselves and for others.

I also wanted to spend as much time as possible with my children. My mother and father were divorced when I was two, and I never knew my father. I vowed that I would do all that I could for my children.[2] I felt an obligation to coach my children's youth sport teams because they were involved.

My motivation for coaching, however, did not lie in giving my children advantages over other children. I believed that I would be a good coach and that my coaching would provide them with a positive sport experience. It was a means of spending time with them. I also hoped I would be able to benefit others through my coaching activity. Doing good things for others was a motivation for coaching.

The Coach's Philosophy is Formed

Will Johnson was once an opposing coach, and his son played on the Force for me for a period of two years. One day he told me, "You are different from any coach I have ever known; and I don't mean that in a negative sense. You have been very successful." My coaching behaviors were the reflection of a philosophy that was developed over three decades as a player, coach and educator.

My coaching philosophy was developed during my years as an athlete. I was an all conference and All State (All-California Interscholastic Federation Southern Section) high school soccer player. I played soccer in college at California State University Fullerton as a freshman. I was a reserve goalkeeper and a broken finger I suffered in the third week of the season assured that. The team placed second at the NCAA Division II National Tournament. During my junior and senior years, I was a member of the University of California at Davis soccer team. I did start in several varsity matches, but was the second keeper. Bursitis, a hernia and a broken hand limited my playing time at Davis. The teams qualified for the NCAA Championship Tournament each of the two years that I played. I also participated on the men's club volleyball team at California Davis.

It was pointed out to me by a club coach that my playing experience was limited and that I was not a successful player because in college I did not start all of the time and because I was not a professional player. My shortcomings should be noted.

As a youth, I was able to make all-star teams in baseball and was able to start on junior high and high school football, basketball, baseball, and soccer teams. I also lettered in varsity tennis. My first organized soccer experience came in high school when I was asked to join the newly formed soccer team by some students who had helped get the team started. They suggested that I play as a goalkeeper. They said that I had good hands and observed that I could punt well.

While attending college, I also served as an assistant soccer coach at both John Glen and Davis High Schools. Each team won a conference championship.

For seven years I worked as a teacher-coach at Crownpoint High School in New Mexico. I received coach of the year awards in volleyball and basketball. As an assistant college volleyball coach at the University of Northern Colorado, I was able to participate in two NCAA championship tournaments. As a head volleyball coach at the university level, I have received two conference coach of the year awards, and my team has won one conference championship.

Though I believe in development and am a proponent of the Pleasure and Participation Model of sport, I value success and performance. I do not believe that sport participation should be all fun and games. It requires a reasonable degree of seriousness and commitment if success is to be achieved, regardless of how it is measured.

At the age of nine, I began playing organized youth sport of my own volition. My parents did not pressure me to play.[3] I had seen kids playing baseball after school on a little league team and thought it would be fun. I played because I wanted to; I cannot even recall peer pressure as being a distinct reason for my involvement. I found success in athletic competition, and it was fun. People paid attention to me because I was successful. Adults that I never had seen before knew me, probably because I was good in sport. In short, sport participation was rewarding to me.

Sport was not something that I had to work hard at in order to be successful. Things came easily for me. I did not have to work especially hard to make the team or to play. I always heard that people had to work very hard to be successful. Coaches said it all the time when I was growing up. I always believed, and still do to a high degree, that you have the physical and psychological characteristics needed to excel, or you don't. I did what I had to do at practice and put forth a good effort, but that came from within me and not because of something some coach did or did not do. My effort came from a love for the games, but I never had a narrow focus on one sport or solely upon sport.

My outlook on winning and losing was formulated at a young age as well. I wanted to win, but winning was not why I played. I never let losing to a superior athlete or team bother me as a player as long as I did my best. I remember playing on a little league baseball team that won only one game in two years. I still had a great time as long as I did well personally. To me the most important thing was the enjoyment that came from playing. Winning happened or it didn't.

My motivation for playing and my outlook on hard work, dedication and winning definitely influenced my coaching philosophy and behaviors. The observations I made as a participant and young coach had an impact upon my coaching philosophy and behavior as well.

I found some of the things that my coaches said and did in order to get players to perform to be humorous and at times frightening. I remember one of my football coaches saying that we were neither excited nor serious enough about playing. He told us that before he played that he would get so excited he would, "piss in his pants" and that we should be the same way. One of my high school baseball coaches would ridicule us in hopes of making us better athletes. He often asked players that shied away from hard-hit ground balls if they, "squat to pee." My football coaches actually encouraged fights at practices in order to enhance our aggressiveness. I witnessed a coach throwing a player against a locker at half-time because the athlete had committed mental errors. Coaches often yelled at players to get them to perform or because they made mistakes. These behaviors and types of comments did nothing to motivate me. Because I personally found them ineffective as a player, I chose not to engage in them myself when I coached. Their comments and actions were the result of their desire to win and because they wanted individuals to engage in behaviors reflective of the Power and Performance Model of sport.

My experiences as a player and a coach, in conjunction with my education and research background, resulted in my rejection of professionalized youth sport, which emphasizes winning as the primary goal (Coakley, 2001, 1994; Dubois, 1980; Leonard, 1998). I saw that winning was something to be strived for but believed that sometimes a team will simply lose because of bad breaks or because another team has better personnel. Other outcomes such as fun, fair play, sportsmanship and citizenship were more important than winning. Those were the primary goals for my coaching. My Pleasure and Participation (developmental) orientation toward youth sport (Coakley, 2001; Dubois, 1980; Eitzen & Sage, 1997) would become the source of conflict with parents as the study continued.

My sport experiences as a participant may have been considerably different than yours. I began participation of my own accord, found success without feeling that sport was work, really didn't care too much about winning and never felt like I had something to prove. My experiences shaped what I believe today.

The Assistant Coaches

Three individuals served as assistant coaches while I coached the Force, though I had no assistant coaches while working as the coach of the Strikers. These men had various reasons for coaching.

Jeff Forrest was my first assistant coach. His son Jackson played with the Force. Jeff had served as an assistant with the Bulls (a rival team of the Strikers) for a number of years and volunteered to assist with the Force. He explained, "I wanted to see the things that you did at practices to get your team to play so well. I also wanted to learn as much as I could so that I could coach my younger son's team and do a good job."

Jeff was very helpful with the team when assigned specific duties during practices. He attended nearly every game because he wanted to see his son play and because he worked directly with the team during practices. Jeff stopped coaching when his son left the Force to concentrate on playing high school tennis. He later served as a coach for his younger son's team. It was successful in terms of wins and losses, but I know nothing else about the experiences of the players or coaches.

The second assistant coach was Paul Jones. Paul had no children involved in youth sports at the time. His son was two years old. He did have a great interest in soccer and was a willing assistant. His attendance was sporadic because of his work responsibilities. He managed two local restaurants and put in long hours. Paul rarely traveled with the team, which was understandable since he had no children that were participating. He assisted for two years and ceased to do so when his son started to play soccer. He coached his son's team.

The third assistant coach with the Force was Jesus Davila. Jesus was a new assistant professor at the university. I discovered his love for soccer at a faculty orientation and found that he had a good playing background. He had, in fact, participated on the varsity soccer team at California Davis. I suggested that Jesus could count working with the team as a part of his community service hours, which were required for merit pay raises and retention at the University. Jesus was a knowledgeable and enthusiastic coach but often was frustrated with the work ethic and level of commitment displayed by most of the players. When I stopped coaching, Jesus' involvement with the team ceased as well.

All three coaches at one time or another expressed dissatisfaction with the fact that I did not delegate enough responsibilities. Why didn't I delegate more responsibility to the assistants? I was responsible for the organization of practice and for the outcome of contests. At the very least I felt that I would be held responsible for them. That combined with my perception that the assistants really didn't know how to work well with kids resulted in my reluctance to turn things over to them.

The assistants did not have much input about what went on in the practices. In order for them to do so, I would have had to spend a lot more time with them to plan what was going to be done in order to get their full input. I did not have the time.

Another concern of all three coaches voiced was the fact that the players did not act as though the coaches had any authority or power over them. After the first month of working with the team, Jesus was ready to quit. He complained, "The kids act like nothing I say is important and as though they just don't care what I have to say." The other two coaches often felt the same way.

The "who are you" attitude of the players was exhibited in my presence and in my absence when practice was given over to the assistants. It has been the same way in the college setting. When I have assistants, the players often ignore them. It happened to me when I was an assistant as well. What I had to say was not as important as what the head coach had to say. Brent Bates, a Force player, stated that he did listen to the assistant coaches and was glad to follow their directions. Based upon the feedback from the coaches and my observations, I believe that Brent was an exception.

A hierarchy of power is expected within the Power and Performance Model of sport. The athletes took what the head coach had to say to heart, but they perceived that the assistants really had little power and responded accordingly.

There was one other volunteer who never really served as an assistant coach. His name was Steffan. He came out to a practice one day, introduced himself to me and declared that he was interested in helping with the team. Nobody knew who he was. He stated that he was new to the country, originally from Liechtenstein, and that he was attending the local community college. It quickly became clear that he really knew very little about soccer and that he had poor skills. He seemed more interested in socializing than in performance. He came to three practices and then stopped showing up. The players thought he was "weird." I viewed him more as a distraction than as a help. Nobody socialized with him. A month later, the local newspaper reported that he was arrested on child pornography charges.[4]

Chapter 2 Observations

Questions and Comments for Parents

Coaches are volunteers.

Individuals have motives for their behaviors. If someone is willing to coach your child's team, he or she has a reason. If you have decided not to coach your child's team, you have reasons as well. In most cases, youth sport coaches are volunteers who have indicated a desire to coach in order to spend time with their own children, because they desire an association with the sports environment, and/or because they were begged by a board member to coach because NOBODY ELSE WOULD.

Many youth sport coaches are not well-trained.

Because you are going to pay money for your child's privilege to participate in organized sport, you may have the expectation that your child will have a well-trained and experienced coach. The expectation often communicated to me by parents in the youth sport and public school settings is that the coach is a knowledgeable and effective instructor. **This is often a mistaken assumption**. Coaching any team effectively requires time, an understanding of the athletes, organizational skills, communication skills and knowledge of the sport. How can you expect a volunteer coach with little or no training in pedagogy, sport sciences, child psychology, sport management and little or no coaching experience to function effectively?

If the individual has not been professionally trained, this is an unreasonable expectation. In reality, even individuals who have college degrees in physical education find their first teaching and coaching jobs very difficult. They realize that, in spite of their education and training, they still have much to learn.

What often happens next in the parent-coach relationship is that the parents become critical of the "poor job" the coach is doing. They complain to their spouses and other parents, often in front of their children. This serves to undermine what authority and "expert" knowledge the coach may have had in the beginning. This results in greater challenges for the coach. In such a case, those engaging in vociferous complaints are contributors to the problems challenging the coach.

How do the coaches respond? My observations have shown me that coaches begin to resent the parents. I have often heard coaches complain about their team's parents, their interference and their negativity. They also complain about the "superstar" image that many parents have of their children. **High school coaches have the same complaints.**

What is the solution to the problem of poorly trained coaches? Boards do attempt to educate their coaches. In most cases they do what they can: many youth sport associations require some level of training for their coaches. They do not, however, require a four-year degree in Kinesiology. In the youth sport environment it is unreasonable for you to expect well-trained coaches, especially in recreational settings. If the coach of your child's team is a beginning coach, you must anticipate that he or she will make mistakes. I would recommend that you be as patient and understanding with the coach as you can be.

Another helpful step is to encourage the board to offer additional educational opportunities for their coaches. You might even collect funds from other parents to purchase educational materials for your child's coach or send him or her to a clinic. Understand, though, that your coach may not have the time or interest required to seriously study. Coaches tend to do what their coaches did: copying the only method they know. That is likely what you would do too! Frequently they resist change because what they experienced worked for them…they turned out all right, didn't they? It is often difficult for us to understand and adopt new ways of thinking and behaving. Some choose not to.

You may have to assist with your child's skill development.

If you find that your child's youth sport experience is not what it should be, utilize your knowledge and experience to teach your child outside of the practice setting. Get out there and teach your child. Practice with him or her. Play modified games that will emphasize performance of skills.

Perhaps you will need to learn more about the sport and its skills yourself. You may even have to practice. However, taking these steps will assist in the development of your child's skills. An added benefit to taking these steps is that you will spend extra time interacting with your child on a personal level. This can be a good thing.

What do I say when my child has a poor coach?

Another thing you should do in addition to accepting the fact that your child's coach may be poorly trained, is to realize that the experience on the current team is not the only thing that will affect your child's love for the game or ultimate athletic development. Do the best you can to help your child through a less than optimal situation with the goal of keeping the experience positive. Explain what is going on. Say things like, "Your coach is doing the best that he can and I appreciate what he is doing."

If you feel that inadequate skill development is taking place, spend time helping your child improve her or his skills as noted above. Do not rely on the volunteer coach. Unfortunately, when I have taken these steps, I have been frustrated by coaches who insisted that my children do things their way. What are your choices when confronted with such a situation? You can tell your child to do it your way (this irritates the coach) or encourage the child to try it the coach's way. You could also speak with the coach about your preferred method of performance and perhaps your child's coach will allow your child to perform as you desire. Tension is likely to result from either action. The coach may disagree with you and should your child perform YOUR WAY, there may be a lot of time spent on the bench. Again, if YOU are the coach, the problem is solved, at least for your child.

Keep in mind this important fact: sometimes your way may not be the best way. There are many subtleties to training techniques that may improve performance. Perhaps you do not know them all.

What if you know better than the coach?

As a parent I was often critical of my children's coaches, of what they believed, who they were as people, their instructional techniques, how they related to the children, their skills instruction, their tactical (strategy) instruction and decision-making during contests. I never recall telling any of them what they should do. I bit my tongue. Why? Because I understand that once my children are in the care of another coach, they must be allowed to experience the influence of another, whether or not these experiences measure up to what I desire for them.

I would explain what was going on to my children, teach what I could, help where I could and then let my child learn from the experience. My children seem to have grown as a result of these experiences, even if they were, at times, negative. I respected the coaches and their positions even if they had not earned it. I understood the time and effort required of them, and I understood how hard it was to work in the sport setting as a coach. I also reminded myself that I had **chosen** not to be the coach of the team (youth sport) and/or that I did not have the opportunity to be the coach. Reminding myself of these facts assisted me in not being confrontational with my children's coaches

Questions and Comments for Coaches

Your philosophy of coaching is your guide.

Why are you coaching? What are your goals for the team? What are your goals for the children? How will you achieve these goals?

Parents will question your motives and your actions. If you cannot answer the questions I posed above, you are likely to act inconsistently and without direction. Parents pick up on this and become concerned as a result. If you think through what is really important in sport and how you will act to achieve it, you will be a better coach. Parents will know what you are actually trying to achieve and will more readily accept your coaching behaviors. You will also be able to explain your beliefs and to defend your actions if called upon to do so. What a great comfort!

It is important to formulate the responses to the questions I posed because those answers will become the foundation of your coaching philosophy: your philosophy guides your behavior. Spend time thinking about what is good, worthy and true. Identify the steps you can take as a coach to achieve these things and then act in such a way that they will be realized.

It is wrong to attempt to justify decisions by stating, "I am the coach"

My last comment concerning this chapter focuses upon something I will call the "Because I am the Coach Card." Often we are tempted as coaches to pull out the card because we can. Coaches do have a position of authority that is based upon the fact that we are the coaches. Traditionally coaches have had the right to make autocratic decisions. Unfortunately, just because we *can* do something does not always make it *right*. Your relationships with players and parents will be better if you can justify the things you do.

Most people are reasonable, and if you can make them understand the basis of your decisions, they can usually accept them, though sometimes grudgingly. I always thought that when there was a problem with a parent or athlete that it was an opportunity for me to test whether or not I was acting appropriately and staying true to my philosophy and goals. This outlook made such situations less threatening to me.

3

THE TEAMS:
THE STRIKERS AND THE FORCE UNITED

Those who have not been involved in youth sport may not be aware of how deeply concerned parents can be regarding the quality of their children's youth sport experience and/or success. Parental goals drive both parent-coaches and non-coaches to engage in behaviors to achieve those goals. One who enters into the world of youth sport may be shocked by what lies beneath the surface of an organized activity that apparently exists for the benefit of youths.

This chapter describes the formation and history of the Strikers and the Force United soccer teams. It is illustrative of how individuals strive to achieve their personal agendas and the inevitable conflicts that arise when individuals adhering to different participation models share the sport experience.

Winning, Losing and Attrition

Many believe that in youth sport, the main focus should be on children having fun and developing their skills. These individuals hold a developmental orientation toward youth sport participation and would seek coaches and teams that emphasize the Pleasure and Participation Model. Indeed, fun, skill development, socialization and health are consistently identified by children as their primary reasons for participating in youth sport (Ewing & Feltz, 1991; Gould & Horn, 1984; Gould, Feltz, Horn & Weiss, 1982; Petlichkoff, 1992). Winning has a place in sport, but an overemphasis on winning tends to contribute to attrition. The importance of winning with youth sport participants is much lower than most parents would believe (Petlichkoff, 1992).

When children enjoy themselves and parents are satisfied with the development of the children's skills, the children will likely return to play youth sport for another season. Low attrition on a given team can be expected if these conditions are met. The child will experience pleasure as a result of participation, development will take place and parents will be pleased with the experience afforded their children.

What factors contribute to a child's likelihood of having fun? Wankle and Sefton (1989) hypothesized that children have fun in youth sport settings if the following conditions have been met:

1. Skill development takes place.
2. Realistic challenges are given
3. Children achieve personal mastery in the sport environment
4. An overemphasis on winning does not exist.

In the spring of 2002, participation in the Overland recreational soccer league was down by over 300 children from the fall season. Shelly Smith, an OSA board member, stated that the people who did not come back were on teams with inexperienced or poorly prepared coaches. The teams exhibited low levels of play, they lost frequently, the children did not develop, they did not have fun and the parents were not happy. Such an observation supports the contention that poor coaching in youth sport may lead to attrition. She hypothesized:

> When parents sign their children up to play, their expectation is that the coaches are trained and experienced. That's not usually the case. The teams that stay together in recreational soccer are the ones that have good and dedicated coaches. The unsuccessful teams lose their players and fall apart. Often the children don't come back. They give up soccer.

Shelly's comments illustrate two important points concerning attrition. First, if coaches are incompetent, children do not have fun as a result of their participation and they may drop out of the sport. The second point is that some parents want their children to develop skills and to win often but when losses are frequent, dissatisfaction is the result; consequently, they remove their children from the setting. In either case, attrition occurs.

As the Strikers played in the OSA's recreational league between the ages of four and nine, twenty-seven different children participated on the team as they matured from age four to age ten. Twenty-one (78%) returned to the team for more than one season. In the first three years of the study, the team had a losing record every season, yet players returned to the team. This was an indication that winning was not the most important thing to the players or parents. The rules of the league did not allow parents a choice of coaches, so this fact should be taken into consideration when examining the attrition rate from my teams.

The success of the team, as measured by wins and losses, improved with each passing year. In its last year of existence the Strikers won the State Soccer Championship. The success of the team in terms of low attrition rates was possibly more significant. It was an indication that my developmental approach was appropriate. The players enjoyed themselves and felt competent. I did not overemphasize winning; instead, I helped the athletes develop their skills, and the level of play improved with each passing year. The kids had fun.

Though parents may have been unhappy with the high number of losses in the first few years, they continued to sign their children up to play on the team. When the team did lose as the children aged from four to seven, they often stated, "Losing isn't that big of a deal. They are out there to improve and to have a good time. It's fun to watch them play. They are so cute!"

My Welcome to Youth Soccer

The State Soccer Association had implemented several rules in an effort to make the initial soccer experience less stressful and more fun for the youngest players. When I went to the first coaches' meeting as the coach of the Strikers, I was informed that coaches were to let all players play in one half of each match, that scores would not be kept, standings would not be kept for championships and that coaches should not "coach" the kids from the sidelines during the matches. Many of the modifications appealed to me, but I did have several concerns.

The day after the coaches' meeting I received a call from Justin Stone, the Under-6 age group commissioner. The Under-6 age group was the one established for children aged four and five. I told Justin that I agreed with letting the children play half of the time, and that not keeping standings was probably a good idea. But I did think that it seemed appropriate to coach the kids and to keep score during games. He told me that, "All the coaches really do coach and everybody really keeps score. Last season my team was 10-0. We outscored our opponents 123-3." The words that Justin spoke really made me wonder what I was getting into. He was a member of the association's board of directors that presumably implemented these rules, yet his focus did not seem to be on Pleasure and Participation.

At the first parents' meeting, I shared my goals for the team and discussed some of the limitations that would be observed in the children as the season progressed. Immediately after the meeting, Samantha Brady called the age-group coordinator and demanded that her son Craig be assigned to another team. The reason? According to Justin, "She believed that you would not be able to teach her son anything about soccer." **Her son was five years old!** She aspired for her son to play in a "serious" environment, and she believed that I would not provide it. Over the years, she exhibited the behaviors associated with an adherent to the Power and Performance Model. I periodically observed her to publicly scream at her son during and after matches because she felt he did not play hard enough or effectively enough.

The Four-Year Olds

Four practices were held before the first game that first season, and since I had never worked with a group of four year olds in the past, I really did not know what to expect in that first match. It turned out to be an unforgettable experience.

There was one child out of the eight who seemed to cry the whole time he was on the field. Renee just stood on the field and bawled. Jenny skipped around the field all the while she was in the game looking at the ground instead of the ball. Justin stood motionless on the field and did nothing when the ball rolled into his vicinity. The game's final score was 11-0 in favor of the opponent.

When the game was over the kids jumped up and screamed, "We won! We won!" I couldn't do anything but say, "You all did great!" I didn't have the heart to tell them that they lost. Did it really matter? I must admit though that the loss was a bit humiliating. I questioned whether or not I knew what I was doing. How could someone with my educational, playing and coaching background have a team that could do so poorly? I tried to stay positive and hide my embarrassment.

Mrs. Garza said that her son Renee wasn't crying because of anything that I had done or said. "I don't understand why he was crying," she said. I didn't understand why he was crying either. I never had a problem with him at practices where he always seemed to enjoy himself.

However, there was a great deal of excitement, yelling and screaming at the games, factors that were not present in the practice settings. Perhaps that is what caused Renee to be upset. Even though the children were placed in the environment "to have fun," the intensity of the parents sent a different message to the children: this is serious and this is important.

For the children, the most exciting part of the competitive setting was an opportunity to receive treats at the end of the game. At every game the children asked with anticipation what the treat would be. They asked before, during and after the game. It was clear that performance was not even close to being a concern for the children.

In an effort to get their children to perform, parents were often heard to offer their children money if they scored goals. Another parent threatened punishment if his child did not meet his expectations for performance. Performance incentives for four year olds!

As the fall 1989 season progressed, the team improved significantly. In the next to the last match of the season, the Strikers played to a tie against the team that they had faced in the first match.

I felt good about the team's progress through the first season. I didn't make a big deal about winning and losing, and I think that was O.K. The kids had a good time and improved as players. That was the purpose of my being there. I never heard the kids cry or complain because the other team outscored us. It should be noted though, that even in the last match of the season, three children cried as they went into the game. The parents sheepishly apologized for their children's behavior and again emphasized, "I don't know what is wrong with him!"

My child never cried at a practice or a game as a four year old, but I never yelled at him or made threats. I just accepted his behaviors during practices and games, unprofessional as they were, as being appropriate for a four-year old kid.

One parent, Dan Dempsey, evaluated the season, "The kids showed a lot of improvement over the season and Sammy [his son] improved a lot." The parents looked for improvement in their children's performance. I also looked for development and signs of enjoyment as the measuring sticks of success. I was able to see the children smile and laugh a lot and that was the greatest reward for being out there. I was most disappointed to see the children crying.

The Strikers did not have a team in the spring season. I chose to coach T-Ball. My son wanted to play T-Ball with his friends in the spring, and I was going to coach. I thought that playing soccer at the same time would have been too much for my four-year old son and too demanding on me as well.

The Strikers from Age Five to Seven

In the spring of the next eight years, I coached T-ball/baseball, softball and soccer. On many days, I had two practices or games with two different teams and there were springs when I coached three teams at the same time. I staggered practice dates and times to enable me to do so. I liked working with the kids, so it seemed worth it.

Because I did not coach the Strikers that first spring, players that signed up were reassigned to other teams. In the 1990-1991 soccer year, the Strikers played both the fall and spring seasons with three members of the original team and five new players. Of the eight players that were on the team in the fall, six returned for the spring season.

I had a positive outlook on the year even though the team won fewer than half of its matches. There were some good matches and some bad ones, but again, I think the kids did well and they had a pretty good time. Most of the kids came back for the second season, but one of them signed up late and that is why she did not get on the team again.

Katy Tharp's mother reported, "I was so upset when I found out I had missed the registration deadline that I could have cried. Katy loved playing on your team. I loved the way you treated her. She really had a great time. Things weren't the same when she played on her other teams." Jane Gilliam played on the Strikers during this period. She was removed from the team when all-girls' teams were formed. Her mother spoke to me at the high school soccer banquet in 2001:

> Jane developed her love for soccer on your team. You treated the kids so well, and I think that is why they liked soccer. I think that year was the best time that she ever had playing soccer. It was in my opinion, for sure.

Apparently the parents were pleased with the team and its performance; most of the players came back and winning was still not everything.

According to Martha Finch and Betty Burrows, parents started to request that their children play on my team, not because we won, but because of how I interacted with the children, because the children improved, and because they had fun. When parents were late in their registration, their child's spot was given to another player. This fact and the season I took off for T-Ball decreased the retention rate for the team during this period.

The 1991-1992 (age 6) and 1992-1993 (age 7) soccer years saw an increase in the size of the field and the number of players on the team. In the Under-8 age group the team consisted of 10 players. The young athletes were still required to play one half of each match. Standings were still not kept, and teams did not compete for championships. Nine of the ten members of the Strikers played in both the fall and spring seasons in the 1991-1992 year. All ten players played both seasons in the 1992-1993 year.

The 1992-1993 soccer year was the beginning of the Strikers' tournament play (at that time only pool matches were played with no champions named) and served as a sign that the team was successful in terms of wins and losses. In the spring, the Strikers were undefeated in league play and against nine tournament opponents. Their record was 22-0. Winning came to be expected, and it happened frequently.

The Strikers at Age Eight and Nine

The Strikers spent the 1993-1994 (age 8) and 1994-1995 (age 9) soccer years in the Under-10 age group. The size of the field enlarged. The number of players on the team increased to twelve, and the dimensions of goals increased. These were the first years that the team could compete for league and tournament championships. During each subsequent year, all twelve players returned for both seasons.

The Striker's local rival was the team known as the Bulls. In the first three years of the study, the Bulls literally ran over the Strikers, defeating them by lopsided margins. In the 1993-1994 soccer year, the Strikers achieved the same level of play and began to surpass them. The Strikers won the league championship in the spring season and placed first in five tournaments over the year.

During the 1994-1995 soccer year, the Strikers won the fall and spring league championships, placed first in five tournaments and won the State Championship. I kept the same developmental philosophy throughout this period, and the team found success in terms of winning. The team's success generally satisfied the parents and players who were proponents of the Power and Performance Model of sport (we won) and those partial to the Pleasure and Participation Model (the players enjoyed themselves and winning was not considered the most important thing).

The state championship was a surprise to some but not to others. My wife Geneva said, "I never thought a team from someplace like Overland would be able to win a state championship. They are just kids, not a bunch of superstar players." Dave Burrows, one of the Strikers' players stated, "I knew that we could do it."

One of my most vivid memories of the state championship tournament involved the presence of Barry Jones' father, Bill, at the games. Barry's mother and Bill were divorced when he was a toddler, and Bill moved to the Phoenix area after the divorce. In the two-year period that Barry was on my team, I had never seen his father or heard mention of him. I understood that he would want to attend the games in order to see his son, and I was told that he had not seen Barry in years.

Bill was not someone I knew, and Barry told me his dad had never played soccer as a youth and knew nothing about the sport. During the games, however, he could be seen running up and down the sidelines yelling instructions to his son. The things he shouted were in opposition to what I wanted Barry to do. It was a strange situation. I quietly reminded Barry to play as I had taught him, and I repeated the same with Bill as I pulled him aside. Clearly Bill was caught up in the excitement of the event and was doing what he could to assist his child.

It was odd to have Bill at the event, and I never saw him again after. I will never forget the look of pride and satisfaction on the man's face or the tears of joy that streamed down his face when the championship was won. He offered a heart-felt thanks for all that I had done for his son. To me, we had simply won a few more games. The significance of winning was shown to be considerably different for Bill and myself. The importance of the competitive situation to each of us resulted in different levels of emotion and in contrasting behaviors on the sidelines.

State Championship Shenanigans

Two negative events took place during the championship match. Brian Harvey recalled, "As we ran by the other guys before the game, a bunch of them cussed at us and said that they were going to 'kick our butts'. One of them punched Jordan as he ran by." The behavior of the opposing players reflected their professionalized attitudes and the belief that intimidation could be used as an advantage. Were they taught these lessons?

During the championship match, I was upset with the opposing coach. One player on his team only played for thirty seconds at the end of the first half and two minutes at the start of the second half. We were supposed to play all the players for one half of the match. He cheated. I felt that he deserved to lose.

The fact that the coach did not play the athlete made the playing field unfair, but it also violated my belief that all of the kids should be able to play and have the opportunity to enjoy participation in the contest. Even though it was a state championship match, it was still a recreational soccer match. How does a nine-year-old child feel when he is told informally (and probably formally) that he is no good? Those holding a developmental philosophy of sport may be outraged. Those with a professionalized orientation might state that, "If you can't help the team win, you have no reason for playing."

I wanted to win, but it would not have been right to deny any of my players the opportunity to play. The rules required me to play them. Letting each child play at least one-half of the match was the right thing to do. Indeed, allowing children the opportunity to play is the primary purpose for the recreational soccer program. Unfortunately, the desire to win and a Power and Performance perspective of sport clouds the picture for many.

Reflecting Upon a State Championship

I felt satisfaction after the Strikers won the championship, but it did not rival some of the other events in my life. I was proud of the boys for the accomplishment. It was not something I had expected to achieve when I started coaching youth soccer, and it was not why I was coaching. I still think the best thing is that the kids were playing good soccer for their age and that they seemed to enjoy playing. I was more excited about seeing my son score a goal than actually winning the championship game itself. Few people would know about the championship today, but it was a great thing for the kids at the time. It was an accomplishment that many children do not have the opportunity to experience. It pleased me to be a part of it.

How could I discount the importance of winning a state championship? It was not what was really important to me. Since I am partial to the Pleasure and Participation Model, the development of the players and the quality of the sport experience were the important things to me. If I were an adherent to the Power and Performance Model, winning the championship would have been more important.

One parent, Gus Reynolds, believed that winning the state championship was the most significant event in the history of the Strikers or the Force. He stated, "It was really a great accomplishment because we were playing for a state championship and because when we won, we basically beat the other teams at their place."

The importance of winning the championship differed between members of the team. Eight years after the fact, my son stated, "It doesn't seem like such a big deal." Brian Harvey, on the other hand, commented, "We were the best, and I think it was a great accomplishment. It demonstrated that we achieved a high level of play and that we were better than anyone else. I will always remember it."

Through the remainder of this study my son continued to play for fun, not recognition. Brian continued to play in hopes of earning a college scholarship and because he enjoyed the attention associated with playing on a high school varsity team, though he did state that he loves the game. The soccer objectives of these two youths were reflective of their personal orientation toward participation. They differed significantly.

The Fury and the Force

Coaches with a professionalized (Power and Performance Model) view of sport view winning as their primary goal and consequently may engage in unethical behavior (Eitzen, 1993; Eitzen, 1992; Stier, 1998). "This would include engaging in rule-breaking behavior. Rules violations occur because they increase the likelihood of winning [which] results in personal and social rewards" (Eitzen & Sage, 1997, p. 70).

Conversely coaches adhering to a developmental view of youth sport, do not hold winning as the highest goal. They view enjoyment, psychomotor development, and the personal-social development of their players as being their primary goals. To them, winning is an outcome to be strived for, but it is not the primary objective. Winning is not worth cheating for. In fact, if a win is gained by cheating, it actually cheapens the victory.

In youth sport settings coaches may compete against one another and despite the differences in the primary goals of their program and the means taken to achieve the desired ends, the coaches may coexist with little conflict. In this study, another coach and I held different orientations. We both wanted to coach a successful competitive team, but philosophic differences would not allow us to work together. Two competitive teams in the 1985 age group were formed in Overland as a result. As might be predicted, we both went about attempting to achieve our goals in different ways, and conflict did take place.

When the Strikers were playing in the spring of the 1993-1994 soccer year, Will Johnson (the coach of the Bulls) made an appointment to meet with me at my office. At the time, the boys were eight years old. Will suggested in the meeting that the best players from the Strikers and the Bulls should join to make a competitive team when the boys turned ten.

Will said that if we combined our best players we would have a team good enough to win a national championship. I thought it was a bit ridiculous to plan so far ahead. I told him I was not sure what I would be doing as far as coaching because it looked as though I would be starting an athletic program at the University. I also thought that it was bordering upon obsession to scheme and plan for a national championship two years hence while the boys were only eight years old. Thoughts like those never entered my mind. Actually, I thought he *was* obsessed. I did understand his goals and intentions, I just didn't think youth soccer should be primarily about winning and that seemed to be his orientation.

Will was always competitive. He had participated in the Pen High School football program and believed in being dedicated to success. Winning was extremely important to him, "I never told you before, but the nights before we played the Strikers and the Force, I would not be able to sleep. I would throw up all night I was so excited." To Will, everything that could be done to assure victory should be done. "I was hard on my players and maybe I did yell at them a lot, but I wanted them to be successful. That's what I thought I needed to do, so that's what I did."

Jeff Forrest recalled that during the years his son played for the Bulls that "Will would ride players unmercifully in order to run them off the team [make them quit]. He didn't want any weak players on his team." Will's behaviors were reflective of a professionalized orientation toward youth sport.

I personally couldn't imagine being so excited about a game between nine year olds that I would become ill. I have not been excited to the point of becoming ill even before state playoff games as a high school coach or before my conference championship games as a college coach. Winning is important to me, but not enough to make me sick.

When I asked Will why he was so focused upon winning and dedication, he replied:

> I am from the old school. I learned my way of looking at sports from my coaches, and to this day I can tell you who they were and what they taught. It is the 60's and 70's Pen football attitude through and through. I grew up being expected to be a part of the program. There was never any question. Questioning a coach or the [process] was never anything I thought about doing.

Will's sport experiences and the expectations associated with them were completely opposite from mine. It is understandable that our views on winning and what was required to achieve it would have differed.

Between the fall and spring seasons of 1994-1995, several of the Strikers' players and their parents told me that Will had called them to ask if they were interested in joining the competitive team he was putting together for the fall of 1995 that would be known as the Fury. At the conclusion of the spring 1995 season, players would be free to join competitive clubs if they were selected. Will was getting a head start, though recruiting at that time of the year was a violation of the state soccer association's rules.

I resented Will's brazen efforts to take away my players but understood his motives. What I thought was important to Will was success. I believe that it was more important to him than the loyalty the parents and kids might have had toward me and more important than how I would feel about losing players I had worked with for a number of years. He was just trying to get the best players he could, but I wish he had started his recruiting after our spring season was over.

A meeting was arranged with Will to discuss the coming soccer year and the formation of a competitive team or teams. Will recalled the conversation we had had a year and a half earlier: "I was under the impression that you were going to be coaching volleyball and that it would prohibit you from coaching soccer. That was why I was talking with your players."

The conversation then turned to who would coach the Overland competitive team if we were able to field only one. I told Will there were several players on my team who would not play for him because the parents thought he was too hard on the kids and that he yelled too much. His response was that there were several of his players that would not play for me. When I asked him why, he said that my players bragged too much and talked trash to some of his players at school. He also said that I didn't seem to take soccer seriously enough. He was worried that I would not have enough time to do a good job. It seemed clear to me that we needed to form our own teams in the coming year, and so we did.

Those partial to the Power and Performance Model of sport believe that coaches and players should exhibit dedication to the cause of winning and devote their time and energies to the pursuit of victory. Other concerns should be secondary. Will's observation was that I was not and would not be committed enough to meet the expectations he had for a competitive soccer team's coach. I coached a college volleyball team, and youth softball, baseball and basketball teams. I served on the board of directors of two youth sport organizations as well. How could I successfully coach a club soccer team effectively? I believed that I would. Will did not. To me soccer would be another thing that I did with my life. Will believed it would be the most important thing in his.

I believed my philosophy of sport and my chosen model were superior to Will's. It is what I desired for my child and for the children I worked with in recreational soccer. In a sense, Will and I would compete for athletes, but our chosen models of sport would also clash.

During the spring of 1995, there were a total of sixty boys playing soccer in the OSA's Under-10 age group. Unless players wished to join a team from neighboring cities, any competitive teams in Overland would have to come from this limited pool of players. "There aren't really many club-level players that are not already on the Strikers or the Bulls. It will be almost impossible to make more than one good team," said Will. Thirty players joined one of the two competitive teams that formed, and eighteen continued to play recreational soccer. The remaining boys stopped playing soccer.

Will's aggressive recruiting resulted in his team, the Fury, having seventeen players. Most of the team members played for him on the Bulls and were joined by players from another team known as the Hot Shots.

Though many of the Strikers' parents thought Will overemphasized winning, his players and their parents remained loyal to him. One Strikers' player joined the Fury.

Brandon White played for the Strikers for two years before joining the Fury. I was concerned about the laissez-faire attitude Brandon had during the two years he played with the Strikers. During the first tryout for my new club team, the Force, Brandon was typically inattentive and disruptive. I told Brandon and his parents that if he wanted to play with the Force, he would have to come to another tryout, be less disruptive and show that he was going to put forth more effort. They never came back, and I was not unhappy to see him join Will's team.

After signing a contract with Will's team, Brandon's mother stated that she thought Brandon was unwelcome on my team and that he would not be allowed to play with the Force. "Will made us believe that Brandon would be a good addition to his team and that he would get a lot of playing time. That entered into our decision [to join the Fury] too."

I did not phone players or parents in order to recruit. I placed an ad in the paper announcing the tryout dates and sent flyers to children in the age group. I did not send announcements to the players on the Bulls because I thought it would be unethical to try to take players away from Will. My players received flyers and phone calls from Will.

After the tryouts and signing date, the Force had signed thirteen players to contracts, one a former Bulls player. A fourteenth player was recruited from the city of El Centro (30 miles from Overland) two weeks into the competitive season. A vignette concerning the fourteenth player is presented in Chapter 8.

Jackson Forrest had played for the Bulls for six years before joining the Force. Jackson's father, Jeff, believed that since the Strikers had frequently defeated the Bulls over the past couple of years that perhaps, "your players were being taught something that Will wasn't teaching." After the first year with the Force, Jeff remarked, "It has been amazing how much progress the kids have made this year without anyone screaming or hollering at them. The kids are a lot looser and seem to have a lot more fun." Jackson was not a highly valued player on the Bulls, but with the Force, he flourished as he improved his skills and gained confidence in his playing ability.

The first two seasons for the Force were difficult. The team participated in the Premiere League. The Premiere League included teams from six large cities in our region of the state. One of them was located four hours from Overland.[1] The league was made up primarily of teams that were one year older than the Force players. Gus Reynolds, a Force parent, stated, "It's incredible how much one year makes. The kids that are one year older are a lot bigger than our kids." Despite the fact that over half of the teams in the league were older, the Force finished in second place out of seven teams in the fall and spring seasons, just ahead of the Fury.

I was pleased with the team's winning percentage as well as with the team's level of play. Throughout the year, the team progressed. They did not lose to a team in their age group in the league. There was little complaint from parents or players. The team won seventy percent of their matches in its first year. That was actually what I had predicted our winning percentage to be before the year began, and I had shared that prediction with the parents before the season began.

After tryouts in July of 1996, the team added one player to make a roster of fourteen. One player ceased his participation in soccer after the 1995-1996 soccer year. The team enjoyed great success placing first in the then age-pure Premier League in the fall and spring and winning five tournaments. The team's record in the 1996-1997 year was 66-4. The success of the Force made the team attractive to Will and several of his players in spite of my coaching eccentricities.

The Force United

Parents must sometimes make an emotional investment in order for their children to achieve success in youth sport (Berlage, 1982). The coach of the Fury found that in spite of his best efforts to recruit quality players and to train them, his team was inferior to the Force. This led to the disbanding of the Fury, and his son joined the Force. The process was an emotional experience for him as well as a personal sacrifice. Individuals committed to success in athletics will do whatever it takes to be successful (Stier, 1998). Will was committed to success and to his son's soccer development.

Will's Bulls team regularly humiliated the Strikers in the first few years of recreational soccer. He recalled:

Fortunately I had my Brian and Jack Coleman on the team, and they were so good that it made me look good as a coach. After the first few years, the Strikers began to kick our butts all the time, and I thought I had better do something. I really had fallen in love with the sport of soccer by that time. I thought I had better athletes and it bothered me that we did not beat [the Strikers]. At that point I started to go to clinics and study the game. I learned a lot more about soccer, but [the Strikers] kept winning anyway.

The Force regularly defeated the Fury during the first two years of competitive team play, though the games were uniformly close between the two teams. In actuality, the Fury had a very good team. Will stated, "It amazed me that the two best teams in [this region of the state] came from Overland, especially when one considers how few players were available." The Fury often placed in tournaments throughout the state in the two years that the team was in existence. They were a very good team that played well with the select teams in the state. They simply could not beat them.

Will discussed the possibility of his son trying out for the Force in the summer of 1996. The "condition" was that six other players would have to be assured a position on the team as well. I told him that Brian [Will's son] would be welcome to join my team, but I did not believe that I could cut a bunch of players to make room for all of his better players. I was not sure that they were all as good as the players I had, and I would have found it hard to cut players that were already on the team. I also reminded him that his team was a very good one and that keeping it together would be the very best thing for the sport of soccer in Overland. Will kept his team together that year.[2]

In the summer of 1997, Will informed me that his son was going to try out for the Force and that several others from the Fury would try out as well. When asked what he would do if only Brian was selected to play, he stated that he was going to do what was best for his son regardless of what anyone else thought. He then added:

> I know we have had our differences, but I hope that they can be put aside. I think it would be best for Brian's development to play with a better quality of players. If he is good enough to make your team, I hope that you will take him.

When questioned how he would feel about not coaching, he responded, "If playing with the Force and working under you can help him to become a better player, I am O.K. with not coaching, but I will miss it." In 2002, Will lamented, "It was really good for me to coach because it kept me active. I really miss working with the kids. I will always regret giving up the Fury."

Will stated that many parents resented his decision to give up the Fury, "To this day [five years later] there are still some parents that will not talk to me." Not only did he have to give up something he enjoyed in hopes of a better situation for his son, but friendships and cordial social relationships were sacrificed as well.

Several parents who wished to remain anonymous believed that Will did not act in his son's best interest at all. Instead, they believed he tried to "live through his son's accomplishments." One coach in the area stated, "He wants to be important through his son's accomplishments. He seeks status for himself in the community by virtue of what his son achieves on the playing field."

I always believed that Will was a driven individual, and he wanted to "drive" his son in order for him to reach his potential. It is, I believe, what he had always done himself in an effort to achieve success in sport or in business. He wanted his child to internalize the beliefs and values that he possessed himself.

Will's son and several other Fury players were very good, and their addition to the team could have made the Force a stronger team. It would definitely make the Force a more athletic team. Will's son, Brian, dominated the play of the Bulls and Fury from age four on. He was creative in his play, had a strong shot and an uncanny ability to focus upon the placement of his shots. David Shultz was a man-child who was so physical in his play that Force players feared him. James Swimley was a physical anomaly in terms of his great size and strength as well. I viewed two other players as being potentially valuable additions to the Force.

I had to decide how to make room for the players, should they actually tryout and wish to join the team. I thought it would be difficult to let eighteen players (the maximum allowed on the roster) get adequate playing time. I didn't know how I would handle additional players or how to make room for them. The thought of cutting players did not appeal to me.

A questionnaire was developed and distributed to the parents and players of the Force to determine whom they thought the weakest players were and to afford them the opportunity to state how they would feel about cutting players who had been with the team. The individuals I thought were the weakest players were also identified as the weakest by the parents and the kids on the team. There was a striking similarity in these rankings.

Improving the team was more important to most of the existing team members and their parents than were the relationships that had been developed over the years. That surprised me.

Tryouts were held. Five Fury players were added to the Force roster. Enough Force players gave up soccer in order to specialize in other sports that only one player had to be cut (a younger player who had been with the team for one year) to make room for the new players. The roster for the 1997-1998 soccer year included fifteen players.

The younger player's father was upset about the decision to not offer his son a contract, but his mother understood why her son was not asked to come back to the team. She saw that her son was less mature and less effective than the other players on the team: "I understand why you are cutting him. Really I think it will be the best thing for him in the long run to play with children his own age. He has not been as successful playing with this team. The other [Force] players are better than he is." The father did not see things the same way and expressed on numerous occasions that his son's soccer development would be harmed if he were to play with children his own age. This was in spite of the fact that his son saw little playing time with the Force. The mother was concerned about her child's pleasure. The father seemed most concerned with his performance and development. I sided with the mother. Of course that made cutting the player easier for me.

In spite of the changes in the roster, the Force did not conquer the world. In fact, they didn't even conquer the Premier League. They finished first in the fall but second in the spring standings. The team did win two tournaments and placed in two others, but there was dissatisfaction among the players and parents for the first time. The Force had *only* won **eighty percent** of their matches on the year.

There were complaints that the team was not aggressive enough, about the player's conditioning and there were complaints about the team's record. The importance of winning suddenly seemed to be greater than it had in earlier years. There were also complaints about the coaching, and all of this weighed on me.

I had never been a dictator when I coached, and I disliked militaristic warm-ups, group responses, and all that rah-rah stuff. The Fury players were used to those things; some of the parents felt that the team lacked discipline and motivation as a result. Since my preferred style was most reflective of the Pleasure and Participation Model, I did not demand high degrees of structure during warm ups. Athletes should have some control over their activities in the sport environment. I felt that the players should, within general guidelines, be able to warm up on their own. A small part of the warm-up was controlled and highly organized. Some parents felt that

I did not exercise enough control and that I did not do enough to "fire up the boys."

If we had won all our matches, I guess the parents wouldn't have complained. The players were kids playing a game; the results of a soccer match did not mean life or death to me, and I don't think it did to the kids either. Sadly, some of the parents acted as though it was. Again, the chosen participation model was important to each parent's perception of what transpired in their assessments of my coaching and their evaluation of the team's performance. If the perception is that the coach should have tight control of the players from the time they arrive for a game until it is over, it is alarming when reality does not meet this expectation: especially if the team loses!

The Force had a similar season in the fall of 1998. The roster ballooned to seventeen players. Playing time for the marginal players decreased as the competition level increased. The team again placed second in its league and won only one tournament. The team won seventy-five percent of their matches during the year, though they played a tougher schedule than they had in any of the previous years.

The Force played in the State Cup for the first time as a club and had a record of 0-2-1 in pool play as they failed to advance. Several parents believed that the team performed well in the tournament, but some disagreed. One parent stated that the team played, "Like shit," and he reported to me that several of the parents felt the same way. I thought the team had played exceptionally well and rationalized the losses (2-1, 5-1) by pointing out that the teams who defeated the Force had bigger, faster and more highly skilled players. Even in the 5-1 loss, we played well; further-more, the teams we played all participated in the state's most competitive and select league.

I don't know what the parents expected. In Overland we had 60 players to choose from and in the larger metropolitan areas coaches had their choice from hundreds of kids in our age group. The best teams get the best players. How are you supposed to beat them all of the time? I cannot make a gifted athlete out of a kid with average size, speed and potential. Even children who excelled in my city were not equal to the elite players on some of the teams we played. One former Classic League coach noted, "The parents are very unrealistic because they rarely get a chance to see what soccer outside of [this region of the state] looks like."

Even though we didn't have a deep talent pool, the team played well, and it was competitive with the elite teams in this region of the country

(Examples: 1-0 loss to the Arizona State Champion, 3-1 Loss to the Colorado State Champion, 2-1 win over the Minnesota State Champion). We didn't play teams at that level on a regular basis and consequently, it was tough to rise to the occasion all the time. It frustrated me to listen to the parents who seemed to believe that I should be able to make their children and the team into national champions. I was there to coach soccer and to do the best I could with the kids I had and be content with that. Some of these parents were never content. I believed they never would be.

Looking back on what his beliefs were at that time, Will reflected:

> At the time, I believed that you were responsible for the team not playing up to the level of the best teams, but I do remember you stating that if the Force did not play at that high level all the time, that they couldn't just turn it on. Several of the players on the team only did what they had to do to win and that wasn't too hard most of the time. The lack of intensity and effort showed against the best teams. You were right. After going regularly to Phoenix when my son was on the Fire [a team based in Midcity], I realized that a person has to play at that level all of the time to do well. Our kids on the Force could have done very well... if we had played in the Classic League.

There was talk in early March that a new team would be forming in the fall, and Will had begun to talk up the new team with Force players and their parents. The Force played well in the spring of 1999, winning one tournament, placing in two others and winning the Premiere League spring championship.

I was frustrated with the discontent among some of the parents and openly wore my emotions to one of the final matches. Will asked, "Why the long face Steve? The team is playing great. They're hustling, passing the ball well and scoring a lot of goals!" I replied, "Then why do you want to break up the team?" Will retorted, "You know why I want to leave. I want to see the boys play in Phoenix."

For three former Fury players and for two of the original Force players that were the primary goal scorers for the team, the perceived lack of success increased their discontentment with the Force and my coaching. Even though the team reached the semi-finals in a major tournament in May, defeating three top-level competitive teams in the state, it was not enough to keep the team together. Players left the Force and joined the

Midcity Fire. A discussion of the formation and early history of the Fire, along with players' experiences are presented in Chapter 5.

Hanging On

Two players from the 1997-98 Force decided to give up soccer so they could play on the varsity tennis team at their high school. Five players left the Force to join the Midcity Fire. It looked as though the Force might have difficulty signing enough players to compete for another season. Three tryouts were held, and only eight returning Force players indicated that they would commit to the team.

On the day of the fourth and last tryout, a group of recreational team players who had played on a team known as the Midcity Renegades showed up. Kenny Hobson, the parent most influential in bringing the players to Overland spoke for the group. "We are looking for a coach who will be more patient with our kids and that will do a better job of teaching than our last coach."

The Renegades' coach had accepted a new job out of the area and there was no one to coach the team. Following the tryout, a total of fifteen players, including eight returning Force players were signed. The Force was given new life for the 1999-2000 soccer year.

The team did well despite the injuries and illnesses experienced by key players and in spite of the fact that many players missed matches because of conflicts caused by other sport commitments or school activities. The team posted records of 19-7-1 in the fall and 13-9-2 in the spring, but the success rate was well below that of previous years. They did not win any of the four tournaments in which they participated, and they placed in only one. In the Premier League, the team placed second in both the fall and spring seasons, defeating the championship team three times.

Several players who had been with the Force from its inception were discontent with the performance of the team. They were accustomed to winning more frequently than they were now, and the losses frustrated them. Jerry Reynolds who played sweeper, bluntly stated, "We suck. Our defense is good, but we don't have any offense. It gets old busting my butt all of the time and being made to feel like the losses are my fault."

I understood Jerry's concerns. They were valid. We lost our offense to the Fire. I thought the team had done exceptionally well considering the players that we lost. Many teams would have been happy to play at the level we did, but it was hard to get the kids to realize that.

Chapter 3 Observations

Questions and Comments for Parents

When is your child ready to participate in organized sport?

When an individual learns sports skills with relative ease and exhibits a motivation to learn, readiness exists (Seefeldt, 1988). Readiness is observed at different times/ages for different individuals because individuals develop at different rates. Learning is more rapid and enjoyable when readiness is present in a child (Good & Brophy, 1990).

When do you feel that a child is ready to participate in organized sport? Just because an organization has made a sport activity available for four year olds, does not mean that all four year olds are ready for participation. A child may not achieve readiness until age six or age nine. Fundamental skill development, adequate physical maturation, sport-specific knowledge, motivation and socialization into the sport role must exist before children possess optimal readiness for participation in youth sport (Aicinena, 1992).

If a child possesses readiness to participate in organized sport, I believe the best indicator is an explicit statement from the child indicating interest. He or she would say something like, "Mom, I want to play T-Ball."

What steps would assist in developing a readiness for participation in organized sport?

1. Encourage the development of basic (fundamental) movement skills such as running, catching, throwing, kicking and striking (batting). Help the child develop balance while standing still (static balance) and while moving (dynamic balance). These are important steps in preparing your child for sport participation. The better your child can move and control his or her body, the easier it will be for him/her to learn the specific skills related to the sport.

2. Play modified versions of the sport with your child so that he or she can become familiar with some knowledge basic to the game before signing up for a team. For example, a child should learn that she or he runs to

a base after hitting the ball or that a person tries to shoot at one basket and defend at the other. By doing this before initial participation, your child becomes familiar with some of the terms and basic rules and strategies. The practice and game environment will seem less threatening if it is familiar.

3. By playing with your child, you communicate the message that the activity is valued. This does not mean that you should force the child play with you. Make it seem as though it is an interesting and valuable activity through your words and actions. Pitch balls and let your child hit (and miss). Stay positive. Reinforce good effort. Enjoy the experience. If your child sees you participating, a desire for participation is more likely as well. Playing with and in front of children socializes them child into the role of sport participant and enhances their desire to play.

If your child is ready for participation, the sport experience is more likely to be positive and learning will be not only more rapid, it will be more enjoyable for both of you. The children I observed crying at age four, five and six at practices and games really exhibited little interest in, or knowledge of the sports. In most cases, the parent simply signed the children up to play and dropped them off at practice. The children were not prepared to participate in organized sport activities.

Although age is the criterion for children to sign up for a sport, the age at which a child is ready for participation in sport differs from child to child. Your child may not achieve readiness until age six, while another may not display readiness until age eight. What is the hurry? There is little objective research supporting the contention that early involvement in organized sport leads to superior performance at the highest levels (Kane, 1986). Delaying involvement in organized sport until age eight or nine should not be a problem for most children in most sports.

What should I do if the yelling at games upsets my child?

Talk to your child before the yelling starts. Explain why people yell during games and be sure the child knows there will be excitement when the games start. These actions will help your child adjust to the environment. Don't yell at your child. This may be the best step in assuring that the noise and excitement will not make the experience frightening or negative.

Don't expect your four-year old (or twelve-year old) to play like a professional.

Children need time, practice, feedback, motivation and physical development before they can play well. These things require time, practice and coaching. I believe that greatness will exhibit itself in spite of our best efforts to stifle it, and that it will happen in its own time. Your child will develop to his or her potential in time. You need not hurry it.

When should I get specialized coaching for my child?

My response to this question comes in the form of another question. What is your child's goal? If it is to be a national champion at age eight, I suppose specialized training is necessary. It is doubtful that many six-year-old children could appreciate what it means to be a national champion. How many young children are driven internally to strive for such a lofty goal? Some would argue that getting professional coaching at a young age is something you should consider doing if you just want your child to achieve his or her potential.

At this point I would like to state that some sports really do require specialized instruction. Sports such as ice skating, gymnastics and diving are good examples. Few Americans grow up participating in these activities at a high level and expertise is needed to teach someone a triple summersault with two and a half twists.

In the movie *Michael Jordan to the MAX*, Jordan stated that he did not participate in an organized game of basketball until he was a junior in high school. How could he have become the best player in the history of the game? He believes that if children just play and develop a love for the game that coaching will be more effective when it is received at an advanced age. Jordan developed a love and an understanding for the sport of basketball before he participated in an organized setting. Coaches have assisted in his development, but not before his junior year in high school.

Regardless of the sport, my question for parents is this: Do the best coaches have the best athletes which results in their high rate of success? Could the best coaches find equal success with inferior athletes? Given a reasonable level of expertise, perhaps coaching success is significantly dependent upon the athletes that come into the program. A good coach will get the best out of the athletes they have. What more can be done? Would paying a coach with more training and a proven track record really get more out of an athlete? These questions are food for thought.

I often stated in regards to my coaching, "You get what you pay for!" Since I coached youth soccer for many years without receiving pay, the message was a means of protection for me. It was a means of stating that your child may not win a championship, but at least you are not paying me a ton of money. Even if the parents paid me thousands of dollars a year, I am not sure how much more effective I could have been in my soccer-related activities. There are no guarantees.

On the other hand, perhaps if I were totally dedicated to soccer, my team would have performed better. I know that I would have been more demanding, less tolerant and less positive. Some individuals do well in such an environment. The majority of children and young adults I have worked with do not.

I want my child to experience success; isn't that important?

What is success? Is it winning every contest? Is it performing well? Is it achieving satisfaction from playing? Success can come in many forms.

Unfortunately for many children, the Power and Performance Model is predominant in this country. Winning is the benchmark of success. There can really be only one winner in a contest, a tournament or league. The reality is that everyone else is a loser. Half of all teams have losing records. Which model of sport makes more sense for our youth? Which makes the most sense for individuals playing in adult recreational leagues?

Even when a group of children experiences success through winning, how it is perceived and remembered is dependent upon the specific child. One child quoted in this chapter thought that winning a state championship was a great accomplishment, while another believed it wasn't a big deal.

How sad to consider the possibility that the greatest feat or accomplishment in someone's life was winning a contest or championship at the age of ten, in junior high school, or high school. The memories are great for some, but what else is to be achieved in life? What greater dreams are possible? Athletic dreams are good to have; they make life interesting. So can other dreams. Encourage your children to have many dreams and not just those related to athletics.

Questions and Comments for Coaches

You can't win them all, but if you treat your players right, usually they'll return.

As a coach, you should strive to win. Failing to do so cheapens the experience. Whether you are a youth sport coach or a high school coach, winning should be a goal, but you must remember that you are there to teach and to serve as an **educator**. I am not sure that winning should **ever** be the highest priority.

Here is a great reason why: you cannot control everything in the sport environment. The ball may take a bad bounce at an inopportune time or the shot may hit the crossbar. Your best athlete may break a leg, become pregnant or suffer from physical abuse at home. All of these situations have occurred in my coaching experience, and they have resulted in my team losing contests, sometimes championships.

If you really do focus upon the development of your players, treat them with dignity and respect, strive for improvement and emphasize performance, you will win your share of contests. Players can have a positive experience even in defeat, and you can teach life skills while assisting them in their personal development. If all of these things can be done, does it really matter what the final record is? The athletes will give you what they can, will generally have a positive experience and will continue their participation. Most parents will be happy if development occurs and if their children are treated well. How could someone ask for more?

If coaches don't win, aren't they replaced?

When my daughter was ten years old, Buddy Ryan was fired as the head coach of the Phoenix Cardinals. The news was broadcast on the radio as we were traveling home over the Christmas holiday. She asked, "Dad, why are they firing the coach?" When I responded that he had lost too many games, she replied, "They should fire the players. They are the ones that must be doing bad. The coach isn't playing."

Her comments made me realize my own attitude. Over the years I had grown to believe that at the professional level, if your teams do not win, you will be fired. I had the same assumption about college teams as well. Students in my college classes also state that they believe coaches will be fired at the high school and junior high school levels if they do not win. I do know for a fact that in high profile sports such as basketball and football, and increasingly in other sports, great pressure is placed upon high school coaches to win. Indeed, some coaches are fired for poor records, but often they find positions elsewhere.

If coaches believe they will be fired for losing records, what is their response? Many adopt the professionalized model and apply it in their coaching philosophy and behaviors. They become **driven** to win. They become obsessed. They live and breathe the sport because their professional lives depend upon it, and they come to expect everyone associated with the team to do the same.

Does being driven as a coach and becoming overly demanding of players really result in greater degrees of success? Do you really have to work sixty hours a week to be a successful coach? Do you have to make sport a priority over your marriage? Do you have to be a stranger to your children? How much good would you be to the young men and women you coach if you are no good to your family and friends? In such a case, you are showing your young athletes that sport is worth sacrificing everything for. You must choose what is ultimately important to you.

If a professional coach attributes success to working longer and harder than everyone else, is there evidence to support the assumption that it *was* the key factor in the victory or is this simply an assumption? How many professional coaches are you aware of who have won four, five or six championships in a row without a cadre of hall of fame players?

Am I suggesting here that you should not be dedicated to your coaching? No, but I am suggesting that when dedication becomes obsession, you are in danger of becoming an inadequate spouse, parent, friend and citizen. I also submit that devoting your life to the success of a team is no guarantee of success.

How can I please everyone that is involved in the sport setting?

These words may not be too comforting, but here they are anyway: you can't. In this chapter, some parents felt the Force won enough. Others felt it did not. Some believed I was serious enough about the sport, but others did not. There will be disagreement concerning your performance as a coach. I believe the only true test of your performance lies in three areas: the achievement of goals, your ability to adhere to your coaching philosophy and in the development of your players.

I once worked for a high school principal who had been a basketball coach at one time. One thing he always said to me was that my players would do better if they used the backboard on their lay ups. They did use the backboard! For some reason he could not see reality. To him, I was probably an inferior coach because my players did not appear to be doing what he wanted them to do.

It seems to me that parents and others involved in sport frequently see what they are looking to see, and it may not be reality. That may comfort you. Some parents look for problems, like to criticize and are never happy. Don't let them get under your skin. Recognize these characteristics and accept the parents as they are. Losing sleep over their judgments would be a waste of time. If you stay true to the things you believe, you will sleep well at night.

You will find out when you get your first coaching job that you have much to learn.

You can read about what it is like to be a coach, but you do not really know what it is like until you assume the responsibility. You will find areas of weakness within yourself and in your coaching behaviors. You will question what is right and wrong. You will learn that there are other approaches to your problems. You will be tired from thinking and from dealing with so many other people and their ideas.

To excel, you will need to grow with each experience. You should read, watch tapes and attend coaching clinics. You would be wise to talk with experienced coaches and observe what they do. You must actively seek to achieve your potential. If you don't seek to become better, you will remain the same. For most coaches, this is a mistake.

What should I do if everyone around me seems to be cheating?

This is not a book on ethics, so my response will be succinct and to the point. You must do what you feel is right.

In this chapter, and as you will see in later chapters, illegal and unethical recruiting practices were engaged in by an opposing coach. He wanted to do all he could to assure his team's success. Many reading this book would agree with such behavior. When winning is paramount to an individual, just about any deed done in the pursuit of victory is deemed acceptable. For some prone to engaging in extreme behavior, placing unreasonable expectations and pushing individuals to the point of abuse would also be considered appropriate. The Power and Performance Model sets the stage for such behaviors.

The Pleasure and Participation Model dictates that individuals follow the rules in the spirit of sportsmanship. The use of unethical and illegal means is not allowed. You cannot do it. When you cheat, you do not play by the same set of rules. Running a player off your team through verbal or physical abuse is detrimental to the development of the individual. You cannot do it.

Your chosen participation model would also affect what you deem to be appropriate behavior in the competitive setting. I have been confronted with opponents' use of illegal tactics in the midst of competitive events, and it bothered me greatly. Examples include: stepping under an airborne-rebounder in order to gain an over-the-back foul in basketball; grabbing shirts during soccer matches; throwing elbows in basketball and soccer events; headhunters used to injure players, etc. Some people do whatever they need to do to win. The event is not played as a contest, but as a war.

How was I supposed to respond? I vividly remember players complaining about such behaviors and then asking me what they should do. Their temptation was to retaliate with the same behavior. This is normal. I often wanted to tell them to go ahead! I never did because I believe in following the rules and did not explicitly approve of similar behaviors. Sometimes we lost as a result of illegal tactics, and the players felt cheated. They were!

The problem is that many of the behaviors I described above become commonplace (convention) in sports, especially at higher levels of play. My players eventually picked up on what was considered convention, adopted the techniques and eventually fit right in. In such a case, the game was played by the same set of rules. I could live with that, though I would never be party to teaching the behaviors. The game would teach them. When the children were very young, I saw that teaching them the "tricks" that were used at higher levels of play would give them a competitive advantage. Because they were not frequently employed by our opponents, I chose not to teach them.

In summary, you will choose how to act based upon what you think the purpose of sport participation is. If it ultimately is to win, you will do whatever it takes. If you believe that lessons are to be learned in a contest and that rules should be followed, then you will not cheat. You will be confronted with situations that present to you a gray area. Contemplate which decision really reflects your orientation toward sport and you will make a decision reflective of your chosen participation model and that is consistent with your philosophy of sport. Coaches come from both camps.

Those who will do anything to win often look at the "goody two shoes" coaches with contempt and consider them to be uncommitted to success. Those who engage in a saintly adherence to the rules often consider their foils weak in character. What do you believe?

What do I do when my team is inferior?

Buy better players. That is what is done at the professional level, and really, it is what happens at the major college level. Money talks.

Most youth sport coaches, high school coaches and small college coaches cannot buy players to quickly change the makeup of their teams. They have two choices. They can accept the players they have and happily go about developing them to their potential, or complain and give up on them. The first response is reflective of the developmental model; the second is reflective of the Power and Performance Model (I would expect these individuals to exhibit a lot of frustration and engage in much abusive behavior before giving up).

Your athletes are your athletes. Accept them where they are and do the best you can in order to maximize their development. Not everyone can become a superstar and not all collections of athletes (teams) are capable of championships. Myth would have us believe otherwise. Why not focus on doing the best you can under the circumstances? Focus upon improvement in performance if winning is not probable. Try to win, but in the event of a loss, find the good in it. You will remain a happier and more effective coach if this is your attitude.

As a professional head coach and as a youth coach (outside of the first three years of youth soccer), I never had a losing athletic team until I coached my first college volleyball team. We had a record of 2-20. I was thankful for each player I had, but several of them were not even starters on their high school teams. Did I want to win? Yes, I did. Was it likely that we would win? Not at the college level. Why should I be frustrated, angry and abusive? Would it have gotten us one more win? If we did win one more game would it have mattered? I was thankful that we won two matches. My philosophy of sport and my adherence to the Pleasure and Participation Model got me through the hard times. I tried to develop each player to her potential.

The rest of the story is that in the following years we won 7, 12, 16, 23, 21, and then 25 matches. Though I saw frustrated players during those first two years, I saw the bigger picture and stayed faithful to my view of sport. The players developed, and we improved. The program became more attractive to more athletes. The teams became capable of greater things. My school does not give athletic scholarships, but it is a member of a conference that grants scholarships. There is no non-scholarship division. Can we be expected to win a conference championship? We have. Can we be expected to win a national championship? We can try, but it is unlikely.

If you were *driven* to win (as opposed to realizing the potential in the players that you have) and believe that winning is what it is all about, how would you function in a setting such as mine? Do you believe that you will be given a steady stream of excellent (skilled physical specimens) and highly committed athletes year after year? What would you do in the lean years? What would keep your motivation and enthusiasm high if you experience a number of lean years? If you are driven to win, my guess is that you would throw in the towel. You would move to another team, school or town. You might even quit coaching altogether because, "the athletes just don't seem to want to do what it takes to be successful."

4

THE END OF THE FORCE UNITED

The primary reasons for ending my youth soccer coaching activity are presented in this chapter. Player attrition, a failure to affect change in attitudes and behavior and fatigue all contributed to my decision to stop coaching the Force.

We are Losers

As children mature, winning seems to become more important. Leonard (1998) observed, "As children attain higher levels of performance and move into more competitive contests, reasons for participating other than winning often fall by the wayside" (p.125).

During the 1998-1999 and 1999-2000 soccer years, players that had been with the Strikers and Force began to experience losses at a rate in excess of what they were accustomed to. Five Force players left the team to join the Midcity Fire in 1999-2000 (Chapter 5), and our best offensive players were among them. Because we scored fewer goals than we had in the past, we lost more matches. Several remaining players said they felt they were now a team of "losers." Being labeled a loser in America is one of the greatest criticisms an individual can receive (Eitzen & Sage, 1997). The fact that our team was no longer the best in our region of the state, made players question whether or not they wished to continue their participation with the team.

My Reasons

I decided that if I could not get ten contracted players to definitely commit to play for the Force again in 2000-2001, I would not attempt to form another team or to coach again. At the conclusion of the 1999-2000 soccer year, I contacted all of the players and parents that were on the team and asked if they planned to play with the Force in the coming year. Though I spoke with the parents and the children, I was only concerned with what the children (actually fifteen year old adolescents) wanted.

When asked what he wanted his son to do in the coming year, Kenny Hobson commented that:

> I have been very happy with the coaching and the way that the team has performed this year, but we would like to play in Midcity if we can. It is difficult to drive to Overland for all of the practices. It was especially disappointing when all of the Midcity players would come to practice and there would be only a few from Overland there.

In Chapter 8, information concerning role conflict is presented. There were many days during the 1999-2000 soccer year that few Overland players came to practice because of conflicts caused by other sport and school-related activities. The players who drove to Overland from Midcity each day were often cheated out of quality practices because of the frequent poor attendance of Overland players.

Several Force players living in Overland stated that they did not know where they wanted to play the following year. I did not count those responses as a "yes"; I did not receive ten commitments. There would not be enough players to keep the Force alive without actively recruiting players from younger teams. I did not wish to be involved in breaking up existing teams, so I decided not to coach the Force any longer.

Objectively, the decision was easy. I had to make many sacrifices of time and money to coach over the years and to retire from youth soccer would be a relief. Also, when the parents and players feel that it is time for them to move on, it probably is a good idea. I could not and would not be willing to stop a player's progress or development. As far as people not wanting to drive here from Midcity to practice, I wouldn't want to do it either.

Furthermore, I simply may not have met the needs of the players who decided not to come back. A professional youth soccer coach in the area stated:

> At some point *YOU* as a coach have to take some personal responsibility in *YOUR* failure to motivate these players. However, the thought does not seem to cross your mind. You always place the blame somewhere else.

When describing what he would have done to keep the players, the coach declared that he would have met with players and their parents to convince them to stay. He would have phoned them several times a week. Those were things I did not have time to do. Nor were they things I wanted to do. If the impression was that things would be better somewhere else, they **should** go.

Player Responses

I wrote a letter to each player stating that I was not going to coach the team any longer and explaining why. Betty Bennett reported that, "Max was very saddened when he read the letter. He liked being on the team, and he had a lot of friends on it. Now he is not really sure where he will be playing."

Max was one of the players who had said he was not sure what he was going to do in the coming year. Four months earlier when I had mentioned that I might take a teaching position in another state, Max was emphatic that he did not want me to leave: "You are my coach. You are the best coach I have ever had. I don't want you to leave." According to Max, for a period of three weeks before the signing date for the 2000-2001 soccer year, he was phoned at least three times a day by parents associated with the Midcity Fire. The coach of the Fire, Carlos Cantu, stated that he did not know what the parents may or may not have done.

When I asked Max why, over the period of a few months, he had gone from insisting that I stay and coach to vacillating about which team he would play for, Max stated:

> I was really confused, so the decision was hard. At that time I really thought that I wanted to be a professional soccer player. Everyone that was with the Fire told me how great the play was there in Phoenix and that playing there would be the best thing that I could do. It really did sound

like the right thing to do. I know now that it was a mistake not to say that I would stay with the Force.

When Brad Cobb received the letter, he said, "Mom, you're not going to believe what happened. We don't have a team this year." Like Max, he was also offered a position on the Fire. His mother Sandy said, "I was thankful to have you work with Brad the past three years, because you came along in a point in Brad's life where he needed a positive influence in his life." Brad's mother believed that I had helped him become a better soccer player and had improved his self-concept because of how I interacted with him.

I had a concern about how my son would feel if I did not coach the team. The previous year (1998-1999), I considered giving up the Force. When the idea was discussed during that summer, Eric accused me of being a quitter. I believed that Eric was serious at that time. When the decision *was* made for me to stop coaching, Eric teased me about it for several months and playfully called me a "quitter." Eric stated two years later that he did not remember his comments toward me during either of the two summers.

All seven of the Force players from Midcity signed with the new Midcity Fire team that would play in the Premiere League and practice in Midcity. It would be known as the Midcity Fire (White). Jerry Reynolds, who had played for the Strikers and Force for ten years, joined the Fire's White team as well. Brent Bates, an original member of the Force, and Brad Cobb joined the Fire's existing team that would be known as the "Midcity Fire (Blue)."[1] The Fire Blue competed in the Phoenix Classic League.

Parent Responses

Many of the Force parents felt a sense of loss over the breakup of the team. Gus Reynolds, Vick Thompson and Jack Bennett said they would miss the people associated with the team. They had made close friendships with the players and other parents. They still call me "Coach."

While at a high school soccer match in the winter of 2002, Betty Bennett told me that soccer matches had been her "social time." At soccer matches she could talk about anything and everything with her soccer friends. Many of the parents felt the same way. Disbanding the Force also disbanded a social network of friends and parents who had been associated with one another and the team for a six-year period.

Concerns over what would happen to the Force occupied much of my wife's thoughts for two months before the decision was made to break up the team. She often expressed her concern for the players, for their families and for my trials. When I finally made the decision, she said, "It is so sad. It's like there was a death." The team was important to her, and when it was broken up, it left a social void in her life.

Betty Bennett said, "When I read the letter, I could not stop crying. I never knew how much the team meant to me." Three weeks after receiving the letter, Teri Reynolds and Sandy Cobb still cried when they talked about the breakup of the team. The soccer team seemed to have meant as much to the adults as it did to the kids, if not more. Debbie Reese explained why the breakup of the team was so much of a loss:

> It *was* harder on the parents than on the kids; at least they get to see each other at school. I've been involved with many teams over the years with John and my other two children, but this one was special. I don't know what it was, but it was different than all of the others. We all looked forward to the games and getting together and traveling with everyone. We travel with the other teams now, but that feeling of family just isn't there.

The Long-Term Fallout

My son reflected on the breakup of the team in 2002 and stated that it is just something that happened, "It was really not that big of a deal. Why don't people get over it?" Conversely, Max Bennett was bitter about the breakup of the team three years after the fact. He blamed Will Johnson for the team's demise:

> When he came and brought those other players, it ruined everything. The years before they came were the best years of my life. The team was the most important thing in the world to me and to my family. They ruined it all.

There were other children and parents who felt the same way. When I told Vick Thompson in 2002 that some people still expressed hurt and bitterness about the breakup of the team, he replied:

> Of course they were bitter. I still hold some animosity toward some of the people, too. Unscrupulous people that are concerned only about them-

selves bother me. I'm not only bitter towards Will, but others too. They expressed loyalty to the team and said things like, "We would never leave Steve." They just left. That still bothers me.

Will was aware that, in the eyes of many parents and players, he was perceived as being a villain for coming and going, and that he was viewed as a negative and self-serving individual. In 2002, he remarked:

I have always tried to do what was best for Brian and to do all I could do to help him achieve his dreams. That meant coaching soccer in the beginning and letting my team go to join the Force. If the Force would have tried to play in Phoenix, I believe that we would have stayed for another year, I really do. When I think about it, I wish that I would have just kept the Fury team for one more year. Maybe things would have turned around...

I also wish that I had been better able to communicate with you and work out some of the differences we had. You could have given a little, I could have given a little and everything could have worked out better for everyone.

You know, the last couple of years that I had the Fury, I acted a lot differently with the kids. My coaching style had changed because of my experiences. I started to use more Biblical stories and I was more understanding with the kids. I even started to ask for their input on things that had happened. Most people don't know that though.

Some parents believed that Will did not act in the interest of his child, but acted instead in an effort to live through his son's achievements. Vick Thompson declared:

I was a national champion in Judo twice, so I didn't feel like I had to have my son excel in sports to satisfy myself. Will wants to live through his son and just wants everyone to believe that he did the things he did for him.

When I told Will that a book was being written about the Strikers and Force, he quickly stated, "Oh no, I am going to be the bad guy." My response to him was:

I have always understood what you have done and why. I just did not agree with you. I have never thought of you as a bad guy, but our paths did cross and you were made out to be the bad guy by some of the parents and kids. I thought that you did what you thought you needed to do. There was really no reason for me to become hateful and bitter about what happened. Some people would think you were deviant because of how you went about things, but there are many that would have done the same thing. Everyone should understand that. I always knew where you were coming from. People were hurt and they responded with anger and bitterness.

The Force Survives

In name only, the Force did survive as a team. Six contracted players from the 1999-2000 team remained, including my son. Several players who had been out of soccer for a period of years joined the Force, and additional players from a younger age group were added to the roster. The team was coached by Dale Burrows. I served as a spectator and parent. Things never did really seem the same.

Chapter 4 Observations

Questions and Comments for Parents

Winning may become more important as your child matures.

For many children, sport is played for enjoyment when they are young. As they mature, winning often gains more importance because they see the sports role as something that begins to identify them.

Success is valued in America, and success in sport is most often measured in terms of wins. Losing is a negative thing in American society. No one, especially adolescents, wants to be thought of as a loser. Even college students do not wish to be associated with losing athletic programs (Sperber, 2000). Consequently, the importance of winning and the desire to win may begin to grow stronger with age. Some children may disengage from their sports participation if they are not successful, while to others, losing may not be problematic. Children who have many activities that define their lives and self-worth may not be as concerned with winning as are those with limited roles.

The child's participation style (chosen model) may be another factor in determining the importance of winning throughout their sports involvement. If participation is all about winning, losing is tough to take. On the other hand, if playing the game and performing is the purpose of participation, losing is merely something that may happen, but it will not deter an individual from participating or lessen the value of the experience.

Should your child desire success from a winning versus losing perspective, it may result in your searching for a team that has a history of winning and that would welcome your child. Competition for positions on successful teams is very great, and the competition for those positions will intensify as children mature.

You may be fortunate enough to be associated with a team that emphasizes relationships.

The parents and players associated with the Strikers and Force enjoyed a closeness that rivaled that of many extended families. For many parents in youth sport settings, such closeness is never realized. There were several caring and outgoing individuals associated with these teams, and that could have been the source of the closeness. Additionally, the team often traveled great distances to participate in competitive events (Chapter 10). This assisted the parents and players in forming close friendships.

Another factor in the formation of close relationships was the length of time the teams remained intact. How could the parents help but develop close relationships when they spent so much time together for so many years (5-11 years)? I coached dozens of other junior high, high school and youth sport teams, and they never approached the level of closeness that existed among the individuals associated with these two teams.

My experience with most teams is that the parents show up for the games over the course of the season and go home afterwards. The contact is brief and inconsequential. Whatever the degree of closeness established between parents and players in a specific youth sport setting, it is a fact that parents, players and coaches are afforded the opportunity to socialize. This is an important function of the youth sport experience for children and adults. For many involved in organized youth sport, the opportunity to socialize makes the sacrifice of time and money seem justified.

Questions and Comments for Coaches

Not all kids will focus upon winning, nor will they be dedicated to the goal of winning.

Some of the athletes in this study wanted to play soccer, but it was not the most important thing in the world to them. Others were willing to do anything to achieve success. If you believe that your athletes will be dedicated to the sport, and in particular to your team, you may often be disappointed. Some will, but others will not.

I will ask a series of questions below, and I would like you to answer them truthfully. When you were a high school athlete, was sport really the only important thing to most of the players on your team? Did most players work to their potential all the time? If the coach gave your team a workout to perform over the summer, did the majority of the players complete it regularly as specified? Did the majority of the players follow training rules (example: no smoking or drinking) throughout the year?

Students in my classes consistently reply to these questions in the negative. My observations as an athlete and as a high school coach cause me to believe that the majority of athletes are not **dedicated** to the team or to victory, though some are.

Here is another question to consider. If you gave your athletes the choice of being able to play in every game, at least to a limited degree, or winning every game and not getting an opportunity to play, what would be their choice? I suspect that at younger ages, playing would be the choice and that at older ages fewer athletes would choose playing over winning. Nevertheless, playing time is still a serious concern for those on my college volleyball teams, especially those athletes who don't get the opportunity to play often.

Naatz (1990) found that 41% of collegiate football players he surveyed indicated that playing was more important than winning. If winning were really the most important thing, why would this be a concern? Why would athletes on any team be upset if they did not get into a game?

You can and will have an influence on the lives of others.

In this chapter, one of the parents said that her child was placed on my team at a very important time of his life. His experience on my team helped him to feel better about himself as a person; it enhanced his self-concept. There is no way of knowing how many people a coach can influence in either a positive or a negative manner. Whether you are a youth sport coach or the coach at a high school, you will influence young people. You will have a greater impact if you stand for something and are consistent in your behavior.

I have not had nearly as many serious discussions with athletes who have participated on my youth sport teams as I have had with my high school and college athletes. Parents of the youth sport players have asked me to speak with their children about the importance of performing well in school, but that is the extent of my "counseling" in the youth sport setting. Perhaps I was seen as a parent by the athletes and was, therefore, not asked for help or input by the athletes themselves.

Here are some of things I have dealt with as a high school and college coach: suicide attempts, drug abuse, alcoholism, homosexuality, pregnancy, school performance problems, domestic abuse, low self-esteem, depression, legal issues, and a whole laundry list of other issues. You may also be called upon for help with such concerns. Both athletes that were suicidal are doing well at this time. How insignificant a win or a loss seems in light of the more serious issues of life.

Considering the length of time I have been coaching in schools and at the college level (21 years), the actual number of such issues has not been high. I suggest to you that similar problems will confront you should you coach for an extended period of time. You will have a significant impact upon these individuals and the impact will be clear.

What is not clear is how you impact others in less obvious ways. You will make some feel competent and worthy because of your influence on them, while you may have the opposite affect on others. You sometimes cannot control the outcome of your interactions with others, but being mindful of the potential consequences is an important consideration and should modulate your comments and behaviors. You can serve as an inspiration to some of your athletes. Others may despise you. What the individuals believe a coach should be like and how able you are to meet their needs will greatly affect their perceptions of you as a coach and as a human being.

There will be times that you are called upon to compromise your values.

As you work with parents and athletes, you will often be questioned. Why did you make that decision? Why is it that I am not playing? Why not cheat like everyone else? Why not let this incident pass by quietly? Why not yell at this player? Coaches do all the time, don't they?

I try to please people, and as a result, I often find myself considering whether to do what I believe is right or do what others are pressuring me to do. Again, a well-thought out and defensible philosophy of coaching will help you out here, but the temptation to cave in to the pressures of others is going to be placed upon you, especially early in your coaching career.

Most of my struggles have come about either because of a desire to win or as a result of a loss. For example, I do not believe I should yell at people. It is disrespectful. In the heat of a closely contested event, errors by athletes are magnified. I, like most people, want to win and occasionally a "stupid" error will be the turning point in the contest. With all of my heart I want to yell. My beliefs concerning why athletes make mistakes, and ultimately my goal of treating individuals with respect, halt me from lashing out.

When I see others cheating, I ask, why not me? Why not? It is because I have thought about these issues and how I will respond to adversity. I want to represent something positive and to do this I must act in a consistent manner.

If you are dedicated to winning and believe that games should be played with the intensity of a war, that there is no excuse for losing, that emotions run high in athletic events and that any behaviors reflecting intensity and devotion to winning are acceptable, you are not alone. If that is how you are and you believe that is the best way to be, I can accept your behavior as long as you are consistent. It is folly, though, to act in such a way and state that you care about the sport, about society and about the athletes' development as well-rounded human beings.

If you clearly state that your goal is to win contests at all costs, people will know why you engage in win-at-all-cost behaviors. I would want to go to a *war* with you, a *real war*, but I would not want you on my team as an athlete, or on my coaching staff. It would not be enjoyable to compete against you, not because I would fear losing to you, but because to me you represent what is wrong with sport and society in general. I believe that concern for the self and a blind devotion to the pursuit of victory without the consideration of how actions will affect others is a growing problem in our society and adherence to the Power and Performance Model increases its prevalence.

Individuals are also entitled to act in response to situations without forethought. However, the consequence of acting in haste and without forethought will be inconsistent behavior. These individuals will not consistently be dedicated to development or to the goal of winning. People will not know what these coaches stand for. Players will find it hard to play for them, and many parents will find it hard to tolerate them.

5

ON TO GREATER THINGS (FOR A COST)

In the United States, there are some parents who will do whatever is within their means to assist their children in the pursuit of their goals and in order to accommodate their children's interests and abilities. In this chapter, members of the Force leave to participate on a team led by a professional youth soccer coach. The players were drawn to the new team in order to have the opportunity to be coached by a soccer professional, to play with higher level players and for the potential to compete against higher level competition on a regular basis. The reality of playing in a professionalized setting was not what most of the players expected. Six of the eight players who left the Force to play on a more select team discontinued their involvement with that team within two years.

The Business of Soccer Comes to Overland

In youth sport settings, winning may become a preoccupation, and in some cases, an obsession (Leonard, 1998). When winning is the goal of youth sport participation for parents, it is difficult to keep them satisfied (Pascoe, 1978). Many parents are willing to make significant sacrifices of time and money in an effort to achieve the title of champion for their children.[1]

I was a volunteer coach. Because of my job, which included teaching, administration of a small University athletic program and coaching a college volleyball team, I had a limited amount of time to devote to soccer. I felt my contribution to the team was reasonable, given all that I had to do outside of soccer and when I considered how seriously most of the young athletes took soccer. Soccer was not the only thing that was important to them, so I felt there was a limit to what I could ask of them in terms of their time. There was also a limit to my knowledge about soccer, and I feel that there is a limit to what I can get out of any individual athlete. I felt like I gave the team and the children on it what I could, given my life's circumstances and my evaluation of what most of the players on the team wanted from their participation. There were players and parents who wanted more than I was able to give them.

Discontentment among the players and parents of the Midcity Sting with their team's performance was great. The Sting was a competitive team that played in the same age group as the Force. They had beaten the Force only three times in a four-year period in over twenty contests. They lost often to the better teams in the Premier League and to the better teams in our region of the state. One parent was determined to do something about the "low level of soccer that is played in Midcity-Overland."

Jeff Wilbanks, a successful local attorney, brought his son to a Force tryout in July of 1998. The Force was the most successful team in our region of the state. Jeff thought that I might offer a better situation for his son than the one that existed in Midcity.

Jeff was not impressed with the tryout. He dismissed me as being a "dad-coach." I took offense to being called a dad-coach. He was not aware of my soccer or professional background. I rarely discussed my playing background or professional experiences with individuals within the soccer community. Doing so may have been a means of self-promotion, but I was never interested in trying to impress others with my experiences and credentials. Compared to some youth soccer coaches, my credentials are lacking anyway. For instance, Carlos Cantu, the coach of the Midcity Fire shared his evaluation of my soccer coaching credentials:

> Soccer credentials? Great for a dad-coach, but very limited within the context of what these kids and parents were looking at. I don't mean this in a negative way; you obviously did very well at the recreational and semi- competitive level (with one team), but competing at the Classic League requires a level of soccer-knowledge far beyond what you have. Out of [all the] Classic League teams, ONLY ONE has a dad-coach. Do

you really think that you are that special? These kids [those on his team] and parents don't...

Mr. Wilbanks, the Midcity attorney, believed that soccer in the area would be best served if a professional soccer coach came to work with the players who desired to play at the highest level possible. The goal was to form four teams the first year, including a boys' team that would be in the same age group as the Force. Hypothetically, the team would take the best players from Midcity and Overland and thus, be able to compete with any team in the state.[2] The coach of the Fire stated that in 2002, his team was competitive with any team in the state, but that it took two and a half years of hard work to get to that point. On the other hand, in the next sentence, he identified three teams that the Fire had never defeated and then stated that he would probably never would.

Mr. Wilbanks and a small group of parents from Midcity and Overland formed a board that hired Carlos Cantu to direct the Midcity Fire Soccer Club. Carlos was well-qualified. He had coached in a high profile club in a major metropolitan area. He had coached state and regional competitive team champions, held a USSF "A" coaching license (the highest awarded) and had been a professional indoor and outdoor soccer player. Carlos came to the area with a guaranteed two-year contract at $60,000 per year.

It seemed to me that $60,000 a year was a lot of money. Coach Cantu defended his salary:

> Before coming to [this region of the state] I was coaching director and a member of the executive committee of a 23-team club. In addition to the 3 teams I coached personally, I was responsible for 20 others, a staff of 12 professional coaches, a total of close to 400 players and an annual budget far exceeding half a million dollars. The Fire is half that size, but has grown every year. This team takes a lot of work because we started from nothing and have had to constantly battle against petty vindictiveness. Currently I coach four teams and supervise a staff of 4 professional coaches and 4 parent-coaches. I am also on the club board. I work seven days a week, and my working hours are longer than yours, yet I do not question your salary or imply that it is a waste of money. This July we will probably grow to 14-16 teams (225-260 players). My elementary school in [Europe] and my middle school in [South America] had fewer students, yet I never would have thought my parents were throwing their money away to the principal.

Will Johnson had known Jeff Wilbanks for several years and was interested in the Midcity Fire as well. He liked the idea of hiring a professional coach, surrounding his son with the best players in Midcity-Overland, and competing regularly against the best teams in the state. Will actively recruited players from the Force to join the Fire during the spring of 1999 while his son was a member of the Force.

I did not like the idea of losing players to the Fire but believed that if the parents and players wanted to compete at a more advanced level, and if they were unhappy with my coaching philosophy and style, it was their choice. I understood there was a limit to my knowledge about soccer and my ability to improve the level of play of each individual athlete. If the parents and players thought another coach would benefit them, they were justified in looking for another coach.

The competition in the Phoenix Classic League is among the best in the nation, and that is where Jeff and Will wanted to see their children play soccer. Based upon how well the Force performed against Classic League teams when we faced them in tournaments (we beat a few of them and were only badly beaten twice), I believe we would have qualified for the league each year, but I was not willing to drive to Phoenix every weekend to play soccer.[3] I couldn't afford the time or the money, nor did I think it would be good for the kids, other than for their soccer development.

It was expensive for parents to have their children on the Fire, though many also stated that it was costly to be on the Force as well. In the spring of 2002, I asked the parents of three former Force players who had children playing on the Fire how much money they were spending for their children to be on the team. In spite of the fact that the coach of the Fire distributed a fact sheet breaking down the specific costs of playing on the team, none of them could state with certainty how much it cost.

Justin Heller admitted, "I have no idea how much it costs. If I thought about it, it would be too depressing." The general consensus was that the players were charged $750 a year to be on the Fire. The actual cost of being on the team was $90 per month ($1,080 per year). This amount paid *only* for the coaching fees. In addition, parents had to pay for their children's uniforms, travel bags, warm-up suits, tournament entry fees, registration fees, travel fees and related travel expenses. In its first year, the team traveled to Dallas, Texas and Las Vegas, Nevada to compete in tournaments. They also qualified for participation in the Classic League and made multiple trips to Phoenix during the fall and spring seasons.

The First Defectors

One of the Force players was given a scholarship to play for the Fire. He did not have to buy his uniform, bag or warm-up suit. His parents did not have to pay the coaching fees. Kent Craft had played for the Force for four years; he was the leading scorer in every season of the team's existence. At fourteen years of age, he stood six foot-one, could outrun any soccer player in Midcity or Overland and he had the gift that is given only to a small number of forwards: creativity that cannot be taught.

The Fire also signed Brian Harvey, the Force's third leading scorer and a valued player. Brian had played for me for seven years (fourteen seasons). According to his dad, Brian left the Force because he wanted to play in the Classic League:

> Brian has decided that soccer is the only activity that he is going to do, and he wants to do all that he can do to reach his potential. He felt badly about leaving the Force because he had played for you for so long, and he knows that you helped him reach his current level of play. He also has friends on the Force, and he feels bad about leaving them.

Brian stated that leaving the Force for the Fire was a very difficult thing to do:

> You had told us at the end of the previous season that if we thought that leaving the Force was the best thing for us, that we should leave and that you would not be mad at us. That was important to me because I did not want to make you upset. I knew what kind of person that you are and trusted that it was OK. That helped me a lot. It would have made it a lot harder if I felt you would be angry with me.

The bottom line for Brian, Kent, and the three others who left the Force to join the Fire that year was that they wanted training from a professional coach and sought a higher level of play that would enhance their development. They sought a more business-like environment than existed with the Force. In other words, they desired instruction from a professional full-time soccer coach, higher levels of intensity from the coach, and they wanted all of the players on the team to be completely devoted to soccer. A more professionalized setting was what they wanted. The coach of the Fire shared his vision for the new team, "I saw it as a group of kids and parents willing to go to great lengths to find out how high they could go and how good they could be."

Recruiting Pressures

The pressure placed upon many children from Midcity and Overland to join the new team was intense. Will Johnson and others associated with the Fire relentlessly pursued players they believed would defect from their teams and assist in creating a highly competitive team. Letters, an endless stream of phone calls and personal visits were used to convince and/or wear down parents and players. Another ploy was to invoke fear in parents and/or players by claiming that it was unlikely their old teams would be able to stay together because of mass defections to the Fire.

James Swimley was influenced in such a way. He had played for the Fury and for the Bulls under Will. With the Force, he improved his skills and was allowed to play in a more comfortable and relaxed manner. He enjoyed playing for me and had stated, along with his grandmother with whom he lived, that he would remain with the Force. The pressure from the Fire was oppressive and comments about the Force breaking up began to wear on James' grandmother:

> Steve, I need to know if you will have a team or not. James needs to play soccer. He has to play soccer. He wants to play with you, but if he doesn't sign with the Fire, and your team does not make, he will be left out.

I could not assure her that I would have a team in the fall because at that moment, I had only eight commitments. If I told her I would have a team at that moment, I would have been telling her a lie.

She apologized to me for not having James sign with the Force. She was convinced that the Force would be no more. She had to do what was best for James. James stopped playing soccer the following year. Maybe joining the Fire was not the best thing for him after all.

If You Can't Stand the Fire...

Five Force players joined the Fire in the fall of 1999 and three others followed in the fall of 2000. Seven of the eight played on the team that played in the Phoenix Classic League and was coached by the professional,

Carlos Cantu. Of the seven, only two stayed on the team for more than one and a half years.

The players found that the coach of the Fire was all business. He took no nonsense from the players and demanded that they follow his mandates and adapt to his playing style. Many players received tongue-lashings at practice and during games.

Brian Harvey recalled, "I had to swallow my pride and do what I was asked to fit in, otherwise I would be on the bench." I liked Brian and felt he was a good, intelligent young man, but he was at times willful. He spoke his mind during practices and games. I encouraged my athletes to do this, but he occasionally said things I did not want to hear. His mother told me that he spent a lot of time running laps before he began to accept his new playing environment. His goal of playing college soccer on a scholarship was so strong that he was willing to do whatever he had to do to achieve it, even if it meant acquiescing to the demands of the coach.

Carlos acknowledged that things were very intense with the Fire, especially in the first year of the team's existence:

> The atmosphere with this team had to be very intense or they would have never reached *their* stated goals. These goals were chosen by the *players*, not the coach.

As you will read below, the intensity and dedication required in the new environment was not something some players were able or willing to give. Consequently, they left the team.

When asked why his son continued to play on the Fire in spite of the negatives associated with the new environment, Justin Heller replied:

> He is focused on a goal. The goal is to play soccer in college, and he sees Carlos and the Fire as the way to achieve the goal, so he overlooks the negative things and keeps focused on his goal. I do not think that there are any perfect situations. It is like my job, there are things about it that are good, but there are also many things I don't like. If I focused on the negative, I couldn't survive. Focusing on the negative won't get you anywhere. It is the same thing here.

Kent Craft did not adjust well to the environment. Kent left the team early in the spring season of his second year with the Fire. His father said to me:

I owe you an apology. I took Kent to the Fire because he said that he
wanted to play in Phoenix with the other good players. That was OK, but
the way the coach treated him was just not right. He screamed at Kent all
the time, and that was embarrassing... You never did that. You were a
good coach. You could get things out of the players without yelling at
them.

Brian Johnson left the Fire after one and a half years. According to his
father Will:

The coach was knowledgeable and that was good, but he ran kids off of
the team all the time. He is not working in Phoenix and players are hard
to replace. He will find that out. He tries to get the kids to play out of fear.
They would play better if they *wanted* to play for him.

It should be noted that ten of the original Fire players were still on the team
at the time of this book's publication. They successfully adapted to the
environment and its expectations.

Brad Cobb also had a negative experience with the Fire. He left the
team after a season and a half:

I thought that it would be fun to play with the team in Phoenix, but I did
not like Carlos' coaching style. He tried to get you to do things by putting
you down, not building you up. Like, he would try to get me to do things
by saying that I was just too scared to do them. All that did was to
frustrate me and make me mad. I hate to say it, but I think that Carlos was
just in it for the money. It was a business situation. We did what we had
to do, not because we loved it, but because we had to.

Carlos explained Brad's experience by stating that he tried every conceiv-
able way to get Brad to develop. He tried being extra attentive and nice and
tried pushing him as well. There are many ways to reach children and one
method cannot work for all of them. It is also possible that the intensity
associated with playing for the Fire was not suitable to Brad's participation
style.

Players and parents told me that members of the Fire were told what to
eat, when to go to bed, and when to wake up when they traveled. Carlos
stated that several children on the team had poor diets and as a result, their
performance suffered. He was hired to assist the athletes in reaching their
potential, and it was his job to inform the parents and players of the eating

and sleeping behaviors that would help them to perform at their maximum. He stated, "It was my job to tell them what they should do. It was up to them to decide if they would follow my advice or not." Meetings were held a minimum of three hours before game time in order to be sure the athletes were awake, fed, hydrated and ready for games mentally and physically. Players were punished for infractions by being benched.

Players were discouraged from visiting amusement parks or malls when the team was out of town. They were to rest for their games. In an earlier version of this document, I made this seem like it was an unreasonable expectation. Carlos asked me, "Would you expect the Pen High football players to go to an amusement park on the day of a game?" Again, it was his job to emphasize the behaviors that would yield maximum performance.

How can parents say that they desire a professionalized, business-like environment and then be disappointed when sacrifices are required and the coach exerts control? Why shouldn't the coach act as a paid professional? Why shouldn't he be intense and demanding?

Perhaps they did not really know what a professionalized environment really meant. Carlos did not understand how this could be possible:

> It was explained to them in painstaking detail because I knew that what they wanted to do was going to be very difficult and possibly different than what they were willing to do. To take a group of 15 year olds who have never competed consistently at the highest level into the top youth league in the country takes a level of sacrifice that cannot be borne by many. I explained this in parent and player meetings. The players and parents still wanted to go ahead. That is why they had hired me.

Sometimes, people do not listen.

Why Didn't More Force Players Join the Fire?

Some of the players who remained with the Force for the 1999-2000 year did not leave because of the cost associated with playing on the Fire and/or because of the travel requirements that were anticipated. Others did not leave because of the *perceived* philosophy of the new club: winning would be the primary goal. The coach of the Fire, Carlos Cantu, stated that winning "has never been the primary goal of *any* team in the club."

Several players remained with the Force because they perceived that playing on the Fire would require them to sacrifice some of their non-soccer related activities because of extensive travel. Brian Harvey illustrated this reality when he admitted:

> It really was hard to play in Phoenix and it still is. You lose contact with friends. They are going out and having fun. We still have fun when we go on trips, but we are told that our fun is to be had on the soccer field. We have to be serious when we play, and the travel really takes a toll on my social life.

Dale Burrows, whose team played in the Classic League for eight years, said that "Looking back, there are a lot of experiences that the kids had to miss when they were growing up that other kids got to have, and there is no way that they will ever be able to get them back."

The financial cost was also an important factor in keeping some players on the Force. It would be cost prohibitive for many of the families to pay the fees associated with the team and the costs of regular travel to Phoenix.

Some players remained with the Force because they had always been with the Force, and they were comfortable with my coaching style. Vick Thompson stated:

> We are not unhappy with the Force or with you. The team does not win all of the time, but they play well. It's unreasonable to expect to win all of the time. Some of the parents that left have unreasonable expectations for their kids.

On a later date Vick observed:

> Our team draws from a pool of about sixty kids. We played head up against teams from [major cities] with pools of six thousand players. We did amazingly well... If you really think about it, my son and a lot of the other players on this team wouldn't have been selected to play on the teams that we beat and played so well against.

Chapter 5 Observations

Questions and Comments for Parents

Coaching your child's team will not be the only responsibility that the coach has.

With the exception of the very few full-time coaches that are found at the elite youth, college and professional levels of sport, few coaches are paid just to be coaches. I know of no high school coaches that are paid to just coach a sport. They will generally have either teaching or administrative assignments as well. Many coaches have families. Often parents expect the coach to be fully committed to their teams, the development of their players and to the achievement of success. Other things get in the way of such dedication. Life outside of sport gets in the way.

If you choose to have your child play for a coach who is solely dedicated to sport, perhaps the same dedication will be instilled in your child. Should life be focused upon sport? You must decide what you would like to see advocated by the coach of your child, especially if you have the option of choosing one. Sometimes you will have no choice of coaches, but if you do, try to match the coach with the participation model held by your child. In this chapter, the players who stayed with the Fire had participation styles that were consistent with the Power and Performance Model. They desired high intensity and were willing to conform to the demands of the program. The players leaving the Fire were not willing to conform, possibly because their participation style was not reflective of the professionalized model of sport.

The most dedicated coaches may choose to let everything else in their lives go in the name of victory, but most coaches do not. They may be less than perfect coaches because they are not totally committed to the coaching role. If you adhere to the Power and Performance Model, such may be your summary judgment. If you believe that sport is but a part of life, you may accept less than total dedication to the cause of victory.

Whichever model you prefer as a parent, most of your children's coaches will be less than totally dedicated to sport. If you wish for a totally dedicated coach, he or she will expect dedicated parents as well as driven and dedicated children. Consider what you wish for. Investigate the coach's beliefs, goals and coaching behaviors before placing your child in his or her hands.

If I have a choice of coaches, how would I pick the best one?

Most likely the best coach for you (though not necessarily your child) would be the one that best reflects your chosen model of sport. I doubt that many parents see eye to eye with their child's coach on all issues, but when the participation models match, fewer conflicts can be expected.

If you consider your child's reasons for playing a sport, his or her chosen participation style should be the primary consideration. The chosen participation style may change with maturation. Say for example that your child simply wants to play a sport and enjoy his or her participation. A Pleasure and Participation oriented coach would be best for meeting your child's needs.

As your child matures, he or she may become more concerned with winning and maximizing his or her potential. This may result in the need for a coach that has a different orientation toward sport. At this point, a coach more closely aligned with a Power and Performance orientation may be more likely to meet your child's needs. In this chapter, the player that had been with me for seven years did well under my coaching, but when he decided to do all that he could to get an athletic scholarship, he was doing the right thing by changing coaches and his playing environment. Children who want to play at the highest level possible need coaches who are dedicated to their team and they must be surrounded with players of a like-mind.

In my response I assume the coaches to be knowledgeable of the sport and that they can teach skills. In other words, if given a choice between a coach who is a good teacher and a coach with little knowledge and a win-at-all-cost philosophy, choose the teacher. Your child will be treated better and will more likely have a more positive experience.

If you have a choice of coaches, get to know them by conversing with them, talking with other parents about the coach and by watching the coach in action during practices and games. I encourage collegiate volleyball recruits to watch my teams play because I know they will be evaluating my behaviors as well. They often remark that they are surprised that I do not express a lot of emotion and that they do not see me yell. That makes my team more attractive to some recruits and less attractive to others. Players with a Pleasure and Participation orientation will be drawn to my team, while those with a Power and Performance orientation will not.

It is worth noting here that coaches can affect change in player orientations toward sport (Dubois, 1980; Harris, 1983). I have gathered enough anecdotal evidence over my coaching career to state emphatically that it is possible, but not in all cases.

Realize that greater dedication to your child's sport will require a greater cost to you and to your child.

Highly competitive sport is expensive. You will be expected to contribute large sums of money to support your child's activities in a high-level youth sport program. You will also have to invest a lot of your time, especially if extensive travel is involved with participation in the program.

Your child may also have to sacrifice his or her time and the opportunity to participate in other sports and activities. Grades and academic achievement may even suffer. When asked if his players' grades suffered during the eight years that his team traveled to compete in the Classic League, Dale Burrows responded, "Well, it didn't help."

The costs, all costs, should be considered before making a decision to join a high-level team or program. Often the true cost cannot be determined until you have actually involved your child in the program. Ask a lot of questions before making a decision.

One last thing to consider before deciding to join an elite program or team is the potential that your child may play less than he or she did on another team. If participation is really important, this should be a serious consideration. Your child may not be the best player in the new environment! If too much time is spent on the bench, the child's primary goal for participation may not be met.

In your community, your child may be a big fish in a small pond.

I often hear parents brag about the talents and potential of their children, especially in the realm of athletics. I do not mean to be offensive, but most of these parents have never been in the presence of truly great athletes. Consequently, their only measure of excellence is that to which they have been exposed personally or that they see in the local environment.

Perhaps a child does stand out in the local community at age eight or ten. The excellent player is easy for parents and coaches to spot. It is difficult, however, to know if the child stands out because of extra practice, special coaching or accelerated maturation (Kane, 1986). It does not mean that the child is "gifted." It is important to remember that early success does not assure equivalent levels of success as children age.

I have watched thousands of children participate in youth and high school sport. I can recall seeing no more than a dozen that were truly gifted. In Overland and Midcity I have seen three. They all received full athletic scholarships to a major NCAA Division I school. They were not just good as child athletes. They were gifted and clearly special. There were no others in my part of the state that I can place into the same category. True athletic gifts and excellence are rare.

Many parents and even athletes themselves cannot assess their abilities correctly because they do not have good measures of excellence in their mind's eye. As parents we often wish to see our children in the best light and can overestimate their abilities and potential as a result. By seeing them as more than they objectively are, we may place unreasonable expectations upon them. Unrealistic assessments of ability and potential contribute to the belief that a college scholarship is just down the road. It results in delusions of grandeur, an aura of elitism and a never-ending dissatisfaction with those perceived to be holding them down: teammates and coaches.

Every year freshmen begin their collegiate participation with memories of having been the best on their team and possibly the best in their conference, while harboring dreams of moving on to the next level. They quickly learn that they are not the best on their new team. They are depressed when they find that they will be a second or third string player. The bigger the pond, the bigger the fish! I see this happen with the dawn of each new athletic season.

A player's self-esteem affects how he or she responds to negative coaching styles.

Some children seem to take criticism and negative coaching behaviors in stride, while others are greatly distressed by the same behaviors. Why is this?

Smith and Smoll (1990) found that children with low self-esteem responded very favorably to coaches who utilized positive coaching styles (were reinforcing and encouraging). They responded negatively to coaches who rarely gave encouragement and failed to provide reinforcement. Interestingly, individuals with high self-esteem were unaffected by a negative or positive coaching style.

In this chapter, Brent's mother said that playing on my team was good for him. I was positive with him. His self-esteem improved. He liked being on my team, and he improved as a player. He left the Fire because he did not respond well to some of the methods utilized by the coach to motivate him. He was not able to overlook how the interactions made him feel. Other players on the Fire were.

Questions and Comments for Coaches

Players may wish to leave your program to pursue their dreams.

Such was the case in this study, and it probably happens in many competitive sport situations. I know of high school players who have moved to other cities and to other parts of a city in order to participate on better teams or to be assured of the opportunity to play on a varsity team. Club players change teams. College players transfer schools, and professional athletes demand trades. Whether the dream is success, a championship, tactical development or riches, people will leave to reach their goals. High school and college coaches frequently move on in search of their dreams.

Though it may be hard to accept the fact that someone will not play for you any more, wish the player well. You can't stop players who wish to leave, and though you may disagree with the wisdom of their decision, it is theirs to make. In this chapter, I lost players to another team because they chose to chase their dreams. I have lost college athletes because they needed to attend another institution for their chosen major and because they wanted to experience the life offered on a Beer and Circus campus (Major Division I college). I have lost players because they became pregnant, by choice. Some athletes discontinued their participation on my teams because they could not stand the pain from injuries any longer.

There may be many reasons for an individual leaving your team. It may even be because of your coaching style. There is no sense in taking their departure from your program personally. Wish them well. You cannot please everyone.

If you advertise that success will be gained through participation in your program, there will be a lot of extra pressure placed upon you, and it is deserved.

If parents place their children on your team in the youth sport setting and the expected payoffs are skill development, winning and the awarding of scholarships, you need to produce. If you do not, parents will look elsewhere. The word will spread throughout the community, and players may stop coming your way. The thing you must realize is that parental and player expectations for production will exist even if you do not have a Power and Performance orientation to sport. It may be a constant source of frustration, tension and discomfort.

The reality, at least my reality, is that in most youth sport and high school settings, there will be a mix of individuals who possess different orientations toward sport participation. If individuals that you coach and/or their parents have a Power and Performance orientation, there will be pressure placed upon you to produce winning teams regardless of your personal orientation.

Your team's success may be greatly affected by how many people live in your community, attend your school or value your sport.

If you are a youth sport coach and want to compete at a high level, the size of your city will have an important impact upon how successful you might be. If there is a large population, there will likely be more participants to select from.

Schools are classified according to the size of the student population when conferences and state championship qualification plans are drawn up. It is clear that the greater the size of the population you can draw from, the more likely you are to have a greater number of good athletes in a specific sport. It is unreasonable to expect schools with a student population of 200 to be able to compete on a regular basis with schools supporting a population of 2,300 students. There may be years when the small school will be competitive, but in most years such an expectation is unreasonable.

In this study, the pool of players in Overland was very limited compared to what it would have been in bigger cities. Many parents did not see the relationship between the quality of the team and the number of potential players from which the coach could select. That frustrated me, and it would frustrate you as well.

A final note concerns the popularity of a sport within your community. If a community is enamored with a particular sport, many children will be driven to participate and excel in that sport. A good example can be found in Overland in its passion for football. In such a situation, even when populations are small, the number of good players may be proportionately greater than in other areas of your state or region of the country. If you live in a small community and the number of children interested in your chosen sport is small, it may be difficult to field a successful team in terms of wins and losses year after year.

6

THE RELATIONSHIP BETWEEN CLUB
SOCCER AND HIGH SCHOOL SOCCER

Many American youths hope to someday participate on their high school varsity athletic teams. As a result of their participation on a varsity high school team, players can gain attention, fulfill social expectations/obligations, find personal satisfaction from making the team, and benefit physically (Bissinger, 1990; Chandler & Goldberg, 1990; Coakley, 1994; Eitzen & Sage, 1997, Holland & Andre, 1994; Leonard, 1998). In terms of the larger social milieu, high school sport can serve as a focal point and source of pride for the community and as a means to socialize participants.

Boys' varsity high school soccer was added to the public school extracurricular sports program in Overland in 1997. It was not uncommon for crowds as large as five hundred to attend high school soccer matches in Overland, but the support did not come close to rivaling that of the Pen High School football team that could attract crowds in excess of 20,000. Generally, those who followed the high school soccer teams were parents and friends of the players and members of the community that had an interest in soccer, such as individuals associated with recreational and competitive soccer teams.

In American sports such as basketball and football, junior high schools support feeder programs that serve to prepare athletes for competition at the high school level. In Overland, Midcity and many other communities, there are no soccer programs affiliated with the elementary or junior high schools. The schools must rely on recreational and competitive soccer programs to develop talent or the high school coaches must develop competitive players between their sophomore and senior years.

In Overland, by the time a player enters high school, he or she may have played organized soccer for a period of twelve years, six at the highly competitive level. Players may have competed in over five hundred organized matches before reaching high school.

What did the players on the Force and their parents feel about high school soccer? Was playing varsity high school soccer an important goal for them? Did they view playing varsity soccer as a means to a college athletic scholarship? What were the thoughts of the high school coach about competitive soccer?

Parental Ambitions

When the players on the Strikers were eight years old, I first heard mention of preparation for high school soccer. Will Johnson suggested that since most of the better players in Overland would attend Pen High, that he expected them to win the 5A state soccer championship.[1]

In addition to Will, the parents of five other Force players spoke about the goal of their children playing high school soccer by the time their children were thirteen. Only three of the Force players ever indicated to me, by the age of thirteen, that playing high school soccer was a personal goal.

Player Goals in the Ninth Grade

By the time the players entered the ninth grade, most of them did not seem to believe that playing high school soccer was important, including Jerry Reynolds who stated, "It's not that big a deal to me." Eric Aicinena said, "I don't really care if I play in high school as long as I can keep playing club." My belief was that most of the players on the team felt that a spot on the high school team was almost assured. Since they believed they would make the team, it was not something they had to strive for or to dream about.

Although high school soccer participation was not a verbalized goal, eleven contracted Force and/or former Force players participated on the junior varsity or sophomore soccer teams at Pen or Overland high school as ninth graders, including Jerry and Eric, who started on their team.

The Soccer Scholarship Fairy

Several parents had hopes that their child's participation in youth soccer would result in their being offered an athletic scholarship. Comments ranged from, "My child will not be able to attend college without a scholarship" to, "It would help a lot if he could get a scholarship. Every little bit will help."

Brent Bates' personal goal was to earn a scholarship. "I am going to do all I can to improve enough to get a scholarship," he promised. Two other players verbalized the same sentiment at some time during my coaching tenure. All three joined the Fire.

In some sports, such as American football, college scholarships are offered as a result of participation and outstanding performance in varsity high school competition. Though college soccer coaches may identify potential players in high school soccer contests, the probability is low according to the competitive soccer community in Overland. Dale Burrows, whose soccer team played in the Phoenix Classic League explained:

> College coaches identify talented players in high-level club tournaments and in the high-level leagues, like the Classic League. If they watch there, they can see a lot of talented players in a short time. It's a waste for them to go to most high school games because they will usually see only a small number of good players at a time.

Chip Brown, the former men's soccer coach at the local university agreed, "High school matches are a waste of time. The level of play in the high schools is typically terrible." Carlos Cantu, the coach of the Fire, echoed Chip's sentiment:

> Every college coach I have ever spoken to in a [nationally] competitive program says the same thing. This is true across the nation. To argue otherwise is folly.

Understandably, the best players in the country are likely to play on the highest profile clubs and in the highest profile tournaments. Coaches at high profile, nationally competitive programs will see these players in abundance in such settings.

Paulo Perez was a club coach in the Overland Flames organization for a period of five years. Paulo also played competitive club soccer in Overland and Midcity for seven years. He was hired after graduation from college to teach and coach at one of the Midcity high schools. Paulo said:

> As a club player and coach, high school soccer was made out to be second rate. I was always told [by club coaches and parents] that college coaches recruited their players from the clubs. High school soccer was just something that people could do between club seasons to keep in shape.

He now sees things differently:

> Since I have been at the high school varsity level as a coach, I've had more college coaches come up to talk to me than I ever did as a club coach. College coaches do see kids play in high school games, maybe not as much in [our region of the state], because we are a long way from a lot of colleges. When we played in the [Bostick] tournament, there were tons of college coaches there.

When asked why he believed the "myth" that college coaches **only watch club players** was so prevalent, he responded:

> The club coaches make up that stuff so that they can keep their jobs. If they told players that they could make it to college without them, they would be looking for jobs.

Paulo's statement may be a bit strong. However, I saw the coach of a nationally competitive NCAA Division II program at a high school match in 2001. The coach had to travel three and a half hours to attend the game. To state that coaches affiliated with competitive college programs do not attend any high school matches is untrue.

Dale Burrows reported that between the fall of 2000 and the spring of 2001, eight of his competitive team's players each received in excess of seventeen letters of interest from college coaches. He attributed the interest to the exposure the players received through their participation in the Phoenix Classic League and high-level tournaments. The majority of the letters of interest were from non-athletic scholarship granting institutions. A total of *two* of his players received any soccer-related scholarship money upon entering college. One player received a half scholarship from a Division II NCAA institution. The other player received money for books. No additional aid was given to any player.

Dale's team was among the best in the Southwestern United States based upon its performance in the Phoenix Classic League and in high profile tournaments such as the San Diego (California) Surf Cup. Most parents would be surprised at how few players on such an excellent team received scholarships. The coach of the Fire was not surprised:

> These were excellent athletes coached by a dad-coach throughout their soccer careers. It is no surprise that they were unable to compete for scholarships (to anyone who knows what it takes to compete at that level).

Another thing to consider is that there is a network consisting of major college coaches, their former athletes and the coaches involved in high-level club programs. Coaches such as Carlos Cantu who have been associated with high-level programs can pick up the phone to place a good word for their players. Because of his association with high level programs and a history of sending elite players to colleges on scholarships, he would be better able to get a major-college coach to look at and seriously consider his players. The athlete's association with the coach of a high-level program may give the player an advantage in the quest for a college soccer scholarship.

Not all soccer players can play on elite teams for well-connected coaches. Consequently, some very good athletes may end up participating in lower-level college programs and fail to receive an athletic scholarship at all. They may not have had the time, money or dedication necessary to participate in a high-level club program or the knowledge of how to market themselves to college coaches. The fact is that some players may choose not to play for high-pressure clubs or college programs. A non-scholarship granting institution may be preferable for these individuals. There is a means to participation in college soccer that does not involve participation in elite programs.

High School Coaches Make Contact
With College Coaches

Each year Coach Cole, the Pen High School coach, sent out packets of information to college coaches about the sophomores, juniors and seniors on his high school teams. The information included physical descriptions of the athletes, their position, grade point average, class ranking and SAT/ACT scores.

At the time this book was written, my son was a junior in high school and he had received seven letters from college soccer coaches before January. I know for a fact that they did not come about as a result of his club "exposure." College coaches often send letters, such as those received by my son, in response to unsolicited contact from players and their coaches. Rarely do they actually express a serious interest in the athlete, instead, they encourage the athlete to maintain interest in their college program. The coaches really do not know the quality of the player that receives the letter; consequently, they hesitate to discourage the player unless they have actually seen the individual play.

I often receive letters and phone calls from high school coaches, dozens every year. I have been contacted only twice by club volleyball coaches in eight years. It seems as though the high school coaches are more proactive in terms of making contact with college coaches and administrators.

In reality, those who play on top-flight clubs are generally interested in obtaining athletic scholarships. My institution does not award soccer scholarships. This may explain why I never hear from the club coaches.

When asked how many club soccer coaches had personally contacted him about players within the past year, Jesus Davila, who coached the women's team at the local university, indicated that none had. He did acknowledge that, "more than dozens of high school coaches have contacted me in the last year." He believed that the number of contacts by high school coaches was based upon a greater personal concern for the individual children and that the high school coaches (who held college degrees) were really more interested in seeing the athletes get a college education. It was also possible, he believed, that the coaches were more often representing the interests of players who could not afford to participate on select competitive soccer teams.

The conventional wisdom in Overland was that if a scholarship was earned, it would be earned through club participation. Further, the players would have to achieve high levels of success as they competed in high-level leagues and elite tournaments. These beliefs resulted in a significant number of the Force parents and players expressing their desire to play in the Phoenix Classic League and to travel often to elite tournaments "to gain exposure" by the time the players were thirteen years of age. These goals led to the formation of the Fire Soccer Club.

Jesus Davila stated that when he speaks to parents during his recruiting activities, the parents all have the same comments:

> It's like a recording. They tell how they are investing in club soccer so that their kids can get a scholarship. Here [in Midcity and Overland] the club parents won't seriously consider my college program because we don't give athletic scholarships. Though they state it is their daughter's goal to receive a scholarship, I think it really is theirs. They really believe that the money spent on club soccer is going to get the girls a scholarship.

During a meeting with the Force parents and players in 1999, I shared the odds of getting a scholarship and stated that, "Everyone would be better off putting money in the bank to pay for college rather than spending it in search of a soccer scholarship." Jane Johnson was visibly upset. Her response was, "How can you stand to take away the dreams of these boys like that? You have no right to tell them that they can't achieve their dreams." I replied, "I'm not saying that none of them can get a scholarship. I just think they should play because they love the game, not because of what they might get later. The odds are against a scholarship regardless of how much money you spend trying to find one."

Coach Cantu, not surprisingly, disagrees with my summary comment:

> The implication that kids and parents are somehow tricked or pressured into something they don't want to do is a bit condescending...But of course, your thesis is that [the parents and players] have all been fooled by the evil club coaches and none of them are smart enough to know any better.

How Many Soccer Scholarships are Available?

You might be surprised to learn that there are a **TOTAL** of 1,431 four-year colleges and universities that support athletic programs and belong to the NCAA or the NAIA (Coakley, 2001). Not all of them have soccer teams.

The following information concerning men's teams was gathered as a result of my Internet searches and phone calls.

- There are 109 junior colleges that offer soccer scholarships according to the National Junior College Athletic Association. These institutions are allowed to offer up to 18 scholarships: 1,962 possible scholarships.

- There are 200 NCAA Division I soccer teams. The maximum number of scholarships that each institution can award is 9.9. This yields a potential 1,980 possible full scholarships.

- There are 169 Division II soccer teams. The maximum number of scholarships that each institution can award is 9. In the NCAA Division II, 1,521 scholarships could exist.

- There are 224 NAIA schools that offer men's soccer. Each school is limited to 12 scholarships. That could yield a possible 2,688 scholarships.

If every school awarded the maximum number of scholarships, the total number of scholarships would be 8,151 within the NCAA, NAIA and NJCAA combined. The fact is that schools don't award the maximum number of scholarships. For example, my institution offers no scholarships in soccer even though we are allowed by NAIA rules to award twelve. When I state that 8,151 are available, this is a **gross overestimation**. Many Division II and NAIA institutions will offer one or two scholarships.

Let us further assume that ¼ of the college soccer players each season are seniors. Their scholarships will be the ones available next year and that a senior in high school would hope to get. That means that during an average, year 2,037 soccer scholarships are available for men in the whole country.

It is rare for an athlete to be awarded a full scholarship. Why? If at the NCAA Division I level 9.9 scholarships are available for a team, a coach must still have 20-24 players on the squad. What the coaches will do as a result is to split up the scholarships into two or more partial scholarships. By splitting each scholarship into halves, a coach can get 19.8 players on the roster. Of course the very best players in the country are offered full scholarships, and that means that some players even at the Division I level may get as little as the cost of their books covered and sometimes nothing at all. These individuals are called walk-ons.

How many people are competing for these 2,037 scholarships each year? It is a big world out there. Remember that some coaches can and do purchase the services of foreign players with their scholarships. In 2000, the NAIA Men's All-American teams consisted of 42 players. Twenty-nine of them were from foreign countries (NAIA, 2000). The North Carolina State men's soccer team had six foreign players on its roster in 2001. How many soccer scholarships do you think go to foreign players nationally?

I can estimate how many American males compete for these 2,037 scholarships. Remember this is just an estimate.

- There were 332,850 boys playing high school soccer according to the National Federation of State High School Associations (2001).

- Assume that 25% of them were seniors: 83,212 soccer-playing seniors.

- There were 2,037 full scholarships that 83,212 boys competed for.

- The probability of receiving a full scholarship was approximately .024 (2/100).

The odds of an individual getting a full scholarship to play soccer in college are very poor. They would be in fact less than 2/100 because many colleges do not award the maximum number of scholarships AND foreign players receive some of them. Further, most scholarships are divided up between two or more players.

Suppose a soccer player received a half scholarship for all four years at my institution. That could amount to a total of $20,000 ($5,000 per year). What if parents invested as little as $4,000 in their child's club soccer participation from the age of ten until the age of eighteen? That is nine years of competitive soccer at $4,000 per year. The total "invested" would be $36,000. You lose $16,000. One parent interviewed for this book stated that he spent ten to twelve thousand dollars in ONE YEAR on club soccer activity. If the expense is considered an investment in a child's future, it is a poor one.

Coach Cantu does not look at the investment as a "waste" in the event that a scholarship is not earned:

Yes the odds of any single young soccer player for getting a soccer scholarship are slim. But the odds of any single sixth grader for becoming a doctor are even slimmer. Yet, you certainly wouldn't discourage any youngster from wanting to become a doctor, would you? Many parents who dream of their kids becoming doctors, lawyers, engineers, etc. invest in the best education for their kids. It is the same when they invest in a professional soccer coach [and high level participation]. In the end, kids may not become doctors or get a soccer scholarship. However, the lessons learned along the way are well worth the parents' investment. That is why there is a growing demand for COMPETITIVE club soccer and *good* coaches.

Perhaps the reason that there is a "growing demand" for competitive soccer and "good coaches" is because parents do not know the facts. It is also imbedded in the psyche of many Americans that if a program is not the biggest and the best, that it is void of any real value. Coach Cantu was incensed by such an explanation:

Just because you had a bad experience coaching youth soccer and ultimately failed in your attempt to coach soccer at the competitive level does not justify your bitterness toward those who do succeed and love what they do enough to do it full time (and are good enough to get paid).

I might add here that if parents are willing and able to spend large sums of money on soccer participation because their child loves to play, I see nothing wrong with doing so. In such a situation, it may be viewed as an expensive but rewarding activity.

Club Soccer and the High School Coach

The Pen High varsity soccer coach, Ward Cole, had some very strong feelings concerning club soccer. He assumed the varsity head-coaching duties at Pen High School in 1999 and was still coaching at the time this book was completed in 2002. When asked to discuss the issue of club soccer, he was very willing to share his views.

He acknowledged that college soccer coaches were more likely to see players in club tournaments and in high profile leagues, but he said that getting a scholarship at any level was a long shot. "We have had only two players get any soccer scholarship in the last four years and that was for only a thousand dollars [the other player received books], and we had some good teams." His teams made the playoffs in two of the four years that he coached at Pen. "For most of the kids that play as seniors, it will be their last hurrah."

Coach Cole also believed that an emphasis upon club soccer over high school hurt the kids:

> They [the parents and club coaches] can't see that valuing both high school and club can make the kids better. There are things I can do at the school, such as working out daily, weight training and plyometric training that the clubs cannot do. They can play high-level competition during the club season. Both of these things can make the kids better and benefit all of us.

There were other things the kids would lose out on if they chose to play competitive club soccer to the exclusion of high school soccer. According to coach Cole:

> In our culture, high school life revolves around high school sports. If kids don't play for the high school, they lose out on that. It might also cost them their fifteen minutes of fame. You don't see the newspaper or television at the club matches, and you do all the time at the high school matches here.

Though Coach Cole had a reasonable degree of success while coaching at Pen high, he did not believe that winning and soccer were the most important things in life. "My main concern is not about winning. It lies with making the kids better people. "

Coach Cantu had strong feelings concerning high school soccer. In his statement below, he uses the term Olympic Development Program. The ODP program is overseen by U.S. Soccer and by the state associations within the United States. Players are identified for ODP participation by coaches appointed by the state's ODP director. Players receive periodic specialized training by state association appointed age-group coaches, and they are eligible for selection to regional teams and national age-group teams. Overland has a player currently with the women's National Team who went through the ODP program. She also played for a number of years on Dale Burrows' club team that participated in the Phoenix Classic League.

Coach Cantu stated:

Here are a few facts, not a selected few to help advance my agenda:

1. High school soccer is a fun experience for the kids, and I encourage all of my players to participate. However, in terms of the competitive playing level, when compared to Phoenix Classic League soccer, [high school soccer] is a joke. Classic League players approach it as such.

2. There are *thousands* of college scholarships available for soccer available to kids across the country... Still, there are many more kids than scholarships and to get one, or a partial one, you have to be <u>very</u> good. Thus, it is almost impossible for Premiere League players to get one. The only way that you are to get a scholarship for soccer as a [player in this state] is if you are on a good Phoenix Classic League Division I team and/or play in the [Olympic Development Program]. I know because I have coached in the Classic League for 13 years. During that time, nearly all of my payers have played H.S. soccer also. I have been an assistant at the NCAA Division I level and have many friends, acquaintances, former teammates, etc. who are college soccer coaches at COMPETITIVE PROGRAMS. A couple of phone calls to some of these programs [not your university], would show you that there isn't a single kid with a scholarship (soccer) that does not come from some sort of COMPETITIVE CLUB PROGRAM and/or ODP.

Coach Cantu did not acknowledge in his remarks that there was any benefit afforded athletes who chose to play at the high school level other than it would be fun. In his response, it is implied that high school coaches do not assist in a player's soccer development.

The High School Coach's View of Parents

I found parents for the most part to be supportive of me as I coached youth soccer. It was always clear that they would be an important part of my coaching experience. Parents can be expected to be important in the high school coach's experience as well. The coach of the Pen High varsity soccer team believes that, "Dealing with parents is part of the job."

Because I followed the high school soccer teams in the community for several years, I overheard many parents complain about Coach Cole and his coaching abilities. Because people talk within the soccer community, Coach Cole would frequently hear second-hand what the disgruntled parents had to say about his coaching methods and game-related decisions. When asked what his feelings were concerning parent grumbling in the stands, he commented:

> You learn to deal with [the negativity], but if the parents know you care about the kids, for the most part they keep the grumbling to themselves. You usually have five or six sets of parents that are happy with everything that you do and five or six sets that are happy most of the time. The rest are unhappy because their kid is not playing enough.

When asked what he thought when he heard that people questioned his decisions, he responded, "Everyone who sees a soccer game believes that he is an expert." I felt the same way when parents questioned my decisions. For the most part, athletic competition is not brain surgery, and that is one of the attractive things about it that leads to the creation of sports fans (Koppett, 1981). The truth is that for every decision a coach makes, there are a multitude of other actions that could have been taken. Armchair quarterbacks are never wrong.

Coach Cole stated that the problems with parents are not consistent. He observed, "It's bad some years and in others it is good. It depends upon the parents. When parents are there to be positive for the teams, that's when the program is successful."

Political pressure can be brought to bear on high school coaches by parents. Not all parents, however, have equal influence. Coach Cole explained:

> After many differences with prominent people in the community, I have found that people with money most often are able to make changes that benefit them disregarding the group as a whole. I have also noticed that less prominent people often times cannot bring about change as easily, even though their needs may be pure. For example, I had a doctor that was able to change my rules that were set up early in the year and that he was aware of well in advance of [his child joining the team]. But with his influence he was able to make a special arrangement through my superiors. Had it been anyone else, I do not feel this would have been the case. I also had a similar problem that a less prominent person brought

before the same [athletic director] and they were unable to bring about a change.

The volleyball coach at Pen High was relieved of her coaching duties in the spring of 2001 after serving as the head coach for several years. She had several losing seasons in a row, and the parents complained in the stands and to the athletic director frequently. I asked her to comment:

> Parents just can't let you coach. They are always trying to influence how you will run your team. If you don't give in to their demands, they run to the administration. I was fired because of parents who could not get their way.

How can parents expect athletes to get along and work together under the guidance of a coach when they consistently put down the coach and question his or her abilities and procedures? She believed that it was impossible.

Coaches at Pen High understand how parents serve to make their positions as coaches more difficult. I asked Coach Cole how they responded as a group:

> The coaches all form their own support group. In the club programs, the coaches are always at each other's throats over athletes. In the high school we have a lot of friendships, and we support each other when we have problems with parents.

To Play or not to Play?

Brian Harvey was offered the opportunity to play on the varsity team his sophomore year but decided not to play at the high school. He decided to train with his club coach instead. Coach Cantu believed that the extra training was necessary to improve the level of play of the Fire and its players. He felt that if the players were to reach their goal of becoming an elite team in the state, that the training was necessary. Brian agreed and chose not to play high school soccer.

Brian decided that he *did* want to play high school soccer in his junior year. Coach Cole had stated that if any players missed high school practices over the Christmas break, they would be booted off the team. It happened that Brian's club team, the Fire, had planned a trip to Florida so that the players could gain exposure to college coaches by playing in a high-profile tournament.

The tournament was to be held over the Christmas break. Coach Cole dug in his heels and stated that an exception would not be made for the Fire players on the high school team. If players missed the school's practices over the break, they would be removed from the team. Brian's dad went to the district athletic director concerning the coach's rule; consequently, an allowance was made for three Fire players.

When asked why he was so intent upon playing high school soccer in his junior year of high school after passing up the opportunity as a sophomore, Brian replied:

> It's probably a superficial thing, but playing at high school is kind of like playing semi-pro soccer. There are a lot of people watching. You know, all the [school spirit] stuff is really kind of neat. It's a great experience and it is fun. High school soccer is fun because it is not as intense as club is. You can relax a little more. Plus, it's a blast to get to travel everywhere with all your friends.

Brian did play in his junior year with the Pen High School varsity team. He scored goals in two 1-0 victories during the season. In each instance, he reveled in the applause, tore his shirt off and waved it as he strutted in front of the crowd. Certainly the experience will remain with him for life.

A Parent's Summary Comment

Spencer Johansen, whose son was a player with the Force and the Pen High varsity team in 2002, summed up his feelings concerning high school soccer and its relationship to competitive soccer:

> It's a shame that high school coaches have to contend with the stuff that was put in the kid's heads when they were ten years old and the fact that they lose some of the top players because they think that something is better than high school soccer.

Five club players who were members of the Fire or the Force and were juniors in high school chose not play with the Pen High soccer team in 2002.

Chapter 6 Observations

Questions and Comments for Parents

Playing high school sports may be important to you, but it is possible that your child may never have the opportunity.

For those of us who participated in high school athletics, positive memories of the experience may still linger. Memories of friendships, travel and the attention we received as a result of our participation remain. For others, disappointments and resentment may be the focus of their reminiscence. For the latter, interscholastic athletic participation may not be something they desire for their children.

If you enjoyed your high school athletic experience, you may wish for your children to have the same opportunity and benefits afforded to them. There is no question that I wanted for my children to become high school varsity letter winners. I was, my wife was, and it was only reasonable to expect that they would. How could the children of a physical education teacher and coach not be able to become varsity athletes? There could be several reasons.

The odds could be against it. My high school graduating class had slightly over 300 seniors. My wife's graduating class consisted of only 23 seniors. My daughter's sophomore class had 1050 students in it. It was more likely for any individual that attended my wife's school to be able to participate in a sport at the varsity level. The small number of potential athletes assured that the odds of making the team were very good. It was less likely for individuals to participate at my high school. It was even less likely for my children to become varsity athletes at their high school.

Should a parent's desires for their children affect the decision on where their children attend school? I know several parents who made decisions concerning high schools based upon the athletic goals they had for their children. They moved because the odds of their child becoming varsity team members were increased.

My wife and I agreed to have our children attend the large high school in Overland in spite of the fact that it would be less likely for them to become varsity athletes. The decision was based upon the following beliefs:

1. If they can't play, it won't be the end of the world.
2. If they really are good enough, they will make it.

Your child may not be talented enough to play. Your children may not be able to make a team or become a starter because they are not talented enough or because they may lack the physical characteristics necessary to beat out 1500 other males or females who may also be interested in playing on the same team or in the same position.

If you were successful, your physical and psychological characteristics may have made it possible to find success. For example, you may have been exceptionally fast, or tall, or fiercely competitive. Perhaps your children will have the same characteristics, but it is possible they will not. My daughter, for example, grew to be only five feet tall. That gave her a competitive handicap in many sports. My son is not exceptionally fast, which handicapped him in some sports and made him less effective in specific positions. It may be possible that your child will not find success because of such shortcomings. There are others.

If a coach has a limited number of spots on a roster, decisions must be made as to who will make the team and who will not. The coach must also decide who will start and how much playing-time each individual will receive. If the coach does not believe your child is talented enough to make the team, to become a starter or to play a significant amount of time, your child may not be afforded the same athletic experiences you enjoyed.

Not all individuals can become varsity high school starters. Fewer can achieve all-conference or all-state honors, and even smaller numbers will achieve distinction as college or professional athletes.

Is it reasonable to expect your child to become a varsity high school athlete? It depends upon the competition for the position and the abilities of your child.

Is it reasonable to expect that your dreams will be shared by your child?

I have often heard it said of some parents that they were trying to achieve their unrealized dreams through their children. In other words, because the individual was not able to achieve the athletic goals that he or she harbored, the child was pushed to achieve the goal for the parent.

Brower (1979) made several biting comments about youth sport parents. He believed that many parents try to live out their athletic fantasies through their children. Bower stated, "They push their children very hard to win because they like to bathe in the reflected glory of their children's victories" (p. 45).

The problem with expecting your child to achieve the same level of athletic success as you, or for your child to realize **your** dreams, is that the dreams may not be your child's! Maybe your child will prefer art or music. Maybe your child will realize that she is not as talented or as gifted in athletics as others in the school are. Perhaps he will grow to be an average citizen and is in reality a less than average athlete. Is it best to prepare our children to pursue their own dreams or to force them to live out ours?

When should your attempts to promote and to protect your child end?

It is natural for us to try to protect our children, and it makes sense that parents will do all that is within their power to give them the best. Parents will do what they feel they must on behalf of their children. This may range from getting involved in attempts to influence high school coaches to crying, pleading and begging a coach to give their child a "break," to going to a school athletic director to overrule a coach's decision or rules. In this chapter, you were given evidence of such activity.

Do parents engage in these behaviors on behalf of their children or on behalf of themselves? Is it appropriate for a child to gain a position because of a parent's influence?

The most difficult youth sport experience I had to endure was my daughter's high school softball career. She started as an outfielder at the varsity level in her junior year and was named co-defensive MVP. She was a part-time starter as a senior, but during both seasons there was ALWAYS discontent amongst parents who had daughters who saw little playing time. I usually sat in the outfield or by myself to watch the games in an effort to escape the negativity. Players believed that they were mistreated, treated unfairly and that they were not given equal opportunities to gain starting spots.

In her senior year of high school, my daughter played less than she and I thought was appropriate. It was most upsetting for both of us. I wanted to protect her and to rush to her aid. I did not. I supported her and tried to help her through her difficult times. I encouraged HER to speak with her coach and for her to express her feelings and to deal with the issues confronting her. That is what I thought best. Wasn't it an appropriate time in life for a young woman to stand up for herself and make her own decisions?

My daughter ended her involvement in organized sport that year with two weeks to go in the season. It was not the end of the world for her or for me, though I must confess that it was an emotional experience for the whole family. It was just sport. She did learn much about herself, about me and about others as a result of the experience. Maybe if I had rushed to her aid and protection, she would have continued to play. What would have been the lesson in that?

If children develop unrealistic views of their talents and abilities, they may cause problems with their coaches and teammates.

Suppose for a moment that your child is a gifted athlete and he or she really does perform better than any other athlete on the team or even within your community. That would be a great thing for your child and would be a source of pride for you. These realities in and of themselves would not cause any problems, except for perhaps jealousy.

The problems develop when you and/or your child begin to believe that their abilities should afford them special attention and benefits. Problems will result when they believe they are above correction and should not be required to do the things required of others on the team or within the community. When such beliefs are present, hubris exists.

If you or your talented child begin to insist on your way and threaten to leave a coach or a team when things do not meet your expectations, perhaps you will be the ones who lose. My feeling has been that my team will be better off without such "stars" and their parents. They are a source of tension and discomfort, especially when things do not go their way.

I once had an incredibly gifted athlete playing on one of my softball teams. She was the best player in the league without a doubt. I found her to be temperamental and at times difficult to work with, but we had no major problems over the course of the season. The next year she had all sorts of problems with the coach, with umpires and with board members. She left games in a huff. Parents threatened coaches and board members. She was not selected to the all-star team in spite of the fact that she was the best player in the league. Nobody wanted to deal with the player or her parents.

The parents came to a board meeting to protest and to give us a "piece of their mind." We were then asked why we wanted to allow the child to be "hurt." They did not see the problems caused by their expectation for special treatment and the belief that her tantrums and outbursts should be overlooked because of her talents on the softball field. She never played softball again.

Is there anything wrong with an individual believing that he or she is a great athlete? No, not unless they begin to believe that they deserve special treatment because of their abilities. Not unless they begin to believe they are more valuable human beings because of their gifts. Trouble begins when these beliefs are fostered and internalized. "Those who do make it in sport are given deference that far exceeds their importance or worth to society" (Lipsyte, 1979, p 15).

Questions and Comments for Coaches

Youth sport coaches are expected by many parents to prepare their children for participation on varsity high school teams.

I was told while coaching a T-Ball team consisting of four year olds that I needed to let a child play in specific positions because he was someday going to play varsity baseball for one of the local high schools. Was that the child's ambition? Would he be good enough? Would he even like baseball by that time? He never did play on the varsity high school team.

What was clear was that this particular set of parents saw participation on the T-Ball team as a link in the chain leading to varsity competition. As unrealistic as this expectation may be, it does exist. In the current study, there was talk about children playing high school soccer several years before the goal was possible. A mother took her five year old off my soccer team because she did not believe that I would help him develop. Parental ambition comes early and sometimes coaches are perceived as being a stumbling block to success even when children are five-years old.

If you are not coaching effectively in the eyes of the parents and/or if you are not placing their children in positions to best highlight their abilities and to facilitate their development, there will be conflict. Again, it is the parents who hold a Power and Performance view toward sport that will be the most confrontational when their children are not placed into a position to succeed or shine. As long as parents have ambitions for their children, coaches may experience conflict with them. You will not be immune.

Verification of a child's abilities is often given when children are selected to all-star and select teams. Pressure is placed upon children to perform so they may be selected, and it is also placed upon coaches. I was once told in a threatening manner by a parent that, "Mary better make the all-star team, or I am going to be one pissed off momma. Marge [her other daughter] was screwed, and I am not going to let it happen to Mary." I am not sure what she would have done if Mary did not make the all-star team that year, but she never did make the high school varsity team.

How may you protect yourself from such conflict? I am not sure you can. These things may help though:

1. Have objective support for your decisions concerning assignment of positions.
2. Be able to provide statistics.
3. Clearly explain what your position is concerning playing time and assignment of position.
4. If you are not concerned with developing high school varsity athletes (as a youth coach), indicate this fact. You may make some parents unhappy, but at least you will have made this fact known. If on the other hand, you believe that the youth sport setting exists for the development of high-level athletes, share this goal with the parents. Whatever your stance, you will upset someone.

As a youth sport coach you may have to deal with large egos. As a high school coach you may have to deal with larger ones.

Because we place value upon excellence in athletics as a society, gifted athletes sometimes believe they are special and that they deserve special treatment. This book is not one that will teach you sport psychology, nor how to deal effectively with problem athletes. I do not believe you do anyone favors by allowing them to believe they are special and as a result are above the expectations that you hold for other athletes. So what can you do when you have an athlete with a large ego?

You have three options. The first is accepting the eccentricities of the athlete and dealing with the behavior as best you can. The second possibility is to try and alter the athlete's perceptions and behaviors. The last is to rid yourself and your program of the athlete. I have used all three approaches.

My experience has been that keeping a problem athlete has **never** paid off unless the athlete was **willing** to change. I coach because I like the sport environment and because I like to see athletes and teams develop. Problem athletes who do not wish to change will not develop, and they will often hamper the development of your team, ultimately stopping it from reaching its potential. The problem athlete will prevent you from enjoying your coaching experience and your other athletes from enjoying theirs.

Why do coaches put up with problem athletes? Often it is because they fear the team will not be as successful, in terms of wins and losses, without them. If this is your primary concern, you likely have a product orientation to sport and adhere to the Power and Performance Model.

The other reason for keeping the problem athlete around is because you wish to help the athlete to metamorphose into a new person. If so, you may be concerned with the process of sport and the Pleasure and Participation Model may be your model of choice. It must be noted here that the athlete may take the pleasure away from everyone else's participation! When I have removed problem athletes from my team, I have **ALWAYS** found that the atmosphere was improved. Often I was surprised to find that the team improved and that we actually did better without the individual.

If winning is more important to you than the quality of the coaching experience and the quality of the participation experience for the others on your team, keep the child with the ego problem who does not wish to change. It is questionable though if you are doing anyone a favor.

Attitudes toward you and your program may be developed long before an athlete participates on your team.

This chapter exposed the fact that high school soccer was not as important to some athletes as the club experience. If you were the club coach, this may be viewed as a positive thing, but I am not sure that the high school coach would agree. Perceptions such as this are developed long before athletes ever set foot on your field or gym floor. It would seem difficult to overcome such perceptions if they have been developed and reinforced within a child between the ages of four and fifteen.

I have heard *parents* speak negatively about junior high and high school coaches **before** the coach even held his or her first practice. Not surprisingly, I also heard their *children* speak unfavorably about the coaches **before** the first practice. It takes some effort and success to overcome these expectations. On the other hand, I have heard parents and children talk about what an honor it would be to play for a specific coach. The point here is that people will come to you with preconceived notions, sometimes reasonable and other times unreasonable. At times you will have to overcome some negative preconceptions of you and your program. You will have to continually earn the positive reputation that you may have developed over the years.

Your job may depend upon young people who are not totally committed to victory.

I have often wondered what it would be like to believe that the performance of my team would dictate whether or not I kept my job. A full-time coach must produce to keep his or her job. I would not take such a job. Winning is not everything to me.

As a high school coach, I was hired as a teacher and could always teach in the event that an administrator believed me to be an inferior coach. Sport was fun for me, an added bonus to my position as a teacher. The athletic environment offered a test that I knew my teams may not always pass. My teams may not always have won, but development took place within the individuals and the teams with which I was associated. As a college coach, I have always felt the same way I did as a high school coach. I am just working with young people who are a bit more mature.

In this chapter, young people stated things like, "Playing high school soccer is not that big of a deal to me." My athletes have also been heard to claim they just played soccer because they liked to play and because it just gave them something to do. These individuals were not **driven** to win. If they played for you, it is doubtful that they would feel any differently. If your main concern is winning, and you place yourself in a position which requires you to win in spite of having individuals on your team that may lack skill, dedication and commitment, I do not understand. If a significant number of your players share these characteristics, how will you assure success for your teams? Would a goal of development be more reasonable?

Everyone is capable of trying to perform to the best of their ability and to work toward improvement. They cannot control the outcome of each contest. World champions are defeated. Tiger Woods loses golf tournaments.

Working for an athletic scholarship to the exclusion of excellence in other areas of life may be a mistake.

College athletic scholarships did not become common until the 1930s in the United States (Sperber, 2000). Sport did not evolve around the existence of athletic scholarships, and I doubt that sport would disappear from our society if they were no longer given.

It is my belief that individuals should play a sport because they enjoy it. If an individual's talents are great enough to result in the offer of an athletic scholarship that is fantastic! However, I do not believe it should be what drives our youth, junior high school and high school athletic participation.

Young athletes should be told to get good grades, to develop interests outside of athletics and to play sport to the best of their ability because it is enjoyable and intrinsically rewarding to do so. The talented will receive scholarships, both academic and athletic. If no scholarships are awarded, perhaps the individual will have achieved a healthy mental and physical state as a result of participation in sport and the full educational process.

7

THE COACH'S SON

According to Justin Warner, a former OSA Board president, "It is rare to get people to coach soccer unless their son or daughter is playing on the team." Although I believe the coaches want to do the right thing and simply want to do the best that they can, they are often accused of favoring their children.

Over the years I heard many parents complain in various sports settings that, "Everyone knows that the coaches' kids play all the time and that they get to play in the [most desirable] positions." I have seen it happen on occasion, but I never felt that the conventional wisdom was a truism. Brian Harvey said when he was seventeen that, "People say coaches favor their kids. Maybe it happens sometime, but I don't see it. Most of the time their kids are good players and they deserve to play."

I also heard the same criticisms concerning parent-coaches in girls' softball. Many times, the coaches could be seen at the softball fields and the parks working with their daughters several hours a week in addition to the normal practice and game functions. I did the same thing with my daughter. Based upon my statistics, the coaches' daughters did perform better than most of the other players in the league. Not surprisingly, the coaches really resented the "you favor your child" comments. The perception that coaches favor their children was prevalent, even if it was not justified.

I was like most other coaches. I coached soccer and other sports because my children wanted to play. Even as I began coaching in the youth sport setting, I was aware that individuals would judge my behavior toward my son. I wanted to avoid improprieties and tried not to treat my son differently than the other kids. It was difficult not to push him extra hard because I wanted him to succeed. It was also hard not to let off of him at times because he was my son. It was a fine line to walk. My son stated at age sixteen, "I don't think that you ever treated me special or differently from anyone else."

Eric was a good athlete, but not a great one. In Dale Burrows' opinion, "Eric's strengths are his ability to control the ball, to see the field and to deliver the ball better than anyone else in his age group. His major weakness is his lack of speed." As a freshman, Eric started on the high school sophomore soccer team that Dale coached. As a sophomore, he started on the district champion junior varsity high school team and at the writing of this book; he was again a starter on the junior varsity team and was a captain.

If he were quicker and more aggressive, I think Eric could be a great player, but he is not. He is a good player that serves a role on the team. He has contributed greatly to the success of his teams over the years. Eric led the Force in assists and was among the top four in scoring every season that I kept track of such information. He was the second leading scorer in 1999-2000.

Because I am cognizant of Eric's limitations, I did not have unrealistic expectations for him. I want Eric to play as long as he wants to play. I have never talked of athletic scholarships, and I never talk about what a good player I was as a means to motivate him. I expect for him to do his best in matches, and that is dependent on his physical and psychological limitations. I tell him when I think he has done well and when I think he did not put forth the effort I expect, but I don't expect him to be perfect. I think he has enjoyed playing over the years.

My expectation is, and has always been, that my son will play primarily for the fun of it. That was why I played. I accept my son's playing behaviors. They are reflective of a developmental perspective of sport and the Pleasure and Participation Model; however, they also reflect an expectation of seriousness in the soccer setting, at least in terms of making an effort to perform.

Eric commented at age sixteen that he plays soccer "because I have played for so many years, I just keep doing it. It gives me something to do."

He did not hold a professionalized orientation toward his participation. In all the years that Eric has played soccer, I think I have only seen him upset about a loss one or two times. He cares about success but is not consumed by it. His attitude reflected mine.

Eric plays soccer primarily because he enjoys it. In fact, he does not like attention in the soccer setting and does not crave recognition, "If people don't know that I am out there, it's O.K. It doesn't matter if I don't score many goals." He plays for his own satisfaction.

Parent Complaints Concerning
My Son's Playing Time

Justin Heller, a Force parent, once told me that Eric received too much playing time with the Force. Though it was suggested that other parents felt the same way, they never confronted me with their beliefs. Will Johnson occasionally suggested that Eric might serve the Force better in another position on the field. He told individuals in Midcity that he was the worst player on the team, but also stated to others that he believed Eric should be on the varsity high school team as a junior. Two other Force parents, Gus Reynolds and Vick Thompson, stated that Eric did not play too much and that the team would not be the same without him.

If Eric's playing time was a problem, it was not a major source of tension for the twelve-year period that I coached. How could a coach really know if his son's playing time really was a problem? If one parent were upset, would it really be problematic?

Eric stated in 2002 that he was unaware that anyone had ever had a concern about his role on the team or over his playing time. Brian Harvey, a former teammate stated, "I never thought that he [Eric] shouldn't start or play all of the time. He always played well." Max Bennett, a Force team member asked, "Who else was better than Eric in that position? Nobody." Brian stated that those who complained about Eric's playing time did so out of personal concerns, "The people that complained were the guys that did not play much and their parents. What could you expect?"

Parents Complain About Their
Children's Playing Time

Parents want to see their children play, and when they don't play as much as they deem appropriate, grumbling and confrontations may be expected. In the spring of the Force's first year, the team traveled to compete in a large tournament in a major city.

In our first match the team's best forward, Kent Craft, was not trying hard in my opinion. As a result, he was taken out of the match. He was given several opportunities when he was placed back in the match to put forth the effort that he was capable of, but for some reason he just didn't. He played little in the second match for the same reason. After the second match, his father accosted me on the way to the parking lot, invaded my personal space and yelled, "If you are not going to play my boy, we'll just get into the car and go home."

This placed me in a difficult situation. If the child went home, his abilities would go with him. On the other hand, if he stayed and did not perform, what good would it do? Another consideration was whether or not it would be worth having the child on the team if he really didn't want to play. I did not have much time to formulate a response. I stated, "I'm sorry that you feel that way, but Kent is not even trying out there, and he doesn't even seem to act like he wants to be here. If he doesn't want to play and you are not comfortable with me, we will all be better off without each other. If Kent doesn't like to play soccer, why should he? If you decide to leave, have a good ride home."

Kent stayed for the next match and played very effectively. We won our pool and lost in the tournament semi-finals. He played as though he wanted to be there. Kent played on the Force for four years and often had days when it seemed like he just didn't feel like playing.

Robert Fishman believed that his son, who was tall, strong, aggressive, and fast, should have been playing more. He made an appointment with me to discuss the matter and told me, "I think you are making a mistake in not playing Jay more than you do. I really think he can help the team if he plays more."

I believed that Jay lacked control on his trapping, had poor control when dribbling and failed to see the field when the ball was in his control. The father apparently could not see that. Robert also looked at the physical attributes of his son (big, strong and fast) as being the important things in the sport. His view of what a good athlete was and what a good soccer player was reflected the characteristics of the Power and Performance Model. Robert was a linebacker on a Division I NCAA football team.

The meeting did not increase the athlete's playing time. I believed that if the boys didn't show what I was looking for at practice, and they didn't show it when they did get into games, it was not there yet. If they couldn't play the way I wanted as competitive team members, they played less than those who could. I think most competitive team coaches feel this way.

Another incident concerning playing time occurred with Bill Davis. His son Terrance injured his ribs in a collision during a Saturday game. On Sunday the Force was going to play with only one substitute. Terrance was still sore. He often stated that he wanted to play striker, and because of the absences, he was going to get his chance. He started the match at forward.

During the first half, he complained that his ribs hurt, and he asked to be taken out. He was put back in a few minutes later because the team needed him on the field. After a brief period of time, he again asked to come out of the game and said that he did not wish to return to it.

After the completion of the game, Bill charged after me across the field with a red face and the veins bulging in his forehead. He demanded to know why his son did not play more in the game. He then aired his frustrations yelling, "He should be playing more than he does anyway and today you hardly played him at all."

I replied, "First of all, Terrance asked not to go back in today. Second, he really isn't that good. He is one of the weaker players on the team, and he has not shown much improvement this season. His ball control is inadequate, and he plays with the ball too much when he does have it. He plays the amount of time I feel to be appropriate." What could the father say to me to make me change my mind?

There were no other emotional discussions concerning playing time with any parents associated with my soccer teams. When playing time (or lack of it) was a problem, parents and/or players would generally ask what must be done in order for the athlete to play more. In most cases a reasonable and specific response was adequate for the parents and/or children. I encouraged parents and players to openly communicate problems and concerns regarding anything.

You should be aware, however, that some parents and some of my college athletes are hesitant to speak with me when they have concerns. Captains and parents who feel more comfortable speaking with me frankly have shared this fact with me. Perhaps my responses are blunt and perceived as unkind or unsympathetic and this discourages some individuals from confronting me.

Justifying Playing Time and Positioning

I always felt that if I could not give a good reason for something I was doing or failing to do, that I probably was wrong for doing it. The fact that people would talk to me about issues was good because that indicated they trusted me. I would be lying if I said they always agreed with me, but my responses indicated to concerned parents that I was reasonable. My willingness to talk and to provide reasonable responses to questions assisted me in doing the right thing. I never relied on my position to excuse my behaviors. I always thought that those shirts that had "I am the Coach" printed on them were funny. What a ridiculous way to justify a decision.

If coaches sincerely attempt to play their athletes where they will best help the team, parents will disagree and conflicts will occur. If coaches play athletes who compete in a manner that best reflects their picture of what an athlete ought to play like, parents will be bothered. Parents have different pictures of what a good athlete is like. Parents are likely to be unhappy with your decisions no matter what you do.

I know my children have both been placed into positions that were out of line with what I thought they were best suited for. I did not agree with the coach. Clearly the coaches saw my children's abilities differently than I did. Sometimes my children spent time on the bench, and I wondered what the coach saw in the child standing out there in my child's spot. What parent would not feel this way?

Ultimately the coach has to decide which athletes play, how much they play and where they play. Objectivity has to be utilized if the right decisions are to be made. Was I objective concerning my son's ability to contribute to the team?

His passing was consistently good concerning control, change of field and breaking down a defense. His receiving skills were excellent. He did not play around with the ball and rarely lost it as a result. He always led the team in assists and those were the things *I* desired in a center half. His defensive play was his major weakness.

In my heart, I wished that he liked to score and had the requisites to be a great forward, but he didn't. I wished that he had the mean streak and anticipation that would have made him a good fullback, but he didn't. I was a keeper, but the position did not interest him. He played where his abilities could best help the team, and I was pleased with his performance.

The parents who criticized his play had a one-dimensional view of what a soccer player should be, and it very much resembled a football player. He used his abilities and talents well and functioned in the position as I desired. Objectively, he deserved the position and playing time he received. He was not asked to join the Olympic team, but no one else was either. He is a good player, but the opinion of what a good player is depends upon the observer's knowledge of the game and preferred style of play.

He Has Always Liked the Game

Eric's fondness for the sport of soccer was expressed very early in his life. In the first grade he was asked to draw a picture about his favorite activity. He drew a soccer field complete with all the field markings. By that time he had traveled with his family to the ocean, gone to amusement parks, played T-ball and done a variety of other things, but he picked soccer as his favorite activity.

In the ninth grade, Eric was asked to write about his favorite activity. He wrote:

> I am the number one tennis player on our tennis team, so I guess I am pretty good at that. I do well in bowling too. I won the city championship. My favorite activity though is soccer. I do well in soccer and I'll probably play on the sophomore team at Pen. The main reasons that I like soccer best are because my family travels together to my games and I spend a lot of time with my dad during soccer activities. He coaches the team.

Eric never meant for me to see the assignment.

Eric continued to play for the Force after I stopped coaching the team. He was fifteen at the time. To him, it did not matter if his dad coached, "I just play because I like to play. It does not matter if you coach." He learned to play under my guidance and continued to play of his own volition. I could not have hoped for more.

Chapter 7 Observations

Questions and Comments for Parents

How you respond to your child's coach is your choice.

How you respond to ineffective coaching in the youth sport environment is your choice. Following are two questions that may guide you. What can you do to make the situation better? How can you avoid making it worse?

If you believe that your child's coach favors his or her own child by playing him or her at a specific position or by playing him or her too much, you are not alone. The coach is in a position to make decisions about who plays, how much and where. There is always the possibility that the coach may make bad decisions. Who are you to complain? You are not coaching, so why even get upset about such a situation? What good would being upset do?

Parents are often upset when they believe their children should be playing more, or when they believe that their children should be in a different position. I often felt the same way when others coached my children in youth sport, in junior high and in high school settings. I never confronted a coach. If my child were one of the best, how would a coach benefit by not playing him or her? Maybe the coach sees something differently than I in another child (the one playing) or even in my own child (the one not playing).

When I did not coach, it was time for my children to experience a separate athletic reality, something different than I could provide. The world is filled with separate realities in the realms of sport, religion, culture and so on. You cannot avoid them.

The only thing I might suggest for parents who have a problem with their child's position or playing time is to respectfully ask the coach for an objective measure supporting the coach's decision concerning who plays, where and when. In other words, what is the batting average, the rate of errors, assists per game, turnovers, etc.? It is astounding how few coaches, even high school coaches, use statistics to make decisions related to playing time and positioning. They would save themselves much grief if they would.

If the coach has no data and operates on intuition, at least you may have planted the seeds for reform. Being angry, confrontational or emotional in such a situation won't often help anything. I can share with you that I suffered for my children when they were hurt in similar circumstances and was often tempted to "tell the coach like it was." I never saw how that would change a coach's mind or make the world a better place. Is your child's playing time or position on the field really so important that it should cause ill feelings, fights or even death?

Is your child really an All-American?

Few children will grow up to be All-Americans. Perhaps realizing this fact will help you when playing time is an issue. I have never seen a **truly gifted** player sitting on the bench on any team unless a game was out of reach. It is hard for us as parents to see our children as average or below average in any way. Most children are capable of mediocrity (average ability), not giftedness (true greatness).

We love our children and want the best for them. Focus on the achievement of your child's potential rather than on an assumption of superiority. Help them to become what they can be, not fail at becoming something they are incapable of becoming. Try to objectively assess your child's current abilities. Make the most of the current situation and perhaps a better situation can be realized tomorrow.

Questions and Comments for Coaches

How do you convince parents that you make sound decisions concerning playing time and positioning?

Parents want to see their children play. Most want to see them play throughout the whole game. Some want to see their children play in the most prestigious positions (examples: pitcher, striker, point guard). How can you play all children in these positions and have a successful team?

When I coached T-Ball, I allowed all the kids play in all positions. The team won the city championship. When I coached older children and the players pitched during games, only those who could throw the ball over the plate were allowed to play in the pitcher's position. Similarly, players had to have a good arm to play third base.

An objective assessment of each athlete's ability to play a particular position was necessary. As a result, I conducted tryouts for all positions. All players pitched 100 pitches and balls and strikes were recorded. Players were hit ground balls and asked to throw to first base from all positions on the infield. Ground balls missed were recorded, the velocity of the throw and its accuracy were judged and recorded. The information was shared with the children and parents; children were accordingly assigned to positions and the season went forward.

Statistics were recorded and shared on a regular basis. Children were allowed to practice at positions they hoped to play, but they did not start there until they could perform better than the child who was starting. By using this procedure, I had little trouble with parents concerning playing time or positioning.

During twelve years of coaching soccer I received three angry complaints concerning playing time, a pretty remarkably low number, I think. I cannot recall an emotional incident concerning playing time or positioning from my youth baseball (4 seasons), softball (5 seasons), boys' basketball (2 seasons), or girls' basketball (5 seasons) coaching experiences.

I believe being objective and having support for my decisions helped me avoid problems. I used the same process as a high school coach (two years football, four years soccer, six years basketball, five years volleyball, four years track) and now as a college coach (8 years volleyball). My best advice to you is to be objective and share your information. It will cut down on playing time and positioning concerns/problems. At the very least, providing objective information will be a means to justify your decisions.

8

THE KIDS

In this chapter, vignettes concerning several of the children who participated on the Force and Strikers are presented. In *Minority Participation in
Overland Soccer*, information concerning minority participation in soccer
within the community is recounted. *The Foreigners* primarily concerns a
Mexican-born child who played with the Force United and how cultural
differences resulted in conflict and his ultimate departure from the team.
Role Conflict and Limited Practice Dates recounts how many of the
children, as well as the coach and parents, felt torn between the demands
of competing roles. *From Early Dominance to Later Mediocrity* illustrates
the frustrations associated with the transformation of a child from a
dominant player in early childhood into an average player by the time he
reached his mid-teens. *The Cut* is a sad account of my decision to cut a
player, the difficulty of the decision, and the consequences of the act. *The
Unwilling Participant* recounts the problems caused by a team member
who exhibited no interest in participating in organized soccer.

Minority Participation in Overland Soccer

A total of forty-one children played for the Strikers or the Force during
the time I served as coach. Eight of them were minorities: two were Black,
one was Indian, one was Native American and four were Hispanic. Two of

the Hispanic children played during the first season of the Striker's existence and never played soccer again.

The public schools of Overland have a Hispanic population nearing forty percent and five percent of the students are Black.[1] Taken as a whole, the proportion of minorities playing for the Force and Strikers did not reflect the percentage of minorities in the community. The curious under-representation of minorities in youth soccer was also observed in a study conducted by Ewing and Seefeldt (1996) who found that Hispanic and Black children were underrepresented. The reason for the under-representation of minorities was unclear.

Data concerning minority participation in youth soccer were not obtained by the Overland Soccer Association. There was discussion as to the benefits and/or negative perceptions associated with tracking minority participation at board meetings. Some believed that tracking the data would be perceived as racist, while others suggested that it would be one way to encourage participation. The OSA decided not to track participation by ethnic/racial background.[2]

Jesus Davila, a resident of Overland, stated that the number of minority children was low in soccer because of the commitment of time required by parents, a lack of understanding by the parents as to how to sign their children up, and because of the cost. Since he was aware of the cost associated with participation in club soccer, he half jokingly commented, "Soccer is definitely not a sport for the lower socio-economic classes. I think I will have to open a bank account for my son so he can play when he gets older."

Juan Gonzales, a former OSA board member, believed that cost was one of the factors that kept Hispanic children from playing. Juan told me the cost "has been a big problem, but it has been getting worse.[3] Soccer is becoming a sport for the rich." But he believed that, perhaps more importantly, cultural differences were influential:

> White coaches have difficulty understanding the Mexican-American children and their parents. That makes the parents and children uncomfortable. The lack of communication results in an environment of distrust. It is also very clear that the Hispanics are disliked because of things they do in their culture. For example, they say that we are obnoxious. When my team plays the fans bring drums and horns and make a lot of noise. When we score, we chant and make a lot more noise. One woman in [a large

city] said, "Why don't you people just shut up." That's what it's like here in Overland, too: "You people."

The Foreigner

A child benefits from participation in youth sport in at least two ways: making friends and having fun (Eitzen & Sage, 1997; Ewing & Feltz, 1991; Gould & Horn, 1984; Gould, Feltz, Horn & Weiss, 1982). If children do not make friendships and they do not have fun, they will eventually quit the sport. One of the players recruited to play for the Force was born in Mexico and came from a culture that was very different from that of the parents and other players on the team. An inability to make close friends on the team, a decrease in the amount of playing time and possibly cultural differences led to a decrease in the pleasure he received from his participation on the team. He chose not to participate on the team for a fourth year.

In the fall of 1995, the Force was only able to sign thirteen players to contracts. The number of players would be inadequate for successful participation over a full competitive season and for tournament events. I contacted Juan Gonzales to see if he knew of any players who might like to play. Juan was familiar with many of the Mexican-American families who played soccer in the area. He served as a soccer official for the OSA and an adult soccer league referred to in the soccer community as the "Mexican League."

Juan arranged for me to contact Raul Sanchez about having his son try out for the Force. Considering the cultural animosity Juan described, I was pleased he was willing to help, but I couldn't help but wonder why:

> I knew that you treated people well and that you cared for your players. I also knew that it did not matter to you what color someone was. I respected you as a coach and a person, and I believed that you had a lot of character.

Richard Sanchez lived in the city of El Centro, located thirty miles from Overland. When I called to speak with Raul (Richard's father) I found that English was not the family's first language, Spanish was. The Sanchez family was from Mexico and had immigrated to the United States to find work and a better life. The adult males found work in the oil fields, and the family had little discretionary income.

Soccer was a family affair in the Sanchez household. Richard's older brothers and several cousins played soccer in the adult "Mexican League." His father coached the "Mexican League" team from El Centro and had played as a child and young adult in Mexico. There was no organized youth soccer league in El Centro. The city did not have a population large enough to support one.

After an arranged tryout, it was clear that Richard would be an important addition to the Force. He was very skilled, but his parents were concerned about the costs associated with Richard playing on the team. The Force's officers voted to waive the $125 per season fee, and Raul agreed to pay the $25 monthly dues to help cover the team's expenses for Richard's participation.

Getting Richard to and from matches and practices was a problem. The adults in the family worked late, so the agreement was to try to get Richard to one practice a week. I agreed to take him to away matches with my family and allow Richard to stay in our hotel room on overnight trips. Richard occasionally stayed at my house in order to make early matches on some Saturday mornings. Richard's family contributed $10 per day when the team traveled out of town. After away trips, I would drive Richard home or meet his family part way to El Centro.

He traveled throughout Texas, New Mexico and Colorado. He also traveled to Minnesota and through several other American states. Trips lasted as long as ten days. At age seventeen, when Richard was asked what he remembered most about his experience with the Force, he recalled the "summer camps we did and the tournament in Minnesota. I got to know places that I'd never been to."

Richard's father believed that having him play on the team was a good experience. He stated through an interpreter, "It made it possible for him to play soccer, and he could not do that here. He also got to see a lot of places with the team's travels."

Richard's mother, Maria, cried when her ten year old left for the first two over-night trips. She said, "I cried because it was my little boy that was leaving to go on long trips." Richard's parents rarely attended his soccer matches. Richard knew that his parents could not often attend games but said it did not really bother him.

Although Richard spent a lot of time with me, he never really opened up or seemed completely comfortable. He had no real friends on the team. He was the only Mexican on the team, his English was not very good, and he came from a different culture than the other players on the Force. He recalled:

> I felt uncomfortable at first because I didn't know you or anyone else very well. I felt better as I got to know you, though. It really wasn't that hard to play [on your team]. Soccer was my favorite sport, so it made it easier. I had a lot of fun.

Richard spent three years as a part of the Force. As the roster size grew larger, his playing time decreased. Because he did not come to practice at all the third year, he did not fit as well with the team tactically. He demonstrated frustration with his performance, as did other players on the team, and he did not return for a fourth year.

In the summer of 1999, after a year away from the team, I asked Richard if he would like to rejoin the team. He stated that he would like to play, but, "Only if one of my other friends from El Centro can play too." This suggested that he felt alienated during his previous play with the Force and that he did not wish to repeat the experience. He said, "It wasn't any fun not having any friends on the team." During his last season with the team he believed that other players started to talk to him less often and believed that they put him aside during conversations. When I asked him if he was also partly responsible for the fact that he was not close to other players, he acknowledged that it "was a little of both."

The whole time that Richard was on the team, I wondered if I was "using" him. I knew that the team needed him over the first two years, and he was vital to our success. I observed that he never really made close friends on the team and that he really came along just to play soccer. There was little I could do to make him fit in better, and I always felt a bit of guilt about that. If he had not been a good player, I don't think he would have been on the team at all, so in a sense I used him. I always tried to justify it to myself by rationalizing that he got to do things he wouldn't have done if he were not on the team.

I take some comfort from Richard's attitude as he reflects on the experience: "I think really that the experience was good for me." I asked him if he would let his children do the same thing when they were ten years old; his response was, "I would let them do it if they wanted to. I'm sure."

As a junior in high school, Richard still participated in soccer. There was no team at his high school, so he played in the "Mexican League" with his family and friends from El Centro. He was on schedule to graduate from high school and worked part-time in an auto parts store. He worked because it was the only way that he could have a truck to drive. He hopes that one day he will be able to go to college and play soccer.

Role Conflict and Limited Practice Dates

Role conflict occurs when individuals must serve in a variety of roles that conflict with one another (Coakley, 1994; Getzels & Guba, 1954; Leonard, 1998). In many cases, the time required to fill a role successfully results in decreased effectiveness in one or more other roles. Role conflict often occurs within teacher/coaches (Bain & Wendt, 1983; Chu, 1984; Massengale, 1980; Sage, 1987). It also occurs in student/athletes (Adler & Adler, 1985).

Today children are often placed into multiple organized programs by their parents. Some believe that American children are involved in too many activities of an organized nature (Elkind, 1981; Popke, 2000). Youth sport is one example. Research into the extent and consequences of role conflict occurring in youth sport is conspicuously absent from the literature. Also missing in the literature is a presentation of the extent and consequences of role conflict upon coaches and parents involved in youth sport. The players and parents associated with the Strikers and Force experienced such conflict, and I did also.

Coaches and children who are committed to one role, such as soccer player or soccer coach, want practices to be conducted with a high degree of seriousness and regularity. Power and Performance adherents desire a professionalized atmosphere, one that encourages excellence, optimal team and individual performance (Hill & Hansen, 1988; Hill & Simons, 1989). Goals such as these cannot be achieved without regular attendance and the requisite degree of seriousness/commitment during practice. Problems occur when committed parents and children are affiliated with teams whose players and coaches are not fully committed to the role of soccer player or soccer coach (Pleasure and Participation adherents). Such conditions were present throughout the course of this study.

Most children who played on the Strikers and Force enjoyed a variety of activities in addition to playing soccer. Several players participated in baseball, football, basketball, track and field, cross-country and choir, **all during the same year.** Some were regularly involved in church activities. Many players attended their siblings' activities, such as dance recitals and choir performances. When the players were very young, they often missed practices and games to attend birthday parties. There were times when players did not attend practice or scheduled matches because they had to study for exams or to complete school assignments.

It always bothered me when players missed practice or matches. I often did not know who would be at practice or for how long. There were days that I organized a practice that focused on midfield play and only one of the five midfielders would show up. I tried to accomplish as much as possible with my teams, but there was always so much more that could have been done if all of the players were dedicated solely to soccer. It bothered me for all twelve years, but I believe that soccer should be a part of life for the players and for me, not the most important part of it. A sport should not be life for anyone.

Though I wanted all the players at all soccer events, I had to accept their absences. How could I say to myself and to others that there are things more important than soccer and then be upset when they missed a practice or game for something important to them?

There were several days the Strikers and Force played with no substitutes and there were some instances when the teams had to play short-sided. My view of the place of soccer in the players' lives assisted me in accepting problems with attendance at practice and matches, but it was never easy. Juggling soccer around multiple activities was not easy for the kids either.

Seth Weber is a good example. He was an outstanding soccer player from the time he was five years old. He was an assertive player, was fleet of foot and had a great shot. Jesus Davila, an assistant coach for the Force in the 1999-2000 soccer year said, after watching Seth accelerate quickly past an opponent to win a ball, "That's not fair." Seth was very fast.

Seth played with the Strikers and Force for a total of thirteen years, from age five to age seventeen. He played for eleven years under my guidance.

His parents signed him up for soccer originally because, according to his father Jeff, "It is something to keep him busy and the running will help with his other sports." Jeff had no experience playing soccer and was not a soccer fan.

Jeff played football and baseball as a child and teen. Jeff's interests had always been with football and baseball. He understood the games well and said on several occasions that he hoped Seth would play football and baseball in high school. Seth played T-ball and baseball each spring from the time he was four until the end of his sophomore year of high school. During baseball season, Seth frequently missed portions of soccer practices and games in order to participate in baseball-related activities.

Seth played soccer to the exclusion of football until he reached sixth grade. In Overland, youths could play organized tackle football through the Boys and Girls Club from fourth through sixth grade. He was torn during those years as to whether to play football or to continue with soccer. Seth's father, his friends, and the community at large placed a higher value on Seth's role as a football player. Football coaches required attendance at practice five days a week, even in the fourth grade. Practices generally lasted two hours each. People in Overland took their football seriously. If Seth played soccer and football, there would be conflicts.

I was not happy about the prospect of losing Seth as a player to another sport. He was an important player on the team, and I was fond of him and his parents. I had known them since Seth was five years old. He had traveled to events with my family, was a friend of my son's, and he came to my home to play on many occasions. He was nearly a part of the family to me. His father once told me "Steve, Seth will never leave your team. He cares too much about you."

Once Seth began to play football in the fall, he came to portions of soccer practices and matches whenever possible. Often he missed entire practices or matches in order to attend football practices or games. This scenario began in the fall of his sixth grade year and continued through junior high. Junior high school basketball, cross-country, track and choir caused additional conflict with soccer activities.

Jeff never encouraged Seth to choose one or two sports to focus on. "I think Seth should do it all while he is young. When he gets to high school maybe he'll have to choose one or two sports, but there's really no hurry now." As Seth entered the 10th grade, he still believed that it was too early to specialize. In his junior year, Seth played soccer with the Force in the fall and spring, as well as varsity football. He did not play high school soccer.

How did Seth feel about participating in so many activities?

> Sometimes it bothered me because I could never really give anything my all. I didn't have the strength or commitment to do it. I think I could have done better if I just focused on one sport, but I did enjoy all of them.

When asked why he continued to do so many activities for so many years, Seth stated, "My dad wanted me to do them all. If I had my choice, I would not have played football. I would rather have played just baseball and soccer."

I asked Seth if he would have his child do as many things as he did, he responded, "With my kids, I'll put them in a lot of things so that they can see what they're like. If they wanted to give something up, I'd let them. I'm pretty worn out." Seth gave up soccer the week that I last interviewed him for this book. He will play varsity football for Pen high next year as a cornerback.

There were ten other Force and Strikers players over the years that *excelled* in soccer and other sports at the junior high school level. Seth's struggles with juggling multiple sports and activities were similar to theirs. Concerning the conflicts caused by participation in multiple activities, Justin Heller, a Force parent, stated with a sense of aggravation:

> I have to accept that some of the players will miss practices, but those of us who get our kids to practice every day are punished in a way. We have to sacrifice to get them here, and our kids have to give up other things to be here. It has a negative effect on how well the team does. It is one of the frustrating things about being on this team.

During the competitive season, practices were generally held only twice a week. I could not conduct more than two practices a week because I also coached volleyball during the fall season and softball during the spring season. I believed holding even one more practice a week would make the time strain unbearable for me. Allocating more time to soccer seemed like a good idea, but I could not do so without further decreasing my effectiveness in other roles.

There were many days I did not want to go to practices because of the pressure and stress associated with my job. There were frustrations associated with missing my daughter's school and sport-related activities and there was fatigue. Usually, once I got to practices, I felt a lot better. Even when I was in a bad mood at the start of practice, it was rare that I didn't leave in a better frame of mind.

The parents of many players experienced role conflict as well. It was most difficult on those with more than one child actively involved in sports. Some children were sent to practice in car pools because of conflicts caused by the activities of their siblings. Often Strikers' players missed practices because parents could not arrange to get the child there. Players on the Force and Strikers frequently traveled out of town with the families of other team members because their parents had to attend events with their other children.

At the end of many seasons I heard parents make statements similar to that made by Terri Reynolds: "I am looking forward to the end of the season so that I can stop running around. I have too much to do, and I never seem to get to rest." It was not unusual for both of her children to practice at different sites on the same day in different parts of town.

Throughout the period of this study, practice time was primarily spent upon technical (skills) and tactical (strategic) instruction. It was unreasonable to believe that significant improvements in a player's conditioning would take place without adequate frequency (how often), intensity (how demanding) and duration (how long) of training, so I spent little time on distance running and sprint training. As a high school coach, I spent a lot of practice time putting my players through conditioning drills. There was a difference in the high school setting and the youth soccer setting because of the inherent structure of public school schedules. With high school teams I could train athletes every day.

From the time the children reached age eleven, parents often complained that the team should be better conditioned. Force parent Justin Flowers' comment was reflective of these concerns:

> The team does great for the first half and then they seem to run out of gas. I think if the boys were in better physical condition that they would be more successful. They play good soccer, but if the kids were in better condition, I can't help but think that they could compete at a higher level.

Another parent, Charlie Harvey, suggested that the team practice more often in order to allow more time for conditioning. My feelings were different. I was not able to spend more time than I did in soccer-related activities, and I did not have everyone at all the practices as it was. The players missed a lot of practices because they were involved in so many other activities.

The only way I could have justified practicing four or five days a week was to make soccer the most important thing in my life and for the parents to make soccer the most important thing in their children's lives. I was not willing to do that and neither were most of the players or their parents. Some, like Charlie, would have been glad to make such a commitment, at least verbally. I didn't believe that his son Brian, who had frequently missed the practices that were arranged because of his other activities (band, choir, church, basketball, tennis, cross country), would make four practices a week. It was a bit of a no-win situation.

Perhaps I could have made attendance mandatory for all scheduled practices, but I would risk losing players who would be forced to choose other activities over soccer. There were not enough potential soccer players in Overland to risk losing the few I had.

Interestingly, in the spring of 2002, I was speaking with Charlie about my life without coaching soccer. The conversation turned to the current Force team's performance. I observed that the team could do better, but from what the kids said, people miss a lot of practice so they are not as well prepared as they could be. Charlie's comment was, "If you would have taken care of the problems with attendance five years ago, they wouldn't exist now." He still held me accountable for players not showing up to practices. Perhaps I was.

Practices for the Strikers and Force never exceeded one and a half hours. When so little time was available for practice, I never believed I could have done more than I did. It seemed unreasonable to practice for three hours a day, so the conditioning was what I let go. It was a decision that parents did not always agree with, but that was my decision, and I would make the same decision concerning practice structure if I had to do it all over again.

The team could possibly have been better conditioned if I chose to make that the focus of my practices, but perhaps they would have been behind where they were tactically and technically. How can you have it both ways without devoting more time to practice? Do you lose because you are unfit or because you are inferior tactically and technically? Pick your poison. The truth was that I masked conditioning in the drills and controlled scrimmage activities (economy of training). The parents did not understand the value of this step, even though it was explained to them.

Role conflict negatively affected the quality of the practice experience for the players, the ability for me to maximally train the athletes, and the parents' ability to follow their children's soccer activities. It was the source of many conflicts among the parents, the children, and me.

Early Dominance, Later Mediocrity

Some children mature more rapidly than others, giving them a physical advantage over other children their age in sports and especially in youth soccer (Malina, 1996; Magill & Anderson, 1996). As they age, later-maturing children begin to catch up and often surpass the early-maturing individuals in performance (Malina, 1996). One individual who played on the Strikers and Force was an early-maturing child who found early dominance and later became simply a good club player.

At the ages of four and five, Dave Burrows dominated the youth league he played in. He was bigger than most players he competed with. He was faster and considerably more aggressive. He had learned to go full speed ahead as long as he was in the match, to kick the ball to open space and outrun opposing players to the ball. Because he played more aggressively than the other children, they would often lose the ball out of fear of being hit.

Dave scored goals at an amazing rate: as many as seven a match. When he played goalkeeper, he could block a shot, dribble the length of the field and score. I saw him do this on several occasions. He was a one-person team. At age fifteen, Dave didn't remember much about playing at age four and five, but he said, "I do remember scoring a lot of goals and winning all the time."

Dave has a brother, Chuck, who is two years older than he is. His father coached Chuck's soccer team, and the sport was a very important part of his family's activities. Chuck was one of his team's key players. Because Dave's family was involved heavily in soccer, he was more familiar with the skills of the game and had a better understanding of how to be successful than did many other players his age. He played with and against his older brother, which caused him to become more aggressive than many of his peers. According to Dale, "I think that when he first started playing soccer, Dave wanted to be the best. That's why he played so hard and did so well. He was around soccer a lot too, and that helped him out."

When Dave joined the Strikers at the age of six, it was a time that the field's size and the number of field players were increased. The playing periods were also lengthened. All of these factors decreased Dave's effectiveness. The ball was not near him as often, and the limitations imposed by his endurance slowed him down considerably. I began to insist that Dave occasionally attempt to pass the ball to teammates and that he play in assigned positions. All of these factors, combined with losses that Dave was unaccustomed to, were a source of frustration for him. There were days that he would cry out of frustration after a loss. According to his dad:

> Dave *was* frustrated. He heard so much about Chuck [his brother] and how good of a player he was. Dave wanted to be as good as he was. I think he was trying to win my approval by being a good player, and when he started to lose his edge, it really got to him.

In spite of the obstacles, Dave was still the best player on the team. He was still big, fast and aggressive. He recalled:

> The thing that frustrated me then was being so competitive [wanting to win so much] and then having referees make bad calls. I remember still being pretty good when I was six and seven. I still thought I was a pretty good player then.

By the age of eight, other players on the Strikers began to surpass Dave in terms of speed and skill. They began to push him off the ball. The kick and run strategy that he used to his advantage was no longer effective: the defenders could now catch him. He made some tactical and technical improvement, but he started to become simply a good player. His dominance had ended. What were his feelings at that time?

> There were other really good players on the team then, and they started to get better than me, and that really frustrated me. I remember that I didn't do as well as I thought that I should do; I didn't score many goals any more. But in my mind, I thought I could do better when I got older.

His father recalled:

> I had several talks with him. I told him he didn't have to be the best player in the world. You know, there are times that you can't be the best.

As a member of the Force, Dave contributed to the team's success, but no longer stood out. He had lost some of his touch on the ball, and he no longer was fast compared to most players. His speed was less than average. His father noted:

He was starting to grow fast and his feet were huge. It was going to take a while for him to get his coordination and touch back. We had a lot of talks like that. I wanted him to know that I did not love him any less because he didn't excel in soccer.

During the years Dave played on the Force, he participated in a number of sports and he found success in them. Dale stated:

Right now [as Dave entered the ninth grade], the football coaches are blowing smoke up his butt. He's 6'3" and filling out. They have him starting at tight end and safety. Because he has not done really well in soccer, I expect him to come home some day and say that he's going to give up soccer to focus on basketball, which he loves, too. It really surprises me that he keeps playing soccer. In fact, this summer he played on three indoor soccer teams when he stayed in Montana.

Betty, Dave's mom, stated that same season, "Soccer is still his first love."

When asked why he continued to play soccer, even though he no longer excelled in it, Dave stated:

I don't get as frustrated any more. It got to be a lot more fun as we played on the Force. There were a lot of good players. There wasn't as much pressure on me, and it was a lot of fun to go on our trips.

When asked why he had changed his attitude to better reflect the Pleasure and Participation Model, he responded, "You helped me a lot and to see that I should just enjoy playing. I just love to play. My dad helped a lot too."

As this book was completed, Dave was a member of the high school junior varsity basketball team and the varsity football team. He played soccer for the Force, but not for the high school. This was in spite of the fact that he served as a back-up goalkeeper for the varsity his freshman year. He chose not to play high school soccer because of conflicts with the coach.

This story is not only about early success and later mediocrity. It is also one of a child's adoption of a product emphasis (Power and Performance) and the evolution of a process emphasis (Pleasure and Participation) as he aged. The evolution was encouraged by his coach, his parents and most likely the his own awareness of the soccer environment and what was really important in his own mind.

The Cut

Some children participate in sports even if they are not big, fast or highly skilled. They do not stand out in any significant way, yet they find satisfaction in playing (Martens, 1978). As teams strive toward becoming more competitive, these children are sometimes cut from a team and denied continued participation in their chosen activity.

Youth sport researchers have stated that cutting youths from sport teams is one of the most serious problems in youth sport (Orlick & Botterill, 1975). The experience of being cut from a team can be painful for the child, but it can also be painful for the parents and coach. This fact is not often acknowledged.

John Reese was a member of the Strikers from the age of six until the age of nine; he was an original member of the Force. He was one of the two smallest players on the team and had less than average speed. He was never a behavior problem and was both attentive and hard working. John's parents were supportive of his play and of my coaching. His mother served as the team manager for most of the years when John was involved with the Strikers and Force.

John was not a spectacular player, but he was steady and dependable. He contributed to the Striker's state championship and in many games with the Force. He always gave his all at practices and games as a member of the Strikers and the Force and demonstrated his joy in being in the soccer environment, at least until he turned thirteen.

At age thirteen, John saw his playing time with the Force decrease significantly. There were many others on the team who were bigger, stronger and faster than John. Some were not as skilled as John, but they made more of an impact on games than he did. The Force rarely played weak opponents, and in some matches he would play as little as ten minutes. He began to appear unhappy at practices and at matches. He became less attentive, and his effort decreased significantly. When asked what made him feel so low, he replied, "I am not getting to play enough." At age sixteen, he admitted:

> It seemed like the other players on the team were stepping up their play and improving a lot more than I was and that made me feel bad, like I couldn't play very well. In a way, that made it no fun. I understand now why I wasn't getting to play very much then, but at the time it was very hard.

The change in John's behavior weighed heavily on me. I knew that the problem had to be the limited playing time. I couldn't blame him. What fun could it have been practicing all the time and not getting to play much in the matches? There were days that I actually hurt because he seemed so sad and disappointed, but what was I supposed to do? Winning isn't everything, but it does mean something, and I felt that I had to play the kids who could perform better a greater amount of time. Playing all players equally did not seem to be a viable option in the competitive club situation.

The following July, after playing for the Strikers and Force for eight years (sixteen seasons), I cut John from the team after tryouts. How could I do such a thing? There were many players who tried out for the team that at the time seemed to have so much more potential than John.

The problem for me was that I liked John, and I was close to his family. I wanted badly to keep him on the team, but his playing time may have gone down even more, and I didn't think that causing him pain for another year would be a good thing. If I didn't feel that keeping him on the team would cause him additional hurt, I would not have cut him. Though I knew John would be deeply hurt if I cut him, I felt that it would be less painful in the long run for him, his family and for me. After struggling with the decision for a period of weeks, I decided not to offer John a contract. John cried, his mother cried and I cried. John did not play soccer that year. He stayed involved, however, in choir and ice hockey.

The following year, John tried out for the Force once again. It surprised me. There was an open spot on the roster, but before it was offered to him, John was asked if he would be content with playing as little as ten minutes a match. He said he would. When asked why, John responded, "I realized how important just being on the team was to me." His mother added:

> Being cut was not going to stop him from trying to play soccer again. He realized afterward that the team was the important thing to him. The team [and his teammates are] the reason he is still playing today [as a junior in high school]. Some kids play because they want to be number one. Others just want to be a part of the team. That's what John is like. The team did well, and he was happy to be a part of it all. Being cut showed him how much the team meant and how much you meant to him. There was no way anyone could have stopped him from trying out the year after being cut.

As this book was completed, John was a starter and co-captain on the Junior Varsity soccer team. He continued to play with the Force as well. He always seems to give his all.

What turned this hurtful event into a positive one was the opportunity for the child to regain a place on the team. A second opportunity was provided. What would have been the outcome if another participation opportunity were not available?

It must be noted as well that tears were shed when this event was discussed in the preparation of this book. The feelings of love, betrayal, forgiveness and hurt are still carried around by all who were touched by this event.

The coach of the Midcity Fire, after reviewing this book stated:

> It seems very convenient to rationalize that cutting this kid was really in his best interest. You seem to judge other coaches by a different standard than yourself. If you do it, it's only because you care about the kids. When someone else does the same thing, they are only concerned about winning.

What was the truth?

The Unwilling Participant

In the early years of this study, children who seemed to be participating only because of their parents' interest misbehaved frequently. As Passer (1996) noted, before children reach the age of seven, organized games (youth sport) are not extensions of what they would do anyway. The fact that they do participate is a testament to the power and influence that adults have over their children.

It is possible that children may find a sport enjoyable once they become involved (Magill & Anderson, 1996). However, it is possible that if they do not have an interest in the sport before initial participation, that the experience will be negative (Aicinena, 1992).[4] Coaches charged with helping such a child fit into a team in this situation can experience frustration and difficulties as well. The following experience illuminates the difficulties and frustrations caused by a child who was an unwilling participant.

Though it was not a part of the activities planned for the day, Trey spent a portion of each practice playing in a dirt pile, running around the area adjacent to the practice field and disrupting the planned practice activities. The parents were not around to help monitor or control his behavior. They dropped him off and drove away. For six seasons (from age seven to age nine), Trey participated on the Strikers.

I always wondered why Trey was on the team. He never once acted like he wanted to play. He did not respond to my attempts to improve his skill or knowledge. He was an unwilling participant. I treated him as kindly as possible. I was as patient as I could be. I used every method I could think of to improve his behavior and interest him in soccer activities. I refused to yell at him. It wasn't his fault that he was dropped off at the practice field with no motivation to play.

The Strikers were a recreational soccer team, and I had the responsibility of taking anyone that was placed on the team. I wasn't going to try and run the child off of the team. Without question, he tested my patience and my character.

Trey stopped playing for the Strikers late in his sixth season with the team. We were in a tournament championship match and the rules of recreational soccer required that we play all of our kids in a minimum of one half of every match. Late in the match he was playing as an outside defender. A ball landed twenty feet away from him. He didn't move to kick it, and an opposing player who was sixty feet away ran to it, dribbled by a motionless Trey and proceeded to score the winning goal. Trey didn't even turn to watch the player dribble by him. He stared at the grass in front of him.

I turned away from the field in an effort to control my anger and disappointment to compose myself. As I did, Trey's dad came to the sideline and said, "Son, you are supposed to run and kick the ball when it comes around you." I snapped inside. I stated without raising my voice, "If he doesn't know that after playing for me for three years, I doubt that he ever will."

I never said anything to Trey and never even displayed my emotions to him. The event was not discussed after the game, but that was the last time I saw him at a practice or match. I am sure that his father was offended.

Trey never played soccer again. His father coached a baseball team that Trey played on the following year. Mr. Adams believed that baseball was good for Trey, "Trey and I had a real good time in baseball. He liked it a lot."

Perhaps the slower pace of the sport of baseball was better suited to Trey. Maybe because his dad was involved as a coach, he was more attentive. Maybe I was not a good coach for Trey. Perhaps he never wanted to play soccer.

Chapter 8 Observations

Questions and Comments for Parents

Organized activities may be good for our children, but when is enough, enough?

Many of us believe that to be good parents, we should place our children into organized activities (Coakley, 2001). In this chapter you read about children who were involved in organized activities involving athletics, church and school virtually every day throughout the year. When is enough, enough?

For many parents that point is reached when they are running around with their children so much they cannot rest. It may come when they can no longer pay to involve their children in additional activities. The parents' inability to get their children to activities will eventually act as a restraining force to a child's involvement in additional activities.

Who would know better than the children themselves that they are involved in too many activities? Is your child tired all the time? Does he or she lack motivation? Is it difficult for your child to do well in any of the many things that he or she is involved in? Does your child tell you that he or she is doing too much? Maybe the child is doing too much.

When my daughter was in junior high, she was asked to participate on a successful and select competitive softball team. I thought my daughter, Sandy, had some ability and believed that playing on the team may be good for her development. I was also flattered that the coaches wanted her to play.

There were problems that I anticipated: It would be costly. I would have to drive her to another city for practices. There would be significant travel involved for competitive events. I was willing and my Visa card was able.

I excitedly told Sandy of the opportunity. What was her response? She said, "I don't want to play." When I inquired why she stated emphatically, "Dad, I want to have a life, you know. None of my friends will be playing. The softball team will play and travel all year. I play volleyball, basketball, run cross-country in school, and I'm playing in the [local] softball league **and** you expect me to have good grades. No." I could have made her play, but why? How could I have argued with her logic? Why would I have tried?

Another problem with being involved in too many activities in our society is the fact that excellence is often expected along with commitment and dedication. How can an individual be dedicated and committed to four, six, or ten things at once? There are conflicts caused by the number of activities and the demands that each places upon the children and parents. Excellence, even as measured in terms of personal excellence, cannot be achieved in such a situation for an extended period of time for most people.

I would like to mention here that many children stop participation in youth sport because of interests in other things (Burton & Martens, 1986; Gould, et. al, 1982; Orlick, 1974; Sapp & Haubenstricker, 1978). There are times when children will choose some activities over others because of a desire for excellence, or in an effort to reduce the demands placed upon their time.

What should I do if my child is highly successful in a sport at an early age?

What I have observed in such a situation is that most of these young "stars" become average as they mature. Here is my advice to parents whose children achieve early success: Enjoy it, and let your child enjoy it.

Out of my state championship team, only five of the twelve continued to play soccer as they entered their senior year in high school, and none of them would I currently classify as "gifted." When they were young, they excelled, experienced success that many never get to experience, and they enjoyed themselves for the most part.

Frequently, I have overheard parents talk of having their eleven year old children play teams comprised of thirteen year olds, or hoping that their ten year old could play in the baseball or softball league with twelve year olds. Most often the parents state that the move would be best for the child's development. Is the child's development as a player (if indeed it is accelerated) worth taking away the precious few years that the child may have been outstanding among his or her peer group? If you move your child up to compete with and against older players, is there a guarantee that the opportunity to be outstanding will ever come along again?

I would like to note here that following the year when our team went 66-4, all of the parents indicated in a survey that they wanted to see our team participate in a league with older teams. I was the lone dissenter. Our team's winning percentage decreased with the passage of the years without playing in a league with older teams. We did play older teams on a regular basis because the number of teams in our age group was limited in our area of the state. What would have been the real value of playing in a league with older players?

I always wanted my children to enjoy themselves. In softball, my daughter's competitive teams (when I was not coaching) often played up an age group, "Because it will be better for their development if they play older teams." I was not in a position to make decisions and never tried to talk anyone out of such moves. I never thought offering my observations would do much good.

My son liked playing baseball because he, "could mess around and it was fun." He did well, but I did not think he was destined for greatness. In the fall before he played as a ten year old, coaches for the major league teams (generally 11 and 12 year olds played on these teams) started to call my house to ask if they could place him on their team in the spring.

The baseball leagues had tryouts after registration. Returning major league players were placed on the team they participated with the previous year. Coaches selected new players through a draft, and first pick was given to coaches who worked with the last place team from the previous year. If a coach was given permission to place a player on his team before the draft, the coach could select another promising player with the draft choice. The number of protected players was limited. There were six major league teams in the Little League in our part of town.

I said no to each of the four coaches who asked if they could place my son on their team. I also stated that my son would only play baseball in the minors. He wasn't that big, and he wasn't that dominant in my eyes. He was more likely to be successful and have fun if he remained in the minor league. He was, after all, only ten.

When I signed him up to play in the spring, I told three board members whom I knew well that I would only allow him to play in the minor league. I also indicated our position on the registration form. It was clear that if he were drafted to a major league team, I would not allow him to play. Not inconsequential to this decision was my son's statement that he did not want to play in the majors.

He was not drafted to a major league team. He performed very well on his minor league team. As the season progressed, I was asked again by three coaches at various times if I would let him play up in the majors.

They had players who had quit and the coaches needed to fill their rosters. I kindly refused. My son was having fun and doing quite well where he was. The coaches honored my wishes.

The rules of the league required that if a child was asked by the player agent to play on a team in the majors, he must or he would be reassigned to another team in the minor league. With two weeks to go in the season, my son's team was in first place, and the city tournament was something that everyone was looking forward to. A coach in the majors demanded that my son play the last two weeks with his major league team. Since his team was in last place, if my son were on his roster at the end of the year, he would not have to use his first pick on the following year's draft to get him.

I asked the coach not to do this. I appealed to the player agent and the board to no avail. He had to go up. Was the rule and were the behaviors of the coach in the best interest of the child? Did anyone really care about the child? He never again was able to dominate a baseball game. What if he had gone to the majors at the start of the season? He may have never been able to pitch, to strike out ten batters in a game or to hit a home run. Aren't those the baseball dreams that children have?

My point in sharing this story is that kids enjoy success. If your child is a dominant player, enjoy it. Let her or him enjoy it. Many children never have the opportunity to stand out. Why take it away from your child by having them play at a higher level for the sake of her or his development?

What if my child is just an average player?

In American society, it is commonly believed that if an individual works hard enough, their goals can be achieved. This belief is rampant in the sports environment. When children are not exceptional players as youths, parents sometimes believe that with the right amount of effort, the individual can become an exceptional player. This may be true in some cases, but how many children are pushed to become outstanding athletes by their parents and coaches? Is it reasonable to push your children to excel if they have average physical abilities?

If your child is participating in sport because he or she enjoys it, practices and participates with a reasonable degree of seriousness and effort, can't this be enough? If the child enjoys participation, why is it important to push her or him to "greater" things? Sport does not have to define the worth of your child or your success as a parent. Is there really anything wrong with realizing that your child may not be a great athlete?

Let me put this into another perspective. All children are not blessed with an IQ of 140. As a result, not all children will learn at the same rate and may not all have the mental faculties to become electrical engineers. Placing your children into an ideal educational setting may help them achieve their academic potential, but it does not assure that they will be as successful academically as the classmate who is brighter. Realizing this does not make you a bad parent. On the other hand, demanding that the children perform at an exceptional level may not assure academic excellence, even with tutoring and coercion. In academics and athletics, perhaps individuals should simply strive to achieve their potential. Ultimately, limits should be acknowledged and accepted. Be content with being the best you can be. This advice is contrary to the dominant social mantra.

Some individuals do mature more slowly than their peers academically and athletically. If your child is predisposed to achieve excellence, if given support, encouragement, a setting in which learning and development are fostered, your child will achieve his or her potential. If your child's potential is achieved later than other children, then so be it. You can only place your child in a good environment, provide support and see what happens.

How can I help my child if he or she does not make a team?

There is no question that being cut from a team may be painful. My children were not cut from teams, so I cannot tell you how I would react. What I would suggest based upon the experiences of others is the following.

First, acknowledge your feelings. You may be disappointed that your child did not make the team. You need to deal with this fact. Acknowledge your child's feelings. Let the child tell you how he or she feels. If you were never cut from a team, don't tell the child you know how he or she feels. You don't. Lastly, make other opportunities for a recreational or athletic outlet available to your child. There may be a void left by the sport that the child may wish to fill. Perhaps other school activities may be a possibility for your child. If he or she is old enough, perhaps entering the workforce would be appropriate. Any loss in our life can be painful. Eventually, the pain subsides. All that we can really do for another in pain is to offer alternatives, our support and friendship.

What should I do if my child does not seem to enjoy organized sport?

When someone asks me this question, I respond with a question. What would you do if you did not like your job? You might find another one. You would move on. You would **quit**.

The concern with my response is that the parent fears that allowing the child to quit will result in him or her becoming a "quitter." It is as though allowing the child out of one negative experience will begin a chain of similar actions.

If your child gives up easily in all situations and quitting is already a problem, there are other factors involved in the behavior that I cannot elaborate on here. It seems ridiculous to me to believe that quitting a sport, as an isolated event, will result in habitual problems.

My son enjoyed baseball when he was eight and wanted to play in a summer league once the Little League season was over. I thought he might get burned out if he did, but he begged me to sign him up. I gave in. The coach never held a parent meeting. I took my son to the first practice, and the temperature was over 110 degrees. Practice was poorly organized, there was little action, and the coach was negative in his interactions with the children. The next practice was the same. The environment was uncomfortable and boring. My son said he did not want to play. I said "great."

Another similar situation involved his junior high eighth grade basketball team. There were twenty-five players out for the team and in the first few practices, which involved only scrimmages. He got on the floor for a total of five minutes. He did not feel it was worth his time, and it certainly was not any fun. He left basketball and went back into the tennis class. What could be the problem with this? He is well adjusted and has found success in a number of other activities. What is the big deal with quitting in such situations?

Am I advocating that people should quit whenever there is a stress, problem or concern? No. In both of the examples I provided, my child did not enjoy the setting and moved on to something else. Kids should enjoy sport. It is for recreation. It is for fun. This is not the same as giving up in a game or not finishing a homework assignment because it is difficult. The sweltering baseball experience was simply no fun, and it was clear that he was not going to get to contribute to the basketball team. How would sticking it out have helped him at all? He had other things to do.

I believe that many times children have negative experiences in youth sport because they don't want to be there in the first place, the parents do.

One evening I saw a little girl who was probably seven years old crying in the on-deck circle of a baseball field. Once it was her turn to come to bat, she started to scream between sobs, "Daddy, I don't want to bat! I don't want to bat!" From behind the backstop, the girl's mother pleaded with the husband, who was the coach, to let her leave the field. He screamed, "No, damn it, she is going to do this!" Why did she have to bat? Why did she have to play? Perhaps the father had his own reasons and maybe they were very good. I am just not sure that I would agree.

In this chapter, I described the effects of an unwilling participant upon the team's success and how the individual posed problems at practice for me. What good did soccer do for that child? If you had a child who did not show a genuine interest in activity, why would you continue to demand participation?

Questions and Comments for Coaches

If you do not care to compete with others for athletes, your team may suffer.

In this study, it was clear that recruiting took place in the youth sport setting. If the player pool is limited in a given area and individuals associated with a team hope to be the best, there will be recruiting pressure on parents and athletes within the community. If recruiting is legal, you should plan to play the recruiting game. If you choose not to, you may not have the best team possible, and you may lose players to more aggressive teams and organizations. I did. I never felt like I pressured a child to play for me or to stay on my team. That was my choice.

As a college coach, I must recruit, but that is expected and is, indeed, required in order to field a team and to be competitive. I do not make players promises I cannot keep, and I attempt to be as honest and open as I possibly can be concerning my philosophy, behaviors and expectations. I do not award athletic scholarships, but I have been able to recruit good players and to find a reasonable degree of success against teams that do offer scholarships.

High school and junior high school coaches may find that they need to recruit within their schools in order to attract potential players. In high school as a freshman, I was called out of a science class to meet with the tennis coach. He tried to convince me to join the tennis team rather than the baseball team. This was before baseball season started. I did the same thing with junior high and high school students who seemed as though they may have an interest in athletics but never after an athlete was involved in another sport. The track coach at my daughter's high school asked her to run track for him. He was simply trying to get numbers out for the team. As a junior high or high school coach, you may need to do the same.

Do I use players to achieve my goals?

As a coach, I must lead players in practices and games. I desire success, and success can only be achieved through the efforts of the young people I work with. The athletes are the means to the team's success. There is nothing unsavory about this fact. In reality, one may observe that the coach is often the means by which athletes achieve their goals. In such an arrangement both the athletes and the coaches benefit.

In this chapter I stated that I thought that I might have been using an athlete in order to achieve success in soccer. Ultimately, I cared for the child and believed that he benefited from his association with the team. I did not benefit solely from his association with the team. When the child and the team both benefit, I cannot see how someone could actually state that a player is being used.

What is a reasonable amount of time for a coach to invest in his or her team's activities?

The answer to this question will differ from sport to sport and from individual to individual. It also differs depending on the context of your coaching activities.

When I coached soccer, I prepared for practices, but for me the task was relatively easy. It may have taken me an average of thirty minutes a day to prepare and fifteen minutes to set up the practice environment before the start of practice. I would spend twenty to thirty minutes before arriving at a match contemplating lineups and substitution plans. Outside of the actual practice and match settings, I spent little time on the sport. I did not regularly scout opponents. I did not break down game films, nor did I do a lot of talking with coaches about upcoming games. Some of the parents pressured me to do these things, but I did not have the time or desire to do them.

You may be different. Your level of experience, your training in teaching, your expertise in your chosen sport and the ease with which you can plan and make decisions likely differ from mine. These factors may require you to spend more time planning for your coaching activities than it does for me. If you believe that you need to be highly familiar with every move your opponent makes, it will take more of your time to accomplish this goal. Football practices may take more time to prepare for than soccer practices, simply because of the number of participants.

Regardless of the sport you are involved in, I would like to give you the following advice: Save time for your family, friends and other activities. I have always held my coaching activity secondary to my family life and my primary source of employment, which was and is teaching. I am a husband and dad first, a teacher second and a coach third. I have always tried to maintain these priorities in this order. I follow my personal religious beliefs. Consequently, I have been happy in my home, in my job, and in coaching. How does this relate to your time? You must make choices. The first priority should be where you focus most of your time.

I know of marriages that fell apart because individuals ignored family responsibilities. The individuals seemed married to their job/sport. The coach slept at the office on many nights because it took too much time to go home. Perhaps some individuals don't mind taking a back seat to a sport, but I don't believe there are many. Where your heart is, so will be your time.

How much time should a coach spend on sport? As much as the individual deems appropriate. I just hope that all coaches reflect on what is important and that they appropriate more time to the things that are really important. You will be able to see when you are spending too much time on sport if you are aware enough and concerned enough to see.

What is a reasonable amount of time to expect athletes to spend on sport?

As was true in the response to the previous question, the answer to this question is dependent upon the individual athlete and the context. Major college basketball players can spend 50 hours a week on their sport-related activities (Edwards, 1984). That would not seem reasonable for most youth or high school athletes.

My general rule was to spend one and a half hours a day in practice with my high school and older youth sport teams. With my college team, I spend two hours a day in practices. For most of the athletes I have coached, this has proven to be an adequate amount of time. There are athletes on my college teams who choose to do additional physical training on their own either before or after practice. I do not require additional time of my athletes because they need time to study, or to work at part time jobs. They also need time just to socialize with others.

My method is unusual regarding the length of my practices. One of my college players noted, "I can't believe how much we have achieved when it seems like we have worked so little. My high school practices seemed more difficult than ours do here. But for some reason, we have improved so much as players. I don't understand." Making the most of the time appropriated for practice is the key.

Another benefit to limiting practice times is that the season does not seem to drag on. My players are rarely tired of volleyball at the end of the season or at the end of their careers. Limiting practice times contributes to this phenomenon.

If an athlete is in a high school or college setting, it seems reasonable to practice daily and to expect an athlete to participate only in your sport during the active season. More and more high school coaches are asking young athletes to specialize in only one sport and training for that sport is expected to take place all year long. However, specialization was not found to be an important factor in the sports careers of professional baseball players (Hill, 1993). Perhaps specialization is not as important as some make it out to be.

Should a youth who has not yet entered high school commit to one sport, train five days a week and play all year long? It could be appropriate, assuming that it is the child's choice. However, as with my college athletes, I believe that all athletes should have the time and the encouragement to develop interests in other activities and to develop their minds to the fullest.

Children serve in a variety of roles just as you do.

You must remember that the young people you are coaching are likely to have many other things going on in their lives. As I noted in this chapter, there were many times that the activities of the players on my soccer teams required them to miss practices and games. The same was true when I coached at the high school level. Athletes missed practices and games for family responsibilities, for other athletic events, for choir, for club activities and a host of other reasons. I have had college players miss games because of family emergencies, weddings, GRE exams, MCAT exams and for a variety of other reasons. Do I like it? Of course I don't. Must I accept the absences? I really have little choice. My response is always one of understanding. People have to do these things. There is no sense in getting angry. For many athletes, there are other activities that take precedence over sports.

What is the best policy concerning playing time?

Certainly if the rules of your league require you to play all players for a specific amount of time, you should do this. Not playing individuals their allotted amount of time cheats the individuals, and it cheats the opponents.

In settings where playing time is not required by rule (club, junior high, high school and college), I have always believed that every player on my roster should have the opportunity to play whenever it is possible.

There are some instances when playing a particular athlete could cost the team a game. I will not allow this, but it is not because I do not care about the feelings of the athletes. It is because when the desire of the majority of the team is to win, the feelings of one or two individuals must be secondary to those of the group. Here I will confess that I do want to win games, but I do feel badly when athletes are not given the opportunity to play when they believe that they should have been. If my team voted to allow everyone equal playing time and/or the players said that winning did not matter to them, I would gladly play all individuals equally. I don't think that this situation is a realistic possibility in present-day America.

Some children mature late. Shouldn't I be sure to play everyone a lot because of this fact?

You must do what you believe is right. On the other hand, I believe that as long as you can keep the child interested in the sport and that the child finds the sport enjoyable, the individual's skills and knowledge can be improved. If the child stays with the sport and becomes one of the better players on the team playing time will come. He or she will have earned it and will deserve it. In the meantime, play the individual whenever possible while striving to meet the team's goals. Never forget that most individuals want to play.

9

GREAT EXPECTATIONS

For the great majority of children, youth sport is not a full time job. There are limits to the length of a season, the frequency of practice and the length of practices. To most children and their parents, sport is not something worth risking one's health for and it is something that, at least theoretically, should be fun. Over time, winning seems to become more important to young athletes. In this chapter, several vignettes are presented to illustrate how differences in parental, player and coaching expectations resulted in conflict involving each of these aspects of the youth sport experience.

Recreational Verses Competitive Soccer: The Players' Perspective illustrates how the Force players came to believe that winning became more important as they moved from recreational to competitive soccer. *Season Length* recaps the changes in the length of the soccer seasons throughout the study and exemplifies the difference in views parents held concerning what amount of time should be spent in soccer-related activity. In *Practices* I describe how the length and demands of practice changed as the children matured. *Requisite Assertiveness* recounts the injuries experienced by the members of the Force and the Strikers and the playing behaviors of those injured. In *Intensity and Motivation* it becomes clear that children have different degrees of intensity and motivation, and these differences can lead to criticism and frustration.

Recreational Verses Competitive Soccer: The Players' Perspective

My coaching objectives were predominantly developmental, even in the club soccer setting. I wondered how the players felt. In 2002, all five original Force players (my competitive team) who were not members of the Strikers (my recreational team) were asked what they remembered most about joining the Force as ten year olds.

The five players questioned all stated that the things that impressed them the most was the skill level of the players on the team and that winning was more important than it was in recreational soccer. The first observation was expected, but the latter surprised me. I did emphasize performance consistently and emphatically. Successfully performing skills and tactics was necessary in order for the individuals and the team to play well, and that is what my goal was. When the team played beautiful soccer, it was like watching a ballet that I had helped put together. I always realized that the performance had to come from within the kids, but I felt I was able to help bring it out.

I did talk about winning, but that was only once a year at our first practice. Winning was not emphasized, performance was. Generally, excellent performance resulted in victory. There were times we played well and lost, but there were also times that we played poorly and won.

Vick Thompson had another explanation as to why the athletes perceived that winning was more important:

> It was because the parents became more serious when their kids started to play competitive soccer. It cost me about $45 a season for my son to play recreational soccer. All of the games were played here in town, and practices were held just twice a week. The mark of success in our country is winning. We had to invest thousands of dollars a year for the kids to play with the Force, and we had to invest our time as well. More pressure is placed on the kids because of the increased time commitment to get them to soccer practices and games. Even if I didn't go on a trip, my money did.

In other words, because the parents invested significant amounts of time and money, they expected something in return. The payoff was expected to be success as measured in wins. The children picked up on these expectations.

Force players who were members of the Strikers were accustomed to winning. My son did not believe, in terms of the emphasis placed upon winning and losing, that there was a difference between his recreational and competitive soccer experiences: "I didn't look at [winning and losing] any differently." The emphasis upon performance and the unspoken expectation of success were consistent in his home.

Season Length

One of the recent phenomena associated with high school sport has been the increase in pressure to train all year long and to compete in high-level events throughout the year (Eitzen & Sage, 1997; Hill & Simons, 1989; Hill & Hansen, 1988; Stover, 1993). In youth sport the same pressures exists (Lord & Kozar, 1996; Popke, 2000). Children younger than age fifteen are encouraged to specialize and for many, there is no such thing as an off-season. Children are expected to pay the price, to excel and to win.

There are several arguments for year-round training and competitive schedules (Lord & Kozar, 1996; Popke, 2000). It may increase the probability of success. The children are less likely to fall behind the competition. There is a perception that year round training will lead to an increased probability of receiving a college athletic scholarship. And finally, it serves to encourage the maximal development of the child's athletic ability.

Year-round training is a symptom of the professionalization of youth sport. The pressure to require year-round training was placed upon me as this study was conducted, and the pressure increased as the children matured.

The season length for the Strikers was ten weeks in the fall and ten weeks in the spring during the first three years of the team's existence (age 4-6). The team averaged twenty-two matches a year. As the players matured (age 7-9), the number of matches increased to an average of forty a year. The season length was extended to twelve weeks in the fall and twelve weeks in the spring.

During my coaching tenure, practices for the Force (age 10-15) began in early August and matches were played through November. The fall season averaged seventeen weeks. In the spring, practices started in early February and matches were played through June and some seasons into

July. The high number of matches in one year was seventy, and the average number of matches a year was sixty-two. The spring season lasted as long as twenty-three weeks. Soccer activities were conducted ten months out of the year from the time the children were ten years old.

Some parents did not feel the Force played enough and that the team should play year around, while others felt that the demands placed upon the families and players was too much. Will Johnson was a proponent of year-round play: "If our kids are going to improve and be competitive, they have to play all year around. Otherwise, they will fall behind the competition." Will often stated that his son had chosen soccer as his sport of choice and that he wanted to dedicate himself to it. Will believed all that could be done to enhance his child's progress and performance should be done. Jeff Weber disagreed, "The kids like to do other things. They need a break from soccer or they will get burned out." Jeff encouraged his son Seth to play as many sports as possible. Soccer would be but one of them.

I believed the children needed a break from soccer in the winter and summer, especially when they were younger than age twelve. When the athletes reached age twelve and thirteen, they could determine for themselves if they wanted to play all year long. I always felt that before that, they would choose to play all year long only as a result of parental pressure. Even as the kids reached age fifteen, I still believed that it was healthy to take a break from soccer for a few weeks a couple of times a year. The break was definitely healthy for the parents and me.

Despite my view that the kids needed a break, team parents organized indoor soccer teams, and most of the players participated, including my son. Beginning at age seven, many of the Strikers and future Force players participated in indoor soccer during the winter and summer.[1] There was essentially no extended break from soccer for the children most heavily involved in the sport from the time they reached age seven until they completed their involvement in soccer.

Practices

As the children matured, there was an evolution in their practice behaviors. The changes that came as they matured closely followed the pattern that would be expected based upon the cognitive and physical development of the children combined with opportunity, experience and appropriate instruction (Coakley, 1994; Gallagher, J., French, K., Thomas,

K. & Thomas, J., 1996; Magill & Anderson, 1996; Passer, 1996; Ruff & Lawson, 1990; Shaffer, 1993; Seefeldt, 1996). At the age of four, children have short attention spans and are easily distracted. As children progress through the elementary school years, their ability to pay attention, to think abstractly and to remember gradually improves. With these improvements, the young athletes were able to achieve higher levels of play and success as they progressed through childhood and into adolescence.

As a recreational team, the Strikers were limited by league rules to two practices a week. Some teams exceeded this limit. As a competitive team, the Force had three to four practices each week before the first match for each season. With the exception of one fall season, practices would begin two weeks before the first match of the season. After the first match, practices were generally held two days a week. When the team did not have a weekday game, a third practice was often held during the week.

Practices lasted one hour in the early years of the study. Over the last five years of the study, practices lasted one and one-half hours each. With very few exceptions, practices were held at Sherwood Park in Northeast Overland.

Practices were not too business-like for the first two years of the study. When the kids were four and five, they were easily distracted. They were not ready to do much more than learn the most basic skills. We took time out from soccer to play tag, to watch ants crawl and to watch airplanes fly overhead. Cones were not thought of as markers, they were a source of amusement to be enjoyed at the end of practice as a reward for being good. I told the kids jokes at the end of practice, and they took turns telling jokes each day. I did all that I could to make the practices as enjoyable as possible.

At the age of thirteen, when he was asked what he remembered about soccer at age five, Seth Weber still remembered having told jokes and playing with cones. He did not recall anything else we did.

As the kids matured (age six and seven), they were capable of learning how to pass and trap more effectively and to employ basic positioning. We watched the airplanes and ants less frequently and spent more time on soccer skills and strategy. Slowly the players began to be interested in performing and competing. They were still kids, and I tried to make things as fun as I could while still working toward their development as players. We still played some silly games and told jokes. In fact, I planned eight minutes at the end of practices for these activities.

At age fifteen, Jerry Reynolds recalled the game called "Revenge of the Big People" that he had played after practice. He could not recall any other activities that were conducted in practices, other than playing in scrimmages (which we rarely did).

By the time the players were aged eight and nine, much more could be accomplished. The children could better understand their roles and positioning. Passes could be made through volition, and they grew in skill and stature. Practices were more businesslike and productive. There were players on the team who still had more interest in ants and airplanes than they did in soccer. We still spent time at the end of practice talking about life and telling stories, but it didn't seem as important during this period. The kids seemed to enjoy the down time at the end of practice, but it did not seem to excite them as it had in earlier years. I believe that this was because more of the players had actually developed a fondness for the sport of soccer.

Between the ages of ten and fifteen, much more could be accomplished at practices. The athletes were capable of following directions and employing tactical and technical behaviors learned at practices in match conditions. Misbehavior decreased significantly. This may have been because most of those still playing soccer in the competitive team setting generally took their participation reasonably seriously. Most of the players were in a hurry to leave practices because they had other responsibilities, activities or homework that they needed to get to. There was less socialization. It was my observation that they were more interested at this time in talking and joking specifically with their peers instead of me.

It was clear that there was a gradual change in the emphasis upon high levels of performance as the study continued. Practices became longer, more complex, and more physically and mentally demanding. This seemed appropriate as the children matured and increased in their skills. Even though I held a developmental perspective throughout the study, the evolution of the practices did not indicate a move toward the Power and Performance Model of sport. The demands were in line with what the participants needed to enjoy the competitive experience. It was needed in order to find pleasure in their participation.

Requisite Assertiveness

In order to be successful in soccer or any other sport that involves contact, the game has to be played with a reasonable degree of assertiveness. Players cannot shy away from contact with opponents. They must be willing to make physical contact as they compete for possession of the ball or they will be unsuccessful. They cannot be afraid of being injured or of injuring opponents (Leonard, 1998). Bredemeir and Shields (1985) stated that in order to be successful in games that require contact, an athlete has to be "bad." Martin and Lumsden (1987) and Eitzen and Sage (1997) have all observed that play in the sport of soccer has become increasingly brutal in recent years. Winning-at-all-costs may include the cost of one's health.

I refer to the desired level of assertiveness as "reckless abandon" because of the need to disregard the potential for injury to the individual or the opponent. As a team, the Strikers and the Force never played with reckless abandon. Tactically and technically, the players were good, but they did not accept or distribute contact readily nor with consistency. This negatively affected the team's performance in some matches. The best way to beat the Force was to play us physically. When that happened, the team began to back away from contact, and we became ineffective both offensively and defensively.

Over the twelve years that I coached during this study, there were nine soccer-related injuries that kept players out of a match. Two required the setting and casting of fractured limbs and three required surgery. No serious injuries occurred in a practice at any time. There were cut lips, bruised shins, and occasional bloody noses due to contact during practices.

Three of the serious injuries occurred to Brad Cobb, the most reckless of the field players. He was a defender who seemed to have little regard for his body or respect for players larger than he was. He fractured his arm twice and experienced a knee injury that required surgery. Brad's mother shared her feelings concerning his injuries:

> After his second arm fracture, after each collision and every time he went down I wondered if he was hurt. I was also concerned when he had knee surgery because of the anesthesia. You have to be prepared that there is a possibility that they will get hurt when they play. Kids get hurt when they play, but they could get hurt just crossing the street.

Even though Brad suffered fractures and was required to have knee surgery, he stated that he never gave injury a second thought once he recovered. He said, "I loved playing so much that it didn't matter."

The only other serious injury occurred to Brent Bates, the goalkeeper, who also played with reckless abandon. Over the years he had many violent collisions with opposing players. He experienced dislocations in both shoulders at different times. The dislocations reoccurred. He eventually had reconstructive surgery on both of them.

I told Brent and his parents that he *would* get hurt if he played keeper. The position requires that you place yourself in positions of vulnerability at times, and there are many times that collisions are unavoidable. Goalkeeping requires that you not have a lot of regard for your safety, and it helps if you have a bit of a mean streak, too. I fractured six bones and had one surgery because of injuries I sustained playing keeper. You can't worry about them and be successful.

Tom and Joan Bates were both physicians, and although they had warned of the potential for injury, they supported their son's play even after his injuries. His mother stated, "He loves soccer and we want him to play. He has given up a lot of things he is good at and that we would like for him to do in order to concentrate on soccer. We just hope that his injuries don't prevent him from playing in the future."

After his shoulder dislocations and surgeries, Brent continued to play. He felt apprehensive about his injuries at first, but eventually the apprehension passed. He loved playing soccer. It was worth the risk of further injury to him.

A few months after his second shoulder surgery, Brent broke his tibia and fibula in his first start in goal as a sophomore on the varsity high school soccer team. The fractures required surgery. At the time his leg was fractured, he believed that he would never play soccer again. As he went through his rehabilitation, he started to believe that he wanted to play again and began to believe that he would, though his feelings were mixed. He still loved the sport and wanted to play:

> I prayed about it and asked for God to show me what I should do. That night I woke up and my shoulder had subluxated [dislocated]. It was clear to me that I should not play again.

He never did. After two shoulder surgeries and surgery on his leg, enough was enough for the fifteen-year old.

Mike Thompson was the only other Force player who was reckless in his play. He was never seriously injured in a soccer match. Although some of the bones in his face were fractured when he was hit with a baseball bat, he participated in a tournament a week later with a protective face cover.

There were no other players who were regularly reckless in their play. I believe that I might have been partially to blame. I was injured a lot as a goalkeeper. It is something that just happens. If you are worried about it, you just don't play the position, or you don't play it well. But as a coach, I was always concerned with the safety of the kids and structured practices so that contact was limited. That prevented injuries, but did little to increase the players' willingness to accept or give contact. I think that the upbringing of the kids on the team had something to do with it too. There were several players on the team who have never been in a fight in their entire lives. They were raised not to hurt others and to avoid being hurt. How can we expect for a child to put aside his or her values just because the game might call for it?

When asked at age thirteen why he did not play more aggressively, Eric stated, "I know that I can go harder to get more balls, but I don't want to hurt anyone." Assistant coach Jesus Davila once observed, "These kids are too nice. They don't want to hurt anyone. When I was a kid, we used to beat the crap out of each other every day at practice, and we loved it. These kids aren't like that." It bothered him when players did not retaliate against overly physical and dirty play that the opponents engaged in. Jesus often spoke of the need for the team to designate someone as an enforcer: someone who would physically assault an opposing player in retaliation for rough play. "When I played, we always had a player like that. It's the only way to stop the other team from injuring your players."

I was often frustrated with the team's lack of aggressiveness, but I believed it was my responsibility to keep the players healthy. I have always thought that either you are aggressive and reckless by nature, or you aren't. Why would you teach someone to enjoy hurting others or to accept injuries willingly? Is it appropriate to teach a child to sacrifice his or her health and the health of others in the name of victory?

As a coach, I was unwilling to sacrifice the health of my players in order to get more assertive play on the field. As a player I decided to place myself into situations that resulted in injury. Nobody taught me to do so. My participation in organized sport through college resulted in three surgeries and 13 broken bones. I did not wish to feel that I pressured a child into experiencing similar injuries.

My concern over the health of my players was consistent with my developmental orientation toward youth sport and my acceptance of the Pleasure and Participation Model. It resulted in us losing more matches over the years than we may have if the team had been more reckless in its play, but it was a choice that I believe was a good one.

Intensity and Motivation

In the professional model of sport the coach is held accountable for the performance of the team (Eitzen & Sage, 1997). This would include being held accountable for the motivation of the team and the intensity the players exhibit in practice and matches. Though coaches may take steps to enhance the level of intensity and motivation of their athletes to perform (Martin & Lumsden, 1987), motivation and intensity may ultimately be up to the individual athlete (Magill & Anderson, 1996). Larry Bird, former head coach of the Indiana Pacers of the NBA and Basketball Hall of Fame inductee, stated in a televised interview that he did not feel it was his job to motivate athletes. In fact, he stated that he could not understand how an athlete could not be excited about playing a game.[2]

Mr. Bird's expectations do not seem to be common in the world of sport. The expectations of parents concerning my role in bringing about intensity and motivation in my young athletes were a source of conflict during the course of this study.

Some of the players, such as Carl Heller, were very intense and worked hard at virtually every practice. His father stated, "I expect for him to give everything he has when he is at practice or a game. If he doesn't, he shouldn't be playing."

Other players went through the motions and periodically gave less than their best. I was generally pleased with my son's performance at practice and in matches but did wish at times that he put forth more effort during some practices. He was out there to enjoy himself. If busting his butt at practice every day was not something that he enjoyed, what was I suppose to do? Scream at him? Make him run laps? Should I have placed so much pressure on him that he would hate playing and quit? What good would that of done?

Though some may have been critical of my son's lack of consistent levels of high intensity, others saw the good in it. Vick Thompson made the following comment about Eric:

... He's a good kid and a good player. I like his ability to play hard and his ability to shake off a loss. He might be upset for a minute or two, but then he's O.K. It's over. With my son [who was very intense] he's upset for fifteen or sixteen hours after a loss and sometimes for days.

The intensity at practices over the last two years that I coached was not what I would have liked, but I felt that the kids had so many other things going on in their lives that most of them viewed soccer as just something else to do. Soccer apparently was not something they cared about passionately, and that's what it takes to excel and to push oneself day in and day out. Can a coach really make an athlete feel passionately about a sport? With passion comes intensity. I often spoke about the need for intensity, but it often wasn't there.

Most parents did not attend practices, so they could not comment on their child's practice efforts, but they were quick to comment on a perceived lack of intensity during matches. Will Johnson once stated, "You really need to do something to get the boys up for the games. They start out too flat." My response to Will's comment was, "It is up to the players to motivate themselves. I can't do it for them. I do expect that on occasion that the kids won't be too excited about a match. They play seventy matches a year for heaven's sake." In regards to intensity during matches, Vick Thompson added:

The boys always came to play. They certainly never went out there with the intention of losing. It came down to whether or not *they* were ready to play. When there was a problem, it was usually because they thought that they were going to win and the other team came out and played harder than they did. You know some days they just didn't play as hard as the day before, but that happens.

When he was fifteen years old, Jerry Reynolds, a player with the Force, said to me, "There is nothing that you can do to make us care more. If we don't play hard or practice hard, there is nothing you can do about it." How can the coach really be held accountable for the intensity of the players when they feel like Jerry?

Jesus Davila had some strong feelings about the team's lack of intensity, "These are just a bunch of spoiled middle-class kids that just look at soccer as another thing to do."

Chapter 9 Observations

Questions and Comments for Parents

Should my child play her or his chosen sport all year around?

I have always believed that children should have some unstructured time for themselves. I also maintain that it is healthy to take a break from a given sport for a period of time each year. Nevertheless, my child ended up playing soccer virtually year-round by the time he was seven. How did this happen?

My child wanted to play with his friends who were playing year-round. There was peer pressure for him to play, and in a way, there was peer pressure placed upon me to allow him to do so. If the other parents associated with my team signed up their children, why would I deny my child the opportunity to play? It almost felt as if I was a bad parent if I didn't let my child play. The thought of my child falling behind the other children did not enter into my mind. The reasons were strictly social, not something driven by a competitive will to win and excel.

If your child really wants to participate in a sport for his or her own enjoyment all year long, why not let the child play? If the idea is strictly yours, I would question your motives and whether the experiences of your child will be compromised. I would also suggest here that at the end of a season, if your child does not seem motivated to participate in practices and games, perhaps a break would be appropriate.

The odds are that your child will be injured during participation in organized sport at some time.

According to the National Youth Sports Safety Foundation, more than five million children seek treatment in hospital emergency rooms because of sports-related injuries (2002). Are you aware that children can be killed during sport participation? Death can come about in sport settings as a result of heat-related incidents, baseballs striking children in the chest, softballs striking children in the head, contact with bats, kicks in the head and a host of other causes. Death is rare in sport, but few parents really contemplate this potentiality when they sign their children up to play.

It is more likely that a child will suffer a broken bone or tears to ligaments or tendons. Most children experience sprained ankles, abrasions, lacerations, bloody noses and black eyes. Things happen in athletic settings that result in injuries, though most are minor in nature.

How should I respond to my child's injuries?

The odds are that your child will experience injuries. How you respond to them will be based greatly upon how you respond to your own illnesses and injuries. I experienced many sport-related injuries and generally played hurt. Pain was something that I associated with participation. As a child, I rarely was taken to the doctor. That taught me to accept my pain, to deal with it and to get on with things.

Other individuals do not play if they feel any discomfort. They were probably told that it would be a bad idea to do so, and I picture them going to a physician often. I suppose that most individuals would fall somewhere in between these two extremes. You will probably respond to your child's injuries much as your parents responded to yours.

In youth sport settings, there are no athletic trainers or team doctors to care for injuries. In most cases, there is a coach, your child and of course, your personal experiences that will all serve to affect how you will respond to your child's injury. I will not offer any specific guidelines for how you should treat or respond to injuries because this is not what this book is about. I will state that how you respond will be affected significantly by what model of sport you adhere to. If you are a disciple of the Power and Performance Model, you believe that people should play in pain and that pain is something that must be experienced by individuals who are dedicated to the game: no pain, no gain. If you are a proponent of the Pleasure and Participation Model, no pain is sane. Injuries should be avoided and participants should not return to action until they are well.

As I noted in this chapter, I played injured, but I did not and do not pressure athletes to play hurt. If an athlete could function at an adequate level, and I believed that participation would not aggravate the injury, I would allow individuals to play with their injuries. It was their choice.

My own children played with minor injuries, and I admired their ability to perform in pain. With few exceptions, they also played when they were feeling ill. I can only assume that my unwillingness to make a large issue out of their or my injuries and illnesses affected their response. I worked when I was sick and participated in athletic activities when injured.

I modeled the behaviors that they adopted. When they skinned their knees as toddlers, I hugged them, patted them on the Pamper and acted like nothing happened. When they were sick, they went to school with very few exceptions. Other parents might think that my expectations and behaviors in this regard were wrong.

Your child will be prepared to deal with illness and injury before he or she enters the sport setting. I think it is important for you not to expect your child to "suck it up" in the athletic setting when you expect him or her to whine, to rest and to recover in response to any other injury or illness. That makes no sense to me and would not make sense to your child.

Should my child play hurt?

That is a decision that you and ultimately your child should make. If the injury is severe, your physician should be consulted. If your child's life, long-term health or ability to function normally is in jeopardy, heck no! Your child should not play.

Some children drop out of a sport because of the pain associated with their participation. I cannot blame them. I wonder how many parents will encourage to the point of forcing their children to play with pain that is ever-present. Why would parents do this?

Other children will, of their own volition, continue to participate in sport in spite of nagging injuries. To them it is worth experiencing the pain. Should parents encourage them to stop their participation?

The position and the sport that your child plays might be more dangerous than others.

As noted in this chapter, goalkeeper is a high-risk position. Individuals that play in the goal are often injured as a result of contact with opponents. In baseball, it would seem that catcher and pitcher would have a higher incidence of injury than other positions. Other sports also have specific positions that are more likely to produce injuries.

One of my greatest fears was that my children would be seriously injured while pitching in baseball and softball. My son was never hit, but my daughter was on several occasions. The pitching rubber was much closer to home plate in fast-pitch softball and there was less time for her to react.

What happened when she was hit? Generally she was swollen and bruised. I recall that one bruise and the related swelling did not subside for a period of six months. I was thankful that she was not stricken in the head. She finished pitching the game, but I am not sure that I could have. She would not likely have received such an injury if she were not playing in the pitcher's position.

Football is an example of a high-risk sport. Insurance companies charge schools that support football higher premiums than they do those that do not sponsor football because the injury rates are high. If your child plays football, an injury that will lead to your child missing a game at some time or another is highly likely.

You should acknowledge that your child's chosen sport and the position that he or she plays can significantly affect the potential for injury.

It does not seem reasonable to expect children who have been raised to be non aggressive and to avoid injury to willingly accept injury and to willing injure others in the sport setting.

When I was a child, I was taught that I should not get into fights. On the other hand, I was also taught that it was acceptable to fight as long as the other person threw the first punch. I participated in several fistfights as a child. In retrospect, I enjoyed them. When it came to my participation in sports, I really did not have much concern over whether or not I would be hurt or if I might injure another athlete. I found it rewarding to play in spite of my injuries, and if I injured another person legally, I felt superior to him. I had no problem engaging in violent acts in my athletic activities.

Today, it is likely that a fistfight is more likely to escalate into something more serious. I did not want my children to get into fights and taught them to just walk away. To my knowledge neither of them has ever been in a fight.

When I observe that my son is not aggressive in the sport setting, and when he stated that he did not wish to harm opponents, it was no surprise to me. On the other hand, it bothered me at times when he would not "let it all out" on the field, to trample someone for a ball or place himself in a position of vulnerability in an effort to make a play. However, I understand that his playing behaviors were a logical consequence of how he was raised.

Are some children able to put aside their normal behaviors when they are on a football field, basketball court or soccer field? Some are, but I believe they have to be encouraged to do so, or they must see on their own that it is functional and beneficial to do so. They will come to this realization and then they will be forced to choose whether to be consistent in their behaviors or to make the behaviors dependent upon the situation. Is it desirable to have children believe that their behaviors should be dependent upon the situation? Why should an individual be willing to injure someone intentionally in a sport setting and not in others? Is it ever really appropriate to injure another person?

I suggest that if you follow the professionalized model of sport that doing whatever it takes to win is desirable, even if it does require one to act differently in the sport setting than is expected in the non-sport setting. Whatever it takes: A person has to do what a person has to do.

Individuals who are proponents of the Pleasure and Participation Model would not advocate setting aside one's values in the name of victory. To do so would not better one's life or society in general.

Questions and Comments for Coaches

Practices should be short, emphasizing fundamental skill development and fun when children are very young.

It makes little sense to emphasize winning when you work with young children. Before the age of seven, children are not generally interested in social comparison or competition as a means of making comparison with others (Passer, 1996). Further, young children really do not understand the complexities of competition until they approach age twelve. Here is another reason why you don't need to emphasize winning with young athletes: parents will emphasize winning whether you advocate it or not. Lastly, to emphasize winning over skill development is a losing formula in most instances.

If children have poor skills, they will often find it difficult to achieve and MAINTAIN early levels of success that they may enjoy. I will acknowledge here that youngsters lacking skills at early ages can find success because of unusual physical characteristics (Cain & Broekhoff, 1987; Haubenstricker and Seefeldt, 1986; Shields, 1986). My observation is that children who are especially aggressive and who play with a high degree of intensity find early success in soccer as well. This success cannot be maintained without adequate skill development as the children mature.

My teams **always** lost to the Bulls in the first three years of this study. The primary reason for their success was the intensity with which the Bulls players participated. The coach was extremely competitive and so were the players. Eventually, my team became superior because they developed superior skills. I never felt that my players were exceptionally driven to win.

If you do not allow young children to have fun and enjoy the youth sport setting, they may grow to dislike sport. In this chapter, I described how the emphasis on fun and enjoyment, aside from that gained from playing, was lessened as the children aged. If the participants develop a love for the sport at an early age, they will maintain their participation longer. As children mature, the value of winning and its association with effort and skill development become apparent. At this point, your practices can become more business-like. I would still advise you to incorporate fun activities from time to time. My college athletes enjoy periodic "fun" practices. I have never been involved with a team at the youth sport, high school or college level that did not communicate to me a desire to have fun occasionally. Generally, after a "fun" practice, my athletes are ready to focus harder during their next practice.

You may want athletes to be aggressive and have a win at all cost attitude, but their attitudes and values may not allow this to happen.

You may find it frustrating when an athlete does not take an opponent out when the opportunity presents itself. You may not understand why an athlete will refuse to "take one" for the team (example: allow herself to be hit by a pitch). In practice you may encourage athletes to do these things, but they refuse. What you need to understand is that the athletes come to the sport environment with beliefs and values that your instructions and encouragement may not change. How should you respond?

Pretend for a moment that you are ten years old and that your parents have taught you to do everything and anything possible in order to win (cheat, hurt others, verbally intimidate opponents). Your coach tells you that these things are improper and punishes you for doing them. How would you feel? I believe that you would feel confused and frustrated.

When children are confronted with beliefs and expectations that are foreign to them, they will be confused and frustrated. The child may change in the direction that the coach desires, there may be no change in the child's behavior, or there may be open defiance. The child may resist your efforts to change his or her participation behaviors and attitudes. The situation may be exacerbated by the comments and actions of the child's parents. I suggest that if the parents desire participation styles that are different from yours, you will have less success in your attempts to change the child.

How you respond to this impediment to the achievement of your goals is up to you. You can allow it to frustrate you and make you angry, or you can accept the situation as it is. Just find a position that best suits the child's personality. I decided long ago that I can attempt to influence parents and children, but there is no guarantee that I will be successful. I can only do the best I can to affect change in the direction that I desire.

Injuries happen as individuals participate in sport, but you can take steps to minimize their frequency and severity.

When I coached soccer, I checked for holes and broken glass on the field before every practice, and I trained the athletes to do the same. If there was a problem, it was fixed before practice started or the problem area was marked with cones. I thought it was my responsibility to do these things in the interest of my players' safety.

I hired a soccer coach at my university. As with all my coaches, I stated that his duties included scanning the field for problems and fixing them before starting practice. He did not believe this responsibility should be his. My question was this, "If you don't actively take steps to maintain the health and safety of your athletes, who will?" I checked the condition of softball fields before practices and games and looked over basketball and volleyball courts for water, dirt, dust and slick spots because I cared for the safety of the athletes. Often times, if you do not do these things, they will not be done and you increase the risk of injury to your athletes.

Because I was concerned about safety, I minimized contact in practices. Injuries were rare on my teams because of this fact. I am thankful that so few injuries have occurred to my athletes over the years. Aside from those described in this chapter, I can recall only the following serious injuries: one knee injury (torn ACL), a few mild ankle sprains, one broken hand, one lacerated chin and one dislocated elbow. That includes teams that I have coached over a period of twenty-eight years, hundreds of athletes and thousands of practices and games. I cannot help but believe that my actions assisted in the prevention of injuries, and if safety is a concern to you, I encourage you to inspect your facilities daily and to anticipate how your drills and practice structure may influence the potential for injury.

Should I allow a child to play hurt?

This is a decision that may frequently confront you. My decision is based upon the best interest of the child when I serve in a coaching capacity. Here is my general guideline. If the parents do not want the child to play, I won't play the child. If a physician will not release a child to play, I will not allow the child to play. If I feel the injury may be worsened by allowing the child to play, I will not allow participation.

There will be times when players and/or their parents will pressure you to allow an injured child to play. If you do not have firm guidelines in your mind, you may make the wrong decision as a result of outside pressures.

Another factor that may influence your decision to allow an injured player to participate is your desire to win. For example, the last year that I coached high school volleyball, my most outstanding player sprained her ankle. She wanted to play before she could jump without favoring it, which was my standard for returning an individual to practice and competition. She was a senior, and we were having a great year (we finished 22-2). She was a major factor in our success. She literally begged me to allow her to play before she was ready and cried in my presence. She missed three matches. I did not allow her to play until she was able to pass my test for the return to participation.

At this time I have a college athlete who has an injury to her shoulder. She will be a senior next year and the only thing that can be done to possibly relieve her pain is for her to have a surgery. She will not do this. Should I allow her to play in pain? I believe that it is her choice. She is twenty-two years old, and her injury will not heal if I have her sit out. The athletic trainer and the orthopedic surgeon have both stated that she can play as long as she can stand the pain. If such a condition existed with a younger child, I would go with the recommendation of the physician as well.

The days when coaches could pressure athletes to play with injuries has passed. If you allow athletes to participate with injuries, especially against the wishes of trainers, parents and doctors, you are setting yourself up for possible court proceedings.

10

TOURNAMENT AND
INTERNATIONAL PLAY

Competition presents an opportunity to test oneself against others. In youth sports programs, this opportunity is provided at the team level as players compete for positions and in contests between teams from the local area. Organized soccer tournaments provide an opportunity for individuals and teams to compare themselves against teams and players from other areas of the state, country and the world. In *Tournament Play* the reasons for participating in tournaments are made clear. Sometimes soccer matches are conducted in adverse playing conditions. Two extreme examples are recounted in *Adverse Playing Conditions*. *International Play* recaps the experiences of the players and the coach as the Force competed against foreign teams.

Tournament Play

Individuals attempt to determine where they stand in relation to others through the process of social comparison (Festinger, 1954). Sport offers children and coaches an opportunity to engage in social comparison as they engage in competition (Barron & Byrne, 1981; Passer, 1996).

Once the Strikers began to win matches frequently in Overland, I wondered how competitive our team would be against teams from other cities. Tournaments provided an opportunity for the players on the Force and Strikers to compete against teams from other cities and to compare their abilities against individuals from other parts of the state, country and the world.

The Strikers and Force played in fifty-one tournaments while I served as the coach. The Strikers and Force won or placed in thirty-one of them. We participated in tournaments held in Texas (Dallas, Abilene, San Angelo, Midcity, San Antonio, Austin, Fort Worth, Overland, Lubbock and Amarillo), New Mexico (Roswell, Carlsbad, Las Cruces, Hobbs and Albuquerque), Colorado (Colorado Springs and Denver) and Minnesota (Blaine). Travel to the tournaments occasionally involved a loss of school time. The expense associated with travel, overnight stays and eating on the road was significant. The average spent on an out-of-town trip by a family was $500-$700 dollars. Players sometimes traveled with other families because of cost or due to their parents' work schedules. I often took players to tournaments along with my family.

The time involved with travel to tournaments, and the fact that parents and players stayed in the same hotels, helped to build friendships among the players and their families. Gus Reynolds's comments on tournaments were reflective of the thoughts of most of the parents:

> I loved going to tournaments. It was good to get to play other teams and to see how people acted and reacted to the games. One of the best parts about traveling was the chance we had to just spend time together and getting to know each other better. At home, we just play a match and leave. During tournaments we got to know each other and a lot of friendships were developed. The tournaments were some of the best times for my family and me.

Each year, the Force parents voted in order to determine which tournaments the team would attend. One indicator of how greatly the parents enjoyed the tournaments and of how close the families were was the fact that each year they voted to participate in a tournament in San Antonio, Texas over Thanksgiving weekend. Thanksgiving weekend is generally a time reserved for families to spend together. Over a period of seven years, Thanksgiving dinners were held at a San Antonio restaurant and shared by all members of the Force and their families.[1]

Bonnie Craft and Sandy Aicinena both had brothers who participated on the Force, and they went on many of the tournament trips. Bonnie stated that she enjoyed going on the trips because, "I liked traveling and I got to see a lot of things. I remember it was neat to go to the Mall of America and to that amusement park in Denver. I got to go shopping on a lot of the trips too." Sandy did not enjoy going on the trips. On some trips, she stayed in the hotel when we went to the games. When she did attend games, she was disinterested. What were her feelings on traveling? She stated, "We got to eat out a lot, and we got to go to the malls. I liked that. I never really watched the games. I might have felt differently if I liked soccer though. I just went because you made me go. But looking back, it was good to spend time with the family."

The players also enjoyed participating in tournaments. At age eleven Seth Weber wrote, "Going to soccer tournaments was a blast." John Reese stated, "I had fun at all of the tournaments we went to." Having the opportunity to compete against players and teams that they had never seen before was an exciting aspect of the tournaments.

Many of the parents viewed traveling to tournaments as an opportunity for the family to spend time together, to see different parts of the country and to see the attractions each area had to offer. Soccer was the reason for the trip, but often it was considered but a part of the whole experience. Debbie Reese stated that, "Traveling to tournaments allowed us to visit historic sites, amusement parks and to do things that we did not get to do at home."

Other parents believed the tournaments were an investment in their child's soccer development. The trips were primarily thought of as business trips. If the children were not "taking care of business" on the field, the trips were considered a waste of time and money. After a disappointing performance in the Colorado Pike's Peak soccer tournament (2 wins and 2 losses), Charlie Harvey stated that, "If the kids are going to play this badly, it doesn't seem worth going on these long and expensive trips." It did not seem to matter that the losses were to the Colorado State Cup Champion and the third place team.

Adverse Playing Conditions

A great amount of time, effort and expense goes into planning and organizing a large soccer tournament. I served as the director for the Overland Soccer Association tournament on four occasions. The OSA had to invest as much as $10,000 to conduct each tournament. We profited

$11,000 in our most successful year when one hundred and twenty teams participated.

The hosting soccer associations generally try to keep matches on schedule because there may be hundreds of matches and referee assignments. It is understood by the tournament directors that a great expense may have been made by teams to come to the events. Failure to provide teams with the matches they anticipate having would decrease the odds of a team returning to the event in coming years. That would be bad business. Because of the reluctance of tournament organizers to vary the tournament schedule in the least, and because of a reluctance to cancel matches, the Force played tournament matches in some very unusual conditions.

The Force regularly played in snow, extreme heat, high winds, occasional lightning and even near darkness. In our region of the country, these conditions were not uncommon, and although we always hoped for good weather, it was never a surprise when inclement weather prevailed. During tournaments we participated in the most severe weather conditions that I have ever had the misfortune to experience.

On the evening before a tournament semi-final and championship date in another city, a cold front blew in from the North. All evening long there was lightning and thunder. The power went off. The temperature dropped to below freezing. The wind was blowing in excess of 40 miles per hour and it was drizzling. In the morning the sky was cloudy, and we could see sheets of white descending from the heavens as we drove to the fields.

When we arrived at 7:30 AM, two inches of water covered most of the playing surface. I questioned whether or not we would play, but was told by the tournament director that the matches would go on as scheduled. My instincts for survival told me we should get into our heated cars and head for home, but we could not abandon the match without the threat of sanctions from the state soccer association.

The boys came out of their cars to "warm up" at 7:45. At that time, it started to rain. Moments later, after soaking us all, the rain turned to ice and it stung as it made contact with our exposed skin. As the match began, the precipitation increased and the wind blew in excess of 45 miles per hour. We completed the first half of the match and had a 5-0 lead as snow blanketed the field. At that point the tournament was canceled. The drive home carried us over roads covered in six inches of snow. It was over an hour before I could feel my feet. I had never been so cold in my life.

Also worth noting was the wind that blew one day in Colorado Springs, Colorado during the Pike's Peak soccer tournament. The tournament is held on the grounds of the U.S. Air Force Academy. It is a picturesque setting and generally the weather is beautiful.

We had a 10:00 AM match and arrived to find excellent playing conditions. The air was calm and quiet as we began to prepare for the match. Toward the end of the warm-up period, the wind began to blow with some intensity from the north, and it did so for most of the first half. We were attacking against the wind and looked forward to having it with us in the second half. As the second half began with the sun shining brightly, the wind suddenly began to blow from the west. It descended from the mountains that protected the campus with great ferocity. We never did get to have the wind with us.

Balls traveled for hundreds of yards when they went out of play. Controlling the ball on the field was an impossibility. The Porta-Potties at the north end of the field blew over and were literally rolled across the ground by the wind. People could stand into the wind at a 40-degree angle and be held up by its force. Yet the match went on.

How hard was the wind blowing? The evening weather report claimed that the wind blew in excess of 75 miles per hour. It is worth noting that the windstorm lasted for only an hour. It stopped 30 minutes after the completion of our match.

International Competitions: Parent and Player Reflections

Over a five-year period, the Force was able to compete with twelve teams from Mexico (losing to one), two from Guatemala (tying twice), one from Brazil (one win and one loss), one from Colombia (win) and two from England (one win and one loss). The Force won most of these international matches and was only "blown out" once.

In the summer of 1996, the Force entered the USA Cup soccer tournament in Blaine, Minnesota. The USA Cup is the biggest soccer tournament in the Americas, and it had over 800 participating teams in the various age groups. The trip required parents to take a week's vacation in order for the children to participate and required a minimum of two days driving each way. Parents also had to pay the cost associated with purchasing meals and lodging for eight days.[2] Two of the thirteen players who were eleven at the time, went with someone other than their families.

The Force played seven matches and placed fourth in the tournament. The team competed against teams from Minnesota, England and Brazil. They defeated the Brazilian team 1-0 in pool play and lost to them 2-1 in the third place match.

The semi-final match against the East Anglia team from England was memorable for all of the players and parents. The comments made by John Thompson, a Force player, are reflective of the impressions held by the players:

> They were really big and fast. They were the best team we ever played. They were really mean, too. One of them asked me if I wanted him to punch me in the mouth. They punched me and held on to my shirt all the time.

The thing that was the most difficult for my players to handle was the physical play. Some of it was dirty based upon the normal play for our age group in our part of the world, but they simply played much tougher than we did. Two of my players cried during the match, and one refused to return after being taken out of the match to rest. The opponents verbally intimidated us as well.

The English won the match 5-0 and went on to win the tournament. The loss was one of the three most lopsided defeats the team had ever experienced. What accounted for the greater intensity and aggression demonstrated by the English children as they played? According to one of the East Anglia coaches, "Some of these players have already been identified as potential professionals and have been signed to [sponsorship] contracts by professional teams."

The following year, the Force traveled to Denver Colorado to participate in the International Friendship Cup. The team placed 1st in the Blue Division and avenged the loss to East Anglia with a 3-1 victory in the semi-finals. It was good to beat the English after being physically beaten and humiliated the previous year. I was happy to see that we had improved in the year since our last encounter. I was also happy to see how much better the players responded to the physical style of play practiced by English. Because they had experienced it the previous year, they were mentally prepared for it and kept their composure during the match.

The Force also badly defeated (13-0) a team from Colombia. John Thompson observed, "They weren't very good and a lot of the players were as small as me."

Why would parents send a team of eleven year olds thousands of miles to lose by lopsided margins? According to one of the Colombian coaches:

We don't bring our kids here to win the tournament. The main reason we come here is to give the kids a chance to see America and to get a feel for its culture. All of the players on this team have parents that are in politics or business, and the kids will have to deal with Americans when they grow up. We hope this experience assists them when they are adults.

As it was with tournament play against American teams, competition for youth teams at the international level served to allow social comparison to take place. It served a variety of other purposes as well. It provided an opportunity to gain exposure to foreign cultures and to prepare youths for competition at the professional level.

Chapter 10 Observations

Questions and Comments for Parents

Traveling with your team to participate in tournaments can have a positive effect upon your family.

In this chapter you read about the tournaments the Strikers and Force participated in. The parents and the players associated with these teams became very close over the years, and the fact that the teams traveled often to tournaments far away from the Midcity and Overland area contributed to that closeness. I do not believe the closeness observed between individuals associated with these teams is typical.

I also traveled to tournaments with baseball and softball teams over the years, and although I did get to know other families, the closeness that developed did not rival that which existed with the Strikers and the Force. The most logical explanation was the length of time the individuals were associated with the two teams. Some individuals were involved with these teams for as long as fourteen years. I do not believe that this often happens in youth sport settings.

One positive outcome that came as a result of all of the travel was that my children developed a surrogate extended family. My relatives live hundreds of miles away from Overland and my wife's family does as well. We seldom get to see them, and the fact that the adults associated with the teams showed concern and care for my children was a positive thing. Another positive aspect associated with travel was that we got to travel together as a family frequently.

A second positive effect was the opportunity for us to spend time together outside of our home environment. My wife, my children and I have always been very busy. When we traveled to tournaments, we spent a lot of time together, much more than usual. We could talk and just experience being together. I will always look back on the trips fondly.

Could we have been taken these trips without the involvement of soccer matches? Yes, but I believe we would have found excuses not to go. The travel was good for my family, and it was good for me.

The travel associated with tournament play can be expensive and can result in conflict.

Because travel was expensive, some children traveled with families other than their own. I know that even as much as we enjoyed traveling as a family to tournaments, there were some heated discussions concerning whether we could afford to go, or if the whole family could go. Since the travel requires a significant amount of time and a great financial commitment, it may cause significant stress in some families.

Traveling to tournaments may demonstrate how your child and your child's team compare to others outside your community, state and country.

I viewed tournament play as an opportunity to gain an accurate assessment of my child's level of play and that of my team as well. Gaining an accurate assessment was valuable to me, to my children and to my athletes in order to assess our abilities compared to individuals and teams in other localities.

Questions and Comments for Coaches

My experiences with tournament play were positive, but you may not experience success, and your experiences may not be as positive.

If your focus is on winning and winning often, participation in tournaments may not be a positive experience for you. It is possible that your team will not win. Further, if parents expect to win and you do not, you are likely to feel their wrath.

Some parents may resist investing the money and time required to participate in out-of-town tournaments if they do not feel the team will perform well. I was involved with softball teams that did not desire to travel far or often because the parents' expectations were low.

The parents associated with my soccer teams were willing to travel to tournaments. Some parents expected us to win all of them. When their goals were not met, they were frustrated, but this was only a small number of parents. If you travel to tournaments and don't succeed, you may well have unhappy parents.

There are professional youth sport coaches who take tournament play very seriously.

When my team played in the USA Cup in Minnesota, there were coaches from as many as four teams watching our match and working up scouting reports. I was surprised. I wanted my team to do well, but I believed my team was there for the experience. It was not going to be the end of the world if we did not win the tournament, nor mean the world if we won it. Frankly, I could not have imagined that my team would be able to finish as high as we did: fourth place. It was an international tournament. My goal was for the team to perform well and overall, they did.

Some coaches demand that their athletes focus on play when the team travels to tournaments.

One of the reasons I felt it was valuable to travel to tournaments was that there were things to do in the cities other than play soccer. I was aware of coaches who prohibited players from going to amusement parks, professional baseball games or hiking in national parks because they might be tired at game time. Would you place such restrictions on your players? Is the only reason for traveling winning? Is there more to life than sport?

Tournaments are exciting for youth players and for collegians as well.

My soccer players enjoyed youth soccer tournaments, and the athletes I worked with at the high school and college level did as well. Competing against teams from other parts of the state or country is exciting.

My college volleyball players enjoy going to different areas of the country and traveling to places they have never been before. Some of my players have been to an ocean and flown on a jet for the first time as a result of playing on my teams. These are positive consequences associated with travel to tournaments. Athletes enjoy them.

11

THE EPITOME OF UGLINESS

Throughout this study, conflicts were caused by differences in the expected and desired attitudes and behaviors of parents, children and coaches. Most differences amounted to little more than minor irritations to the parents, to the children or to me. In this chapter, the incidents causing me the greatest sense of pain, disappointment and sorrow are presented. In these situations, emotions ran out of control within an environment of youth sport that became the crucible for a volatile mix of participation models and intolerance.

The Original Cause of Concern and Sensitization

In the summer before I began to coach soccer, I was participating in a sand volleyball tournament at Sherwood Park. I had lived in the community for only a few months. I noticed there was an evening game going on at the Little-League baseball field and took my wife and children over to watch an inning or two before going home for the night. Since I believed that some day our children would be involved in organized sport, I wanted to get a feel for what went on.

On the very first play at first base, there was an argument over the call. As is usually observed in major league baseball games, the coach flew out of the dugout to argue the call. The first base coach soon became involved in the brouhaha, and shortly thereafter, the third base coach came running to add his two cents.

Faces turned red with rage and veins bulged on their necks. Voices were raised and threatening postures were assumed. Fists started to fly, and by the time the fight had moved to the pitcher's mound, the public address announcer had started to yell for them to stop. Shortly thereafter someone turned off the lights to the field, and the scuffle broke up. Yelling continued as the combatants headed for their cars. Without warning, one of the coaches started to charge after his nemesis, and the fight resumed.

I wanted to see what youth sport was going to be like when I went to watch the game. I saw perhaps eight pitches and one play at first and then all that happened. The thing that I remember the most was how sick the incident made me feel. I remember asking myself if I really wanted my children to be involved in youth sport. The hatred and ugliness was unlike anything I had ever been involved with personally as an adult.

I decided then that if I were to involve my children in youth sport that I would coach as often as possible. I hoped that I would be able to prevent incidents such as this from happening under my leadership. My means of attempting to reach this goal involved emphasizing fair play, respect for opponents, respect for officials' decisions and communication with the parents and players.

The commitment to my goal was strong enough that during games I gave feedback to players and parents concerning their behavior. I also directly asked parents to modify their behavior when they became too vocal or too negative.

I asked parents to control themselves during matches and to avoid yelling at their children, the officials or opponents. Many parents had years of doing all three, so I had to work on them for a long time before they significantly improved their behavior. I made these appeals at the start of every season at the first parent meeting with every team I coached.

Vick Thompson was one of those parents. During the first year of his involvement with the Force, I often asked him to "let it go" after something happened on the field that got him excited. I reminded him and the other parents that they were role models for their children and that yelling would most likely make the players more upset than they might be than if they would just let the transgression made by the opponent or the officials go by. Though he never completely exhibited a saintly adherence to my mandates, he improved dramatically:

I must admit that before joining this team I was highly vocal. You said that you didn't appreciate it, so I thought it was in the best interest of the team, John and myself to be quiet. I don't get on to the referees nearly as much as I used to.

At times, when officials pointed to the area where Vick stood as being the source of their torment, he would quickly indicate that he was not the problem. He usually wasn't, but he did have a reputation with some of the officials in Midcity and Overland based upon his actions over the years.

Vick's son John was a fiery player who displayed his displeasure with officials' calls and non-calls. During contests, he often made retaliatory fouls against opponents. He received more yellow cards (cautions) than any player who had been with the Strikers or the Force. His behaviors seemed to have reflected his father's, and although John tried to control himself at times, he never mastered his emotions. Sometimes they got the best of him. According to his father:

Youth sports are one of the greatest things in the world. It can build character, the ability to work with others, and it can also be humbling. My son's behaviors improved, and I like to think that I helped him. I had nothing to do with his soccer playing improvements, but I hope I influenced him in other ways to develop. I'm not even sure how much of that came from the coaches he has had.

The Strikers rarely received a yellow card (warning for rough or unsporting behavior). There were entire seasons during which three or fewer were issued to my players as they competed in competitive soccer as the Force.

One way that I acted to lessen the chance of players receiving cards was by removing players from the game if they argued or displayed displeasure with the officials. My view of inappropriate "jawing" with the officials was different than the view of some parents. Will Johnson once told me:

I agree that the boys need to have good sportsmanship, but there are times that it is appropriate for them to get upset and say something to the officials. Sometimes the other team is holding them and fouling them. It's the only way to get [the referees] to do anything.

Many coaches, regardless of the level of play, view it as part of their "job" to "work the officials." I refused to do it whether I was a high school coach, college coach or youth sport coach and did the best that I could to prohibit parents and players from doing so. At times it seemed like I was trying to keep the leaking boat from sinking by bailing out the water with a teaspoon, but I tried anyway. Winning was very important to me, but I felt that the priority was being a good human being who had control over my emotions.

Hatred of the opponent was not used as a means of motivation, and there were many times that I would take angry children aside and remind them that it *was* just a game. It was often hard for the players to tell if fouls were intentional or not, especially when they were younger. The typical reaction was for them to assume there was intent naturally resulting in their own desire for revenge.

I did not want fights, injuries and ugliness in my life. There was enough ugliness in the world as it was. Throughout the years of my coaching tenure, violent incidents were infrequent and minor. When they did occur, I viewed them as teaching/learning opportunities. However, over the years there were two incidents that assaulted my fragile belief that my attitudes, values and behaviors had an influence on the parents and players associated with my teams. The second was influential in my youth sport coaching "retirement."

The Guatemalans

In the fall of 1995, a team of ten year olds came to Overland from Guatemala as a cultural and athletic experience. The individual in charge of the trip was Edward Costillo, a Guatemalan native who lived in Overland. He regularly conducted business in Guatemala and thought it would be good for the children to visit the United States:

> I brought the team here to give the children from both countries the opportunity to learn something about each other. It gave the players from Guatemala the chance to go out of their culture and economic distress to see something different. Soccer is looked at, especially by the young people, as the number one solution to making their lives better. Here the atmosphere and attitudes are different. People look at other avenues for improving their lives.

I also believed that the international exchange of cultures was good. I had stayed in Mexico for periods as long as three months at a time, and I learned a lot about myself as well as others during these trips. Seeing and experiencing various cultures has helped me better understand myself and others.

One of the Guatemalan children stayed at my house on the first night of the team's arrival. When Pablo found out that I spoke some Spanish, he was very happy. The next night two additional players stayed at my home. The three of them stayed with my family for three nights.

I brought the group with me to work twice and arranged for the children to attend school with my son for one entire day. They played baseball at the little league field and did a variety of other things as a group.

The Force played the Guatemalan team, and the game ended in a 1-1 tie. It was well played, and there were no behavior problems.

In the spring of 1999, the Guatemalan team made a return visit to Overland. Many of the players were new to the Guatemalan team. None of them stayed with my family, and there were no opportunities to socialize before the match. None of the travelers stayed with the families of any of my players.

The Force players seemed to take the game more seriously than any other it had played in recent years. When we played the East Anglia team from England the second time, my team was determined. This game had the same intensity for some reason. Many of the players remembered the tie from the previous contest and wanted badly to beat the guests. I was surprised at how important the game was to them. The players talked up the game as they had never done before.

The game was very hard fought, literally. Both teams played physically, an anomaly for the Force. The Guatemalans were highly skilled, proud and they played well together. They were physical, and they were easily inflamed by contact and body language. The Force players made "ridiculous fouls" and often pushed and verbally assaulted their opponents. Seven yellow cards were given to the Force. One Force player received a red card for a vicious foul that took pace in the penalty area. I believed the foul was intentional. Players I interviewed could recall the foul four years after it had occurred.

By the middle of the first half, parents of the Force players started to demand that the game be ended. Some stated that the game did not mean anything and that since there was an important tournament coming up that weekend, it was not worth the risk of having anyone injured. I thought it was better to have the players try to overcome the adversity presented by the environment of the match, and it continued on.

The game ended in a tie and upon its completion, the linesman yelled at me when I met the officials at midfield after the match: "That was the most pitiful display that I have ever seen. You are a disgrace to soccer." Harry held me responsible for the behavior of my team.

The fact was that I could not control what was going on. The emotions of the players were out of control. Some of the fouls were retaliatory; some were accidental. On several occasions it looked like fights would break out. Players from both teams questioned and disputed calls that were made and those that were not made. Taking players out of the game and having them cool off did nothing to defuse the situation.

The contest was nothing like the previous one. I felt nauseous through the entire event. I grieved over what I had been a witness to and by association, a part of. It was one of the saddest days of my life. Why couldn't I get control? Why was there such hate?

Edward offered this explanation:

> If you ask me what caused the problems, I believe it is because how important soccer is in Guatemala. The model the children have is that of the professionals, and the game is played like it is a war. The smallest thing can become a big thing, like a comment or a foul. Then there is the American mentality: wining is everything. A lot of bad things can happen when these two sets of ideas come together.

Both teams exhibited a professionalized attitude in this match. Civility was less important than winning and pride.

The Land of Enchantment

In May of 2000, the Force participated in the Sandia Cup Soccer Tournament held in Albuquerque, New Mexico. The third place match of the tournament was the last time that I served as the coach of the Force.

In the third place match, the Force faced a very good team from El Paso, Texas. The Force players were loose before the match and felt they would win. That soccer year, the team did not place in any tournaments, but the team had played very well in this one, the last event of the soccer year.

The opposing team was composed entirely of Hispanic players. They spoke Spanish between themselves before, during and after the match. The Force players viewed them as foreigners.

The match started out intensely, but the opponents were quicker and more highly skilled as a group. They scored in the first ten minutes and again shortly thereafter. The Force players were frustrated by the shirt-pulling and the fouling they believed was overlooked by the officials. My players could be heard yelling at the officials and at each other. The opponents were apparently having a good time.

After a collision and as he got up, Hans Shultz kicked one of the opponents in the head and received a red card. The parents, who by this time had also assumed the role of outraged victim, applauded the young man as he left the field. He received high fives of support from his teammates as he left the field. When I confronted him about the kick to the opponent's head, he denied that he meant to do it.

I could not believe what I had seen. These were nice kids, and their parents were nice people. The match and the events surrounding it seemed to transform them into strangers engaging in alien behaviors.

From that point on, things actually deteriorated. Force players assumed that the opponents were speaking derogatorily about them when, in fact, they weren't. The Force players started to say things like, "Why can't they learn to speak English?" They started to curse at the opponents. Parents yelled at the officials and the opposing players. I knew enough Spanish to understand what the El Paso players were saying. They were talking about strategy, teasing each other and congratulating each other. Their conversations had nothing to do with our team at all. I never heard a curse word spoken in Spanish during the game. There were many uttered by my players in English.

Three goals, one red card (two total) and seven yellow cards later, the match was over. The talk amongst the players was over who got the best shot on the opponent, who had caused the most pain and how great it was that everyone pulled together. I felt like an outsider.

There was really no post-game talk. None of the players wanted to listen to what I had to say. I left the field feeling as though I had failed. My spirit was grieved by what I had just been a part of. It was the first time I had felt like crying over a youth soccer match. I felt responsible and yet powerless concerning the events on the field.

Chapter 11 Observations

Questions and Comments for Parents

It has been my observation that athletes generally reflect the behavior of their parents in regard to opponents' actions and officials' calls.

It was rare for children who have played on my youth teams not to react much like their parents in response to the actions of their opponents (fouls, gestures and language) and to officials' calls. Most often, if parents responded negatively and vocally to something in the environment, so did the children. A lot of effort was required on the part of the parents, children and me if change was to take place in their sporting behaviors.

As a parent, I would like for you to consider this question: Do you want your child to compete with a spirit of sportsmanship or with a disdain for sportsmanship? If you have a win at all cost attitude and look at opponents as an obstacle to your goals, you may look at the calls officials make "against" your child's team as an obstacle as well.

If you are focused solely upon victory, anything that happens that may hamper the achievement of success will be viewed as a purposeful and unjust act. Collisions will be the result of intent. When a referee makes a call you disagree with, you believe it was made against you on purpose. It must be hard for individuals to enjoy the sport setting if such PERCEP-TIONS are made. If your PERCEPTIONS are that everyone is out to take advantage of your child and the team, and your child is taught to PER-CEIVE things the same way, how will your child ever really be able to enjoy participation? How will you ever enjoy watching your child play?

Sometimes things are just not fair.

Are things unfair in the sport setting? Of course they are. Opponents are sometimes bigger, stronger and faster. If you think about it, it does not make for a fair contest. I have often heard parents complain about how unfair it was when a child who was big, strong and fast dominated a contest (soccer, baseball, basketball and softball). What good did complaining about it do? The situation was not going to change. Perhaps looking at such a situation as a great challenge or test would be a more appropriate response. If this is the approach that you take, the game and the challenge can be the focus instead of how unfair things appear.

I have seen parents and coaches demand to see the birth certificates of players during tournaments, even though they were verified during the check-in before play began. Girls have cried in front of me because they were harassed and questioned so often at softball tournaments. In all of the years I have been associated with sport, I can only recall two cases when an illegal player was used out of THOUSANDS of contests. What good do the accusations and the complaining do anyone?

The sport setting is filled with imperfections. How do you want your child to respond to them?

I often observed children who threw their bats and cried after striking out in baseball and softball. I have seen major leaguers break their bats, throw their bats and smash water coolers in response to striking out. Such behavior may come about as a result of frustration or embarrassment. Children may see this behavior exhibited by others and consequently believe it appropriate. Is it?

If you believe that an individual should be upset after striking out or failing in some other way during sport participation, you will look for **proof** that your child is upset when he or she is not successful. Throwing a "tantrum" and making visible indications of anger and disappointment indicate that an individual is upset. You will likely communicate to your child that you expect success and when it does not come, that it should be upsetting. I have heard parents ask their children if they were bothered after failure. When the children responded yes, I have heard their parents respond, "Well it doesn't look like it to me!" It does not surprise me when these children begin to throw tantrums and argue with officials and coaches. It is what their parents want: A visible sign of discontent!

It no longer shocks me to see parents yelling at children, at officials and questioning the decisions of coaches out loud. They believe these responses are appropriate and indeed required of an individual who possesses the requisite degree of seriousness.

I have always thought and still believe that sport is supposed to be fun. If I chose to gripe and complain about the officials, coaches and how my child played during and after each contest, I do not know how I could have enjoyed my children's participation in sport. If my displeasure filtered down to my children on a regular basis, I question how they could have expected to enjoy it either.

I wanted my children to keep things in perspective. No one is perfect. Officials are not perfect; coaches are not perfect; my children are not perfect; I am not perfect. Why not understand this reality and participate in sport without dwelling upon the imperfections? If a child strikes out, what could be done to decrease the likelihood of striking out next time? Maybe focusing on the future instead of the disappointing failure would be a superior response. Why not have your children focus on how to do better instead of how disappointed YOU are? If an official blows a call, realize that calls are sometimes missed or made the wrong way. Why assume the call was made purposefully against you? The call was missed. There are many flaws in the athletic setting. If individuals keep control of their emotions and understand that errors will occur, the sport environment can be more positive. Cannot the same be said about life?

My children were told after they each saw their first tantrum that if they engaged in such a behavior, they would be taken out of the game and sent home. I told them they would fail on occasion and that when they did, that they should consider how to do better next time and not dwell on their frustration. I laid out my expectations, explained why I believed as I did and let them know the consequences of tantrum-throwing should they choose to go against my expectations. Neither child ever had to be taken out of a game or admonished for such misbehavior during a contest. It should be noted here that my children would have been more likely to violate my expectations within the sport setting if I failed to follow through with consequences for non-compliance outside of it. I also modeled the behaviors I expected to see from them.

When bad calls were made during a contest, we would talk about it, and I would again emphasize that people make mistakes, that the world is not perfect and that dwelling on mistakes would not make them go away. We can only do the best we can, and we cannot control what others do.

My response to mistakes and flaws is reflective of a developmental perspective of sport. This perspective, for better or worse, carries over into all aspects of my life. I try to do the best I can as a parent, teacher, coach, administrator and husband. I do not serve perfectly in any of these roles, but I strive to do the best I can. I apologize when it is appropriate. Then I try to alter my behavior for the better and move on. I am not especially hard on others or myself.

Are win-at-all-cost people more likely to look for and reinforce anger and discontent, to argue with others and to complain? Are they more likely to dwell upon imperfections and to make individuals feel inadequate because of them? I believe that they are. They want to win in sport and in life. In their quest for victory, they run into obstacles that frustrate, confuse and stifle. Their lives are often unsettled and they become angry. They are not content; they are not happy, and I do not believe they ever will be. They bring sadness to others and to themselves through their actions. How could they possibly want their children to live their lives this way?

When you yell at children on the field, it bothers them and creates a negative environment.

I was watching a high school soccer match and a group of parents, as was typical of them, yelled suggestions to the players on the field, as they had since the children were four years old. One of the players who had previously played for me turned to the bleachers and yelled to the parents, "Shut the hell up!" The athlete was a junior in high school, and his words were reflective of his frustration. He had played soccer for fourteen years. Does he need to be told what he should be doing by a bunch of parents? I don't think so. If he is frustrated, will he play better? How could he?

I understand that parents want to help their children if they can, but I'm sure that yelling at them during a game is not appropriate. There is tension and pressure associated with games. Perhaps your child will be more receptive to suggestions at other times. If you recall, in this study when the children were young, some of them cried during games. I believe that it was a result of all the instructions and all of the yelling that was associated with the event.

Many children do not appreciate their parents' suggestions, especially as they mature. Several of my athletes have told me so on several occasions. You should also understand that there may come a point when the children may actually know as much as you about the sport, and they will not be receptive to your suggestions because they disagree with you or because they do not view you as an expert. Yelling suggestions out during a game would likely do little good in such situations. Perhaps these actions are best left for the coach. In fact, most coaches would tell you that they prefer parents not coach their children during contests (Strean, 1995).

Officials miss calls and at times make incorrect calls. Get over it.

Sometimes officials do seem unfair. I have been an official (high school basketball and volleyball, youth soccer and softball). I have been questioned, booed and yelled at because of calls that I made or "missed." I can assure you I never made a call in an effort to hurt one team or to favor another. Contrary to popular opinion, I was not blind; I knew who my father was, and I never wanted to see one team win more than another. Given my orientation, why would anyone believe for a moment that I tried to be unfair? It was because they chose to perceive it to be so! It is easier to blame a loss on an official than it is to acknowledge that the team, your child or your coach turned in an inferior performance.

Questions and Comments for Coaches

You set an example for the players and their parents

When we are in the presence of children, we set examples for their future behavior whether we wish to or not. Most coaches claim they want to set a good example for their athletes. They often speak about demonstrating respect for officials and showing good sportsmanship. When things are going well and we are not under a lot of stress, these behaviors are easy to engage in and to model.

The true test of your belief in the importance of respecting officials and sportsmanship comes when things are not going well. It is unreasonable for you to expect your athletes to participate with respect and in a spirit of sportsmanship if you do not. In times of stress, you will need to reflect upon what is really the most important thing: winning and having everything go your way, or participating with an attitude of respect and sportsmanship.

I am often upset when I feel things have not gone my team's way and when I feel a call has gone unfairly against us. At these times, I take a deep breath, realize that mistakes happen and then think about how to overcome the transgression. I remind my team to focus on the next play and move on. Screaming at officials over a bad call does not demonstrate respect or a spirit of sportsmanship. It also distracts the team from focusing upon what is important: the future instead of the past.

You can affect change in parents' and players' sporting behaviors.

If you choose to decrease the frequency of negative behavior in the sporting context, it can be done. You must set standards for the parents and the players and model them yourself. Point out when you have decided to not yell or carry on concerning a bad call or event. Provide feedback to parents and athletes concerning their responses to negative situations. Hold parents and players accountable for their behavior.

What do you want the sport environment to be like?

Do you want your athletes to demonstrate a win-at-all-cost mentality? If you do, you may feel free to harass officials over bad calls and scream every time you believe the opponents are engaging in unfair play. Act like the game is a war. Your parents and athletes will do the same thing.

When many young coaches enter the competitive environment, they will see that often, poor sportsmanship is the norm. Coaches yell at officials and their players, and some of these coaches are successful. It is easy to accept these behaviors as convention (normal) and to believe that to be competitive, they must do the same thing. If you can't beat them, join them.

The alternative is to be distinctively different. It is your choice. I do not understand how hostility and anger as it is found in the sport environment serves to make society better. If important values, attitudes and behaviors are learned in the sport context, I fear what these angry and aggressive individuals are like in their work and their home environments.

Officials aren't out to get you!

I do believe—on one occasion in my entire coaching career—that officials really did cost my team a win: one time. At other times, they may have made a call that I disagreed with that resulted in a key score, but that was just one play during an entire contest. The reality is that many plays constitute a game, and there is any number of possible plays my team could have made that might have resulted in a score. As I coach, I choose to focus on those plays rather than the error of the officials.

Why don't more coaches, players and parents do this? Perhaps it is a lot easier to blame a loss on an official rather than upon inferior play. Blaming a loss on the shortcomings of my athletes or the team places the responsibility for a loss squarely on my athletes and me. At times, that is a difficult point to acknowledge. It is easier and more comforting to blame someone else. To do so does not admit our inadequacies, nor does it require us to improve or develop as individuals.

12

THE SOCIALIZATION OF PARENTS

Parents are a powerful factor in the socialization of children into their role of sport participant (Coakley, 1994; Eitzen & Sage, 1997; Kenyon & McPherson, 1987; Leonard, 1998). When children take part in activities their parents are unfamiliar with, children may serve to socialize the parents as well (Hasbrook, 1982).

At the commencement of the current study, most parents of the participants were unfamiliar with the sport of soccer. Parents became more familiar with the rules, skills and strategies associated with the sport as the study progressed, and some became fans and consumers of the sport. The parents also gained familiarity with normative international fan and player behavior as a result of their children's participation.

Only two percent of the parents whose children played on the Strikers or Force had played organized soccer before their own child's initial participation in soccer. Two of the fathers of the forty-one children had played soccer as children or adults before their children took up the game. None of the forty-one mothers had participated in organized soccer. Four of the fathers joined adult indoor leagues after their children began playing.

Coach, Maybe You Should...

Throughout the years of the Strikers' existence (as the children matured from age four to age nine), I was never directly questioned about player positioning, strategies, playing time or training. Parents often said they were unfamiliar with the sport. Jeff Weber's comments were reflective of parental comments:

> Shoot, I really don't know if they're doing what they are supposed to be doing or not. All I know is that they are supposed to kick the ball and try to kick it in [the goal]. I can tell if they are trying hard or not, but that's about all.

Comments from parents concerning play were most often very general in nature, such as, "They played really well today."

By the time that the boys had reached age thirteen, the parents knew more about the game. Two parents in particular were quick to express their displeasure with the Force's performance after losses. They would offer opinions about what was wrong with the team or individual players.

There were times their observations were valuable. There was only so much that I could see, but much of the time they were simply wrong. They never played the game and did not study it. They did not understand the players as well as I did. There were many things they did not understand.

Their suggestions often irritated me because of their ignorance or lack of insight. Their suggestions frequently involved changes in strategy and/or would have required the team to change its style of play, things that could not be done on the spur of the moment. These factors made the suggestions appear ridiculous in my view.

I was frequently angered by the comments and had to consciously hold my temper and my tongue. My restraint did not stop the comments from coming, but it did serve to maintain good relationships with the parents.

From Ambivalence to Soccer Fan

Some parents, such as Vick Thompson, became soccer fans as a result of their child's participation in the sport:

> I was a die-hard football fan before my kids started to play soccer. I had no interest in soccer. Now that I understand more about the game, I realize that there is a lot to it. I even watch soccer matches on T.V. instead of football. If you told me I would be doing that a few years ago, I would have said you were crazy.

Gus Reynolds declares that he now loves watching soccer. "Before Jerry started to play, I knew nothing about it. Now when the boys don't play for a while, I miss it."

The Creation of Soccer Consumers

Parents became familiar with soccer equipment and supply manufacturers as a result of their children's participation in the sport. They began wearing shirts, warm-ups, hats and jackets with Diadora, Umbro or Reebok Soccer stitched or silk-screened on the products. Often the parents ordered the same shirts and warm-ups as the players. They also ordered clothing from soccer catalogues when they placed orders for their children. The parents were socialized into the role of soccer supply consumers as a result of their children's participation in soccer. Wearing the same clothing as the players also expressed solidarity within the group.

How Does a Soccer Fan Behave?

The parents were unfamiliar with the behavior of soccer fans from other cultures. In many countries, fans sing songs for much of the match and the scoring of a goal is cause for great singing and celebrations. This is uncommon in American sport.

In 1984, my wife and I attended a soccer match at the Los Angeles Olympics. She had never been to a soccer match and was literally frightened by the behavior of the boisterous fans, their chanting, singing, and flag waving. Nothing was unusual in my opinion, because I had attended international matches before and had seen how the fans acted during televised matches.

While the Strikers were participating in a tournament match against a team from El Paso, the opposing team scored a goal and the parents burst into song and danced on the sideline. To add additional flair, the celebrating players formed a caterpillar and danced about the field as one. All of the players and the parents from the opposing team were of Hispanic origin.

The response of the opposing team's parents was a far cry from the Strikers' parents' and players' own shouts of, "Good shot!" or "Way to go!" The Strikers' parents were indignant. "What poor sportsmanship!" "I have never seen anyone get so excited about a stupid goal!" "They ought to be ashamed of themselves for acting that way!" They didn't know that the opponents' parents weren't rubbing the goal in their faces, which is what they thought. If I did not know that in other countries such behavior was typical, I would have thought so, too. I got the parents' attention and explained what was happening. They still didn't think the celebrations were appropriate. One parent retorted, "This is America for heaven's sake. You just don't do that. It just isn't right."

Five years following the event described above, the parents of the Force players had still not become accustomed to or accepting of the celebrations of the players and fans from other cultures. In similar situations, they mimicked the opposing player and fan behaviors in a derogatory fashion. Some parents still were heard to say, "Why don't they just shut up?" Tolerance did not come about as a result of exposure and education. Differences seemed to be exaggerated, not glossed over.

Taking a Dive and the Magic Water

The normative behaviors of athletes differ from sport to sport, from country to country and even from one part of the country to another. The parents and players involved in this study observed that soccer players from other areas faked injuries and fouls in order to receive favorable calls from officials. This behavior was not deemed appropriate by the parents or players of the Strikers and Force. I did not teach or encourage such behavior.

The response of the Strikers and Force players to an opponent's faked injuries was ridicule. They would not say anything to the opponent, but they would be heard to say to one another things such as, "They are a bunch of babies." Parents also made fun of the "injured" players amongst themselves. They would observe the "injured" player make a "miraculous" recovery after receiving attention. They remarked that the "magic water" (water rubbed onto or consumed by the player) must have been responsible for the "miraculous healing."

From the time the Strikers' players were four years old, they were told by parents to "be tough and suck it up" when they experienced a minor painful injury. When the players reached age ten, I would not allow them back into a contest if they embellished the seriousness of an injury.

The players and parents considered faking injuries and fouls as cheating. They also considered it to be reflective of physical and emotional weakness. Nevertheless, faking fouls and injuries to receive favorable calls and to disrupt the flow of the match is normative behavior in high-level soccer. As this study was completed, the players on the Force still did not engage in such behaviors. The behaviors were often observed in players on other teams.

Chapter 12 Observations

Comment for Parents

If you are not familiar with your child's sport, you should learn as much about it as you can.

Some coaches effectively assist parents in learning about the game while others do not. In order to really understand a game, I believe that you have to experience playing it. The next best thing is to watch the game as it is played throughout the country and the world. Understanding that there are differences in how the sport may be played in different localities may serve to decrease the conflict that occurs when competitions are held against individuals outside your community.

Comment for Coaches

It is important for you to teach the game and its nuances to your athletes and their parents.

Failure to teach the game to parents and players may result in unnecessary conflict. The biggest problem may come when parents do not know the rules. Often parents complain loudly about the unfair referees when they do not even know the rules! Teach your parents and players the rules.

Likewise, normative player behaviors should be taught to the parents and athletes as well. Taking these steps can minimize conflicts with officials, players and opposing parents.

13

THE PLAYERS' COMMENTS
AT AGE ELEVEN

Following are comments made by the players on the Force at the age of eleven. After reading the previous chapters, you should have an idea of my coaching philosophy, and you know that the Force and Strikers had a reasonable degree of success. The comments have been included so that you may read what the children thought about the team and me. Following their comments, I have placed in italics an update on each of their current athletic activities.

The comments were written by the players and placed into a scrapbook along with pictures of all of the players by Debbie Reese. I looked at the scrapbook and read what the young players had to say as I completed this book. I was overcome with emotion.

Coaching took a lot of time and effort. I experienced many difficulties concerning the use of my time and in dealing with the problems associated with parent and player personalities. Through all of my difficulties, I tried to keep in mind why I was there. I was there because I wanted to help the kids develop as soccer players and as young men. I fought to keep winning and losing in perspective and to maintain a developmental attitude that was reflective of the Pleasure and Participation Model.

Even though I did not coach until these young men all completed their soccer participation, their comments suggest that I have had some effect upon their development. I am thankful for that, and it made my efforts worthwhile. In another life, I would coach these children all over again. I would do it the same way.

Coach,

> Thank you so much Steve for being such a great coach. You've taught me more things than all of my other coaches put together. You've taught me that in order to have a good attitude in games that I have to have a good attitude in practice. And a good attitude is a key to success. Thank you for all of your hard work and encouragement. *Max Bennett*

Max was on the Pen High School Varsity in 2001 and started for the team in 2002. He still plays with the Force.

Dear Steve,

> I have been playing on your soccer team ever since I was seven years old. It's been a lot of fun. I have had several different coaches, but you have been the best. I want to thank you for all the time you have given to the team. I like being on your team because you don't yell at us and make us feel bad. Instead you are patient and tell us what we did wrong and how to make it better. I have played on your team for five years or more and I have had a lot of great memories. Thanks for everything. *Sincerely, Jack Jones*

Jack stopped playing soccer two years after this note was written to focus on tennis, choir and his church-related activities. He graduated from Pen High in May of 2002. He plans to become a minister of music with the Baptist Church.

Coach Steve,

> This season has been great playing for the Force United and you have been a wonderful coach. Through your leadership, I have learned patience, determination, and a desire to improve my skills. I like the positive attitude and the questions you ask us to make us think about what we're doing. Thank you for all of the time you spend with us. *Sincerely, #15, Kent*

Kent left the Force in order to play with the Fire. He stopped playing soccer a year and a half later. He no longer participates in any sports at the high school or in organized youth settings. He works at a local shoe store and has a keen interest in his Firebird.

Steve,

Thank you for being my coach. I've really had a great year. I'm very proud to be on the Force United. I've learned and improved a lot while being on the team, and will try to play for the Force United as long as I can. Thanks for all of the time you have given the team. *Jackson Forrest*

Jackson left the Force to focus on tennis three years later. In his junior year of high school, he started on the Overland High varsity soccer team as a sweeper.

Steve,

Thank you for helping me to become a better player this season. Each day, soccer becomes more fun because I have you to teach me the correct way to play the game. I love not only to play soccer, but to play for you. *#1 Keeper, Brent Bates*

Brent stopped playing soccer after he had his third soccer-related surgery. He was on the Pen High varsity at the time of his third major injury. He participated in academic decathlon competitions at Pen high in his junior year.

Dear Steve/Coach

I just wanted to say what a great coach you've been. Being a coach must be hard; players not listening, not trying, goofing off, but most of all, you take four and a half hours a week and devote it to us. That's just a few bad things about coaching that I named so not to make our team look bad. You have coached our team for several years and in those years you taught me almost everything I know. I wrote this to say thanks for all the years and hopefully years to come of your coaching. *Brian Harvey*

Brian started on the Pen High varsity team as a junior and was key in two of the team's wins. He continues to play with the Fire and hopes to earn a soccer scholarship as he enters his senior year of high school.

Steve,

This is one of the best years that I had played soccer. I had learned more on my sport. Thanks for taking me to all the tournaments we went to. *Love, Richard*

Richard enjoyed playing soccer with the Force, but left the team because he had no close friends on it. He works after school in order to pay for the expenses associated with his truck and to have spending money. He plays soccer on the "Mexican League" team located in his hometown. There is no soccer team at his high school.

Steve,

Soccer is a lot of running, kicking, passing, dribbling, shooting, blocking defending and scoring goals. It is a team sport. Steve, thanks for being my soccer coach all these years. I have really enjoyed playing and learning soccer from you. You made soccer fun and going out of town was a blast. Force United #1 Strikers #1 Force Rules. *Love, Seth Webber*

Seth gave up soccer in the spring of 2002 in spite of his being one of the most highly valued players on the team. He stated that he was just, "worn out." He is listed as a starter on the Pen High varsity football at the cornerback position going into his senior year. He will play in front of 20,000 people.

Dear Steve,

Thank you for a great season. I had a lot of fun. I have liked being on your team for all 6 years that I have been on it. I look forward to another great season. *Thanks, Jerry Reynolds*

Jerry continues to play for the Force as a sweeper. He does not participate in any sports at the high school. He participates in choir and enjoys racing cars at the local speedway. He stated that soccer at the high school would interfere with his classes.

Dear Steve/Coach

I have enjoyed all of the years that you have coached me. You have been a special friend to me and I learned more than just soccer from you. Even when you get mad at me I know you are just trying to make me a better player and person. I hope to stay together for many more years. *Your Friend Always, Dave Burrows*

Dave plays with the Force and enjoys his participation. He was on the junior varsity basketball team as a sophomore and is listed as a member of the Pen high varsity football team for next year. He is being pressured by his soccer friends to join the soccer team at the high school next winter. He is undecided at the present time.

Dear Steve,

I appreciate the things you have helped me with this year. This year was great. I learned more about how to play my position. I had fun at all of the tournaments we went to. It's been a wonderful year with a great coach. I owe most of my thanks to you. I am looking forward to another great year. *Thanks, John Reese*

John played and started on the Pen junior varsity soccer team in 2002 and was brought up to the varsity team for the playoffs. He also participates in the choir at Pen high. He still plays with the Force.

Coach Steve,

I liked being on your team this year. Your coaching is a lot of why we are so good. Your coaching brought the best out of us. I wanted to be on your team for a long time. Then I finally got a chance to play on your team. It has been a great year. Thank you for giving up your time to coach us. *Mike Thompson*

Mike Thompson is still a member of the Force. He played on the varsity soccer team at Overland high school in 2002.

Dad,

Thanks for all of the memories, and all of the time you gave to the team.
Love, Eric

Eric played on the Pen High junior varsity soccer team in 2002, and was
elevated to the varsity team for the playoffs.

14

CONCLUDING OBSERVATIONS AND COMMENTS

This book was written in order for you to gain insight into the youth sport experiences of individuals who were associated with two youth soccer teams. My goal was to provide enough information to allow you to reflect upon what the youth sport experience should be, whether you are a parent or a coach. My hope is that as you read, you were at times either, amused, surprised, or outraged.

It is important to me that I make every effort possible to be fair with everyone. There are two sides to every story. Throughout this book, I have tried to allow my beliefs and those contrary to mine to be expressed. Much of what I have presented may have come across as being very critical of youth sport and youth soccer. Celebrating only the good does not serve to make things better.

It should be made clear here that I would go through the soccer coaching experience all over again. I enjoyed it. Coaching was, and is, rewarding. There are problems, however, associated with youth sport, and I have tried to address many of them within the pages of this book. Talking about the positive aspects of coaching will do little to assist you in dealing with the conflicts involved with youth sport participation as a coach or as a parent.

Conflict Occurs Due to Differences in Participation Model Orientations

It was my belief that differences in the chosen participation models and desired participation and coaching behaviors of parents, coaches and athletes leads to conflict in the youth sport setting. Below are the major findings from this project that would support my contention.

The Level of Commitment Held by Participants Varies

Some parents wanted me to devote more time to coaching than I could or would be willing to give. Comments that the parents made in regard to my level of commitment resulted in my becoming frustrated. My unwillingness to devote more time caused some of them to seek another team.

Athletes on my teams also differed in the level of commitment they had toward soccer. Some individuals attended virtually every practice and game, while others came only at their convenience. This frustrated my ability to develop players and the team to the level I saw possible. Some parents blamed the team's level of play partially upon practice attendance.

Many of the athletes on my teams participated in multiple school activities, both athletic and non-athletic. For some, fatigue was a problem and the players' ability to focus only upon soccer was impaired. This limited the development of the individual athletes and the team.

In the Power and Performance Model, excellence is demonstrated through success. Success is obtained in this model through dedication, hard work and sacrifice. Commitment to these valued means to success was in short supply. This upset those individuals who adhered to the Power and Performance perspective. The Pleasure and Participation Model, however, does not require total dedication, heavy amounts of hard work or great sacrifice in order for personal or team success to be achieved. There were players and parents associated with the team who were not frustrated with the team's performance. Differences in an individual's perspective on what success is and what is required to achieve it affected our perceptions. Commitment, or a lack of it, was a source of conflict.

Active Participation is the Goal for Some, but not for Others

In recreational soccer, all children were guaranteed the opportunity to play at least one half of every contest. In competitive soccer, they were not. The expectations for playing time differed in the two settings on the part of the parents, the players and me. Though every child wanted to play often in all games, athletes did not get equal time. To have allowed this most certainly would have reduced the probability of success as measured in wins and losses. Though winning was not everything with the Force or Strikers, it was important to the parents, players and to me.

Because some children played less than others, parents and players periodically expressed disappointment; parents claimed that some of the less effective players played too much.

The Pleasure and Participation Model holds active participation as a primary goal. If children are not actively playing, this goal cannot be met. Conversely, in the Power and Performance Model, only the best should play because inferior players reduce the chance of winning. These opposing views of the importance of playing time resulted in conflict.

Not all Individuals Agree Concerning Decision-Making

I allowed players to make decisions in many cases concerning practice activities, warm-ups for contests, eating, sleeping and participation decisions, etc. I did not try to control the behavior of my players off the field. I encouraged them to make decisions and to live with the consequences. I was a guide for them, not a dictator.

If I had exerted more control, the team may have performed better at times, but teaching the athletes to make decisions and live with the consequences may have been a better learning experience. These behaviors are associated with the Pleasure and Participation Model and were upsetting to those holding a Power and Performance perspective.

A Child is not a Machine

I was concerned with injury from the time I began working with the children at age four, until I stopped coaching them at age fifteen. I wanted to minimize the frequency of acute injuries in practices and games as well as injuries that may have occurred due to overtraining. My view was that injuries that could be avoided should be avoided. Further, I believed that the participants should be emotionally healthy. I did not yell, disparage athletes, blame individuals for losses, etc. These behaviors were consistent with the characteristics of the Pleasure and Participation Model. In the eyes of some, I did not demand enough of the athletes, place blame when it was appropriate or actively drive the athletes toward victory, but there were limits to what I was willing to demand of the athletes. There were also limits to what I was willing to do in order to motivate them to perform. This caused conflict with Power and Performance adherents.

Excellence is Demonstrated Through Success

In the United States, there is little chance to escape the belief that excellence is best reflected by a person's win-loss ratio. I believe that winning is important. It simply holds a lower place in my hierarchy of measures of success.

When I found myself being tempted to yell at players or to act in a way that was contrary to my philosophy of coaching, it was due to my ego. If my teams did not win, it was a poor reflection upon me, even if I did not believe that I was always ultimately responsible for the play of my team.

As noted earlier in this book, there were times when I thought my team played exceptionally well in defeat and at other times played poorly in victory. In fact, I recall being extremely pleased with my teams after specific losses, even to the point that I was elated. At the same moment, I could look at individual players or parents and see disappointment or even disgust in their eyes. I was applauding their skilled performance and trying to instill in the players the intrinsic pleasure that results from performing well in spite of the final score. Differences in the measures of success resulted in some being pleased in defeat and others feeling disappointed, frustrated and willing to look for other competitive teams.

At younger ages, most parents and players looked for development and did not seem to focus as much on winning. In this study, the importance of winning and proving oneself as a superior or elite athlete seemed to grow as the players matured, not only for the players but for the parents as well. These individuals left my team. Objectively, this was a reasonable step for the parents and players to take. On a personal level, I was disappointed to lose players who had been on my teams for as long as ten years. People change.

Strength, Speed and Power are Emphasized

The Power and Performance Model of sport holds strength, speed and power as the essence of a good athlete and the measure of their worth. In this study, many children participated on my teams. Some were bigger, faster and stronger than were others. However, having these attributes does not automatically guarantee an individual athlete will also perform at a superior level; appearance can be deceiving. There is more to soccer and to most sports than being big, strong and fast.

When children who were not big, strong and fast played more often than those who were, it caused conflict between the parents, some athletes and me. The fact that training at my practices did not include a lot of time devoted to the development of sheer speed or power was also linked to conflict

Other Observations

In reflecting upon the events described in this book, I could not help but make many observations concerning youth sport in my community. I also observed some trends that trouble me. Some of these observations are presented below.

The prevalence of professional coaching will continue to grow at the youth sport level.

In the United States, winning is the most common measure of success (Coakley, 2001). Further, a desire to be the best is also ubiquitous in America. As parents and their children strive toward personal excellence, hiring professional coaches is a reasonable, even logical, step. In my community, professional youth soccer coaches did not exist at the start of the study and at this time, there are at least four clubs in the area with coaches who are paid for their services. That is a significant change.

Professional baseball instruction has become available for youths in my community. In the past fourteen years the number of sports camps available to youths has increased exponentially. Last night, I saw a commercial on the television for a business in town that offers "professional" physical and skills training. Youths were shown receiving instruction in agility, hitting, kicking soccer balls, and shooting basketballs. The children appeared to be between the ages of eight and ten. If the proliferation of professional youth sport instruction in this community is any reflection of what is going on nationally, I would expect to see an increase in the number of individuals making a living in the youth sport environment. There is obviously a demand for specialized sport instruction for youths. There is money to be made. Youth sport has become big business.

I see nothing inherently wrong with this. There are many good professional coaches affiliated with youth sport programs just as there are many good coaches associated with high school and college programs. On the other hand, some coaches are self-serving and do not perform in a manner that is developmentally appropriate for young children. Abuse is more likely to occur when performance is measured by winning, and coaches can only keep clients when their teams win. Therein lies the problem.

Certainly there are volunteer coaches in youth sport who have a win-at-all-cost mentality who engage in abusive behavior, and there has been for generations (Ralbovsky, 1987). The main point is that paid youth sport coaches will continue to increase in the youth sport setting. More pressure will be placed upon children to perform at younger and younger ages by both their coaches and their parents. Sport will be work for more and more children at younger ages. When will they have fun?

High School sport will become further discounted in its importance to parents and athletes in selected sports.

It was clear in the attitudes held by my players and their parents that high school soccer was not generally valued as highly as club soccer. In fact its importance was discounted. It was described as being inferior. I was a high school coach, and I teach individuals that are or who aspire to be high school coaches. To me and to them, this idea is problematic. It denies the high school coach status with some of his or her players, removes some very good athletes from the varsity team, and it undermines the traditional importance of participating on high school teams.

As more and more athletes come to view the club setting as being more legitimate than the high school environment, fewer athletes will participate in high school sport, and those who do may discount its contribution to their lives. High-level play may not be the single or most important contribution of high school sport to the lives of the participants. If there are values other than the development of high-level players in the high school setting, those who choose club sport instead may be denied those benefits.

The poor will be more often excluded from playing high-level sport.

Some excellent athletes who do not have the funds to participate in privatized high-level sport will be identified and given scholarships by those associated with these programs. Performance is valued in high-level sport, and the most talented will often have the opportunity to play at the highest level. Others who may develop later or who choose not to sacrifice their time and money will be excluded from reaching their potential.

To me, the problem is that as society comes to believe that it is a waste of time if one is not playing at the highest level, opportunities to participate at lower levels of competition will become less prevalent. If the love of the game is not sufficiently valued to encourage individuals who are not talented enough or who cannot afford the price of playing at a high-level to continue their involvement as players or as coaches, the existence of the Pleasure and Participation Model may be threatened. Such a change is not a positive one.

The importance of success and development increases with age for many young people.

As I noted previously, some children and their parents became more concerned with winning and high-level play as the children aged. The majority of the individuals who demonstrated an adherence to the Power and Performance Model were more likely to become more concerned with winning and high-level play in this study. This is an observation, not a condemnation of their desire to achieve their soccer dreams. The individuals who maintained a Pleasure and Participation orientation seemed less concerned with winning and high-level development as the study progressed. Six of the original Force players were on the team as this study concluded, and the team had a losing record. There are reasons for playing other than winning.

Sport becomes more professionalized as children mature.

The demands placed upon athletes increase as children mature. If the level of play increases as children mature, the skill level and tactical development must increase if children are to enjoy participation. The environment becomes more serious as a result. What was once fun may become something much different as an athlete goes through the system.

How serious things become can affect the experience of the athletes. The experience of one of my students as she participated in basketball serves to illustrate this point quite well:

> From a personal experience, I played organized youth sports for the enjoyment and because my parents wanted me to increase my social and motor skills development. As I made my way through elementary school and middle school, I felt like it was still organized youth sport. However, I started to notice a change once I got to my senior year in high school. Winning was everything and there was more pressure. As I made my way to college, there was a drastic change. College basketball was definitely turned into a [professionalized] sport. I got paid to play (college scholarship)… There was definitely a lot of pressure to not only play well, but to win too. In a sense, the "fun and relaxation" of the game was no longer present.

> As I did the readings, it was as if a light turned on and I suddenly defined what had happened between playing basketball when I was in elementary and middle school, to when I played in high school and in college. It was more stressful than I had thought it would be. Sometimes I even found myself thinking back to how basketball used to be when I was playing at home in my driveway without any pressures. Those memories helped me to realize why I was playing in the first place.

It would be wrong if I failed to acknowledge that some individuals might find their experience in a similar situation to be quite rewarding. It seems unlikely that the majority of our youths would find it to be so. We all respond to life's situations differently. This should be understood and appreciated.

I hope that your experience in sport will be as rewarding as mine was. My wish is that as a coach and as a human being that I could have pleased everyone. Such is not possible in sport or in any aspect of life. For me, the key to an enjoyable experience is to understand your goals and expectations as well as the goals and expectations that are held by others. Understanding why differences exist can assist you in changing and/or accepting a given circumstance. I have usually been able to minimize conflict and in doing so, I have made the sport and life experiences more pleasant and rewarding for the people around me as well as for myself. It is your choice to be accepting and tolerant of the goals, expectations and behaviors of others or to be confrontational and intolerant. To a high degree, your youth sport experience will be what you make it. Life is what you make it.

APPENDIX

SPORT PARTICIPATION MODEL EVALUATION SCALE

The items appearing in the questionnaire below were created from the characteristics of the Power and Participation and the Pleasure and Performance Models of sport participation as described by Coakley (2001) and my modifications of his characteristics. It may be used to assess your current view concerning specific attitudes and behaviors in sport settings. The questionnaire possesses content validity. The questionnaire was given on two occasions to thirty-seven individuals. Scores were subjected to statistical analysis through the SPSS statistical analysis program. The Average Measure Intraclass Correlation was .9506. The aggregate scores of the thirty-seven individuals changed very little when they completed the questionnaire each time. In regard to individual item reliability between tests, the Equal-Length Spearman-Brown Coefficient was .7038. The questionnaire is reliable and valid and can be used for research purposes based upon the criteria set forth by Ferguson and Takane (1989).

Instructions

For each of the statements below you are asked to select either agree or disagree. Your responses should reflect how you feel about sport in general (youth sport, school sport), not what you feel should be done at the professional and international levels.

1. Winning **is not** the most significant measure of success in the sport experience.

    Agree ___ Disagree ___

2. My opponents **should be** respected.

    Agree ___ Disagree ___

3. Performing to one's capabilities is the most significant measure of success in sport.

    Agree ___ Disagree ___

4. Athletes **should** take legal performance-enhancing drugs in the pursuit of success.

    Agree ___ Disagree ___

5. Only the best should be allowed to play.

    Agree ___ Disagree ___

6. An individual must work **very hard** in order to experience success in sport.

    Agree ___ Disagree ___

7. Individuals can be successful in sport without allowing other aspects of their lives to suffer (Examples: relationships can be maintained and excellence can be achieved in other areas of life).

    Agree ___ Disagree ___

8. Only coaches should make decisions during contests.

    Agree ___ Disagree ___

9. I **do not** consider success in sport more valuable if an individual experiences pain during a contest.

   Agree ___ Disagree ___

10. Athletes that are poorly skilled **should not** get the opportunity to play.

    Agree ___ Disagree ___

11. It is the coach's responsibility to complain to officials when calls are often made against his or her team.

    Agree ___ Disagree ___

12. Losing **should be** a painful experience.

    Agree ___ Disagree ___

13. Televised sporting events **do not** provide good examples of behavior for coaches and athletes.

    Agree ___ Disagree ___

14. The greatest measure of success in sport is whether or not an individual enjoyed the contest.

    Agree ___ Disagree ___

15. An individual can decide not to participate in a contest when injured and still be committed to success.

    Agree ___ Disagree ___

16. Sport participation should be very hard work.

    Agree ___ Disagree ___

17. Individuals who are not willing to sacrifice their short-term health are not committed to success in sport (Example: not willing to break a bone)

    Agree ___ Disagree ___

18. All individuals should strive to play like the professionals.

    Agree ___ Disagree ___

19. Opponents are my friends.

    Agree ___ Disagree ___

20. Winning is more important than my honor.

    Agree ___ Disagree ___

21. Coaches **should not** set training rules for athletes (Examples: don't smoke, don't drink alcoholic beverages).

    Agree ___ Disagree ___

22. Individuals unwilling to sacrifice their long-term health can experience success in sport.

    Agree ___ Disagree ___

23. Opponents stand in the way of my achievement of success.

    Agree ___ Disagree ___

24. It is **not necessary** to utilize current information from the sport sciences in training sessions to be successful in sport (Examples: Exercise Physiology and Biomechanics).

    Agree ___ Disagree ___

25. The win-at-all-cost philosophy common in professional sport is unacceptable for youth and school sport.

    Agree ___ Disagree ___

26. Individuals should strive to win by as much as possible, even if the opponents are embarrassed.

    Agree ___ Disagree ___

27. Athletes **should not** take illegal performance-enhancing drugs in the pursuit of success.

    Agree ___ Disagree ___

28. Athletes and coaches should regularly study game films of events in order to find success.

    Agree ___ Disagree ___

29. Large sums of money should be sacrificed in the pursuit of athletic success.

    Agree ___ Disagree ___

30. It is acceptable to break the rules in order to win.

    Agree ___ Disagree ___

31. It is **not necessary** for athletes and coaches to study game films in order to find success.

    Agree ___ Disagree ___

32. It is important for athletes to use the latest technology to find success in sport (Example: high tech equipment).

    Agree ___ Disagree ___

33. It is appropriate to participate in sport and **not reflect** the behaviors of professionals.

    Agree ___ Disagree ___

34. Coaches should make all decisions concerning the training of the team or individual athlete.

    Agree ___ Disagree ___

35. It should be clear to anyone watching that the coach is in control.

    Agree ___ Disagree ___

36. Competitors keep me from achieving success.

    Agree ___ Disagree ___

37. Coaches should make all decisions during competitive events.

    Agree ___ Disagree ___

38. Winning is the most significant measure of success in the sport experience.

    Agree ___ Disagree ___

39. Opponents are my enemies.

    Agree ___ Disagree ___

40. I believe that if an individual overcomes pain in the pursuit of success that the achievement is even more valuable than if pain were not experienced.

    Agree ___ Disagree ___

41. Televised sport events provide good examples for the behaviors of coaches and athletes.

Agree ___ Disagree ___

42. Sport participation should be fun.

Agree ___ Disagree ___

43. All athletes should be given an opportunity to play in all contests.

Agree ___ Disagree ___

44. Even poorly skilled athletes deserve the right to play.

Agree ___ Disagree ___

45. Athletes should be allowed to make decisions during contests.

Agree ___ Disagree ___

46. Individuals should strive to win, but should be careful **not** to embarrass opponents.

Agree ___ Disagree ___

47. Athletes should take illegal performance-enhancing drugs in the pursuit of success.

Agree ___ Disagree ___

48. If an individual is not willing to compete in pain, he or she lacks commitment to success.

Agree ___ Disagree ___

49. Losing **should not** have much of an affect upon an individual.

Agree ___ Disagree ___

50. Both my competitors and I can achieve success in a contest.

Agree ___ Disagree ___

51. The win-at-all-cost philosophy common in professional sport is acceptable for youth and school sport.

Agree ___ Disagree ___

52. Individuals **should not** be willing to sacrifice their short-term health in pursuit of success in sport (Example: break a bone).

Agree ___ Disagree ___

53. It **is not** important for athletes to use the latest technology to find success in sport (Example: high tech equipment).

Agree ___ Disagree ___

54. The greatest measure of success in sport **is not** enjoyment.

Agree ___ Disagree ___

55. Athletes **should not** take legal performance-enhancing drugs in the pursuit of success.

Agree ___ Disagree ___

56. My honor is more important than winning.

Agree ___ Disagree ___

57. Athletes should have input into their training.

Agree ___ Disagree ___

58. Individuals can experience success in sport without working hard.

    Agree ___ Disagree ___

59. It is acceptable if the coach does not seem to be in control at all times.

    Agree ___ Disagree ___

60. It **is not** acceptable to cheat in order to win.

    Agree ___ Disagree ___

61. The coach **should not** complain to officials concerning calls that are made against his or her team.

    Agree ___ Disagree ___

62. Performing to one's capabilities **is not** the most significant measure of success in sport.

    Agree ___ Disagree ___

63. Coaches should set training rules for athletes (Examples: don't smoke, no alcohol).

    Agree ___ Disagree ___

64. Individuals should be willing to sacrifice their long-term health in the pursuit of success (Example: life-long joint pain).

    Agree ___ Disagree ___

65. My opponents should be hated.

    Agree ___ Disagree ___

66. Athletes should have input into decisions during competitive events.

    Agree ___ Disagree ___

67. In order for individuals to be successful in sport, they must dedicate themselves to the point that other aspects of their life may suffer (Examples: sacrifice relationships and the achievement of excellence in other areas of life).

    Agree ___ Disagree ___

68. The latest information from the sport sciences should be utilized in training sessions (Examples: Exercise Physiology and Biomechanics).

    Agree ___ Disagree ___

69. Opponents assist me in achieving my success.

    Agree ___ Disagree ___

70. Individuals **should not** sacrifice large sums of money in the pursuit of athletic success.

    Agree ___ Disagree ___

Response Key

Instructions:

For each response that you made on your evaluation, give yourself one point every time your answer is the **same as the key**.

For Example:

- If the key indicates Agree and your response is Agree, give yourself one point: +1

- If the key indicates Agree and your response is Disagree, give yourself no points: 0

When you complete scoring your evaluation, add up the total number of points and then go to the next page.

1. Disagree	26. Agree	51. Agree
2 Disagree	27. Disagree	52. Disagree
3. Disagree	28. Agree	53. Disagree
4. Agree	29. Agree	54. Agree
5. Agree	30. Agree	55. Disagree
6. Agree	31. Disagree	56. Disagree
7. Disagree	32. Agree	57. Disagree
8. Agree	33. Disagree	58. Disagree
9. Disagree	34. Agree	59. Disagree
10. Agree	35. Agree	60. Disagree
11. Agree	36. Agree	61. Disagree
12. Agree	37. Agree	62. Agree
13. Disagree	38. Agree	63. Agree
14. Disagree	39. Agree	64. Agree
15. Disagree	40. Agree	65. Agree
16. Agree	41. Agree	66. Disagree
17. Agree	42. Disagree	67. Agree
18. Agree	43. Disagree	68. Agree
19. Disagree	44. Disagree	69. Disagree
20. Agree	45. Disagree	70. Disagree
21. Disagree	46. Disagree	
22. Disagree	47. Agree	
23. Agree	48. Agree	TOTAL Score:
24. Disagree	49. Disagree	
25. Disagree	50. Disagree	_____

What Does My Score Mean?

The highest possible score is 70. The lowest possible score is 0. The highest score in my testing population of 37 college students was 48. The lowest score was 8. My score was 11. The average score for the testing population was 21.

The testing population was composed of students that had just completed a Sociology of Sport course. My assumption is that scores would have been somewhat higher had the subjects not taken the course. My goal in the course is to move the students toward the Pleasure and Participation end of the continuum. In the class, students were asked to think about sport in ways that they never had and engaged in frequent discussions concerning what the meaning of sport was to them and what sport should be. Change in their attitudes concerning desired goals and behaviors may have occurred over the course of the semester. After the completion of the course, many students have told me that their beliefs had changed.

The closer your score is to 0, the more you lean toward viewing sport from the Pleasure and Participation Model. If your score was between 0 and 10, I believe that you would be likely to have conflicts in the sport setting with individuals who lean toward the Power and Performance Model of sport.

- You are more likely to view the achievement of one's potential and development as the greatest measures of success in sport. Winning is not the most important thing in sport.

- You are more likely to believe that there are limits to what someone should do in their pursuit of excellence.

- You are less likely to believe that it is acceptable to make great sacrifices in the pursuit of excellence.

- You are less likely to believe that technology should be used in training and competition.

- You are more likely to believe that athletes should make decisions concerning training and competitions.

- You are more likely to view opponents as needed and valued in the quest of excellence.

- You are more likely to view opponents as needed and valued in the quest of excellence.
- You are more likely to believe that all people should have the opportunity to participate in sport and that accommodations should be made to accomplish this objective.

The closer your score is to 70, the more you lean toward viewing sport from the Power and Performance perspective. A score between 31 and 70 would indicate that your beliefs and expected behaviors in the sport setting may be at odds with those who are partial to the Pleasure and Participation Model.

- You are more likely to view winning to be the most important measure of success in sport.

- You are more likely to believe that regardless of what must be sacrificed in the pursuit of winning, it is worth it.

- You are likely to believe that if sacrifices are made in sport that victory is even more meaningful.

- You are likely to believe that training and competition should be enhanced through technology.

- You are likely to believe that coaches should be in control

- You are likely to look at opponents as obstacles and sometimes feel as though they are enemies.

- You are likely to believe that sport is for the skilled. Individuals who cannot contribute to a team's success should not play.

If your score falls in the neutral range (11-30), you believe that various aspects of each model are appropriate in the sport setting. Individuals who are extreme in their beliefs may cause conflict with you.

- You are not likely to be extreme concerning what behaviors you may expect from coaches or athletes.

- You would be likely to "go with the flow" in most cases, though you may feel strongly about particular issues.

- You may be unsure about what is ultimately important in sport and what must be done to achieve success.

- Your behavior as a parent or coach may be perceived by others as being inconsistent. This may result in conflict.

AUTHOR NOTES

Chapter 1

1. The precise number of participants cannot be determined because many youth sport programs do not belong to national sport governing bodies.
2. Data obtained from the Overland Soccer Association records from 1999-2000.
3. Recreational soccer was not offered through the OSA after 1998 for children over the age of eleven.
4. Players could play on teams in tournaments as guest players with the coach's permission. Children moving from the area could receive a release upon appeal to and approval from the North Texas State Soccer Association.

Chapter 2

1. As a member of the Overland Girls Softball Association Board of Directors, I had the same difficulty in recruiting coaches. The backgrounds of coaches were not checked. They were discussed, but the primary qualification to coach was willingness.
2. My father and mother were divorced when I was two. He spent time in correctional facilities and in drug rehabilitation. I never knew him.
3. I had two step-fathers.
4. It is unusual for youth sports organizations to run background checks on coaches. The cost would be prohibitive. The OSA required coaches to fill out a form stating whether or not they had a criminal past. Backgrounds are not checked. The softball board once discovered that a coach had been arrested and tried for murder, a fact unknown until a month after the season began.

Chapter 3

1. I was present when the Premiere League was formed, served on the Board of Directors for four years and served as its President one year.
2. "Will" spoke of the expectation of having a state championship team at Pen high. By the time this book was published, there were only seven remaining "85" competitive soccer players still involved with high school soccer at Pen. I thought at the time that "weeding out" thirteen-year old players would hurt the numbers in high school. My concern appears to have been justified.

Chapter 4

1. Eight former Force players played for the Midcity Fire "Blue."

Chapter 5

1. Two children who joined the Force at age 12 received their very first, first-place trophies.
2. The team was very competitive; however, it was demoted to the second division of the Classic League in the spring of 2000. The team re-qualified to participate in the first division in 2001.
3. The drive to Phoenix requires a six-hour one-way drive. Some parents of the Fire players flew to matches in 1999-2000.

Chapter 6

1. The 5A classification is the highest in the state. Classifications are based upon the number of students attending the schools. Pen High School had a student population of 2,122 in 1999-2000 (grades 10-12).

Chapter 8

1. Overland School District enrollment figures.
2. I was present at the board meeting when this discussion took place. I assisted the board by serving as the director for the annual soccer tournament on four occasions.
3. The Board of the Premiere League voted in the fall of 2000 to charge a player a fine of $25 for red card infractions. A second red card during

the year would result in a $50 fine. Such fines would be beyond the means of many families to pay.

4. It was not unusual for younger children to cry when their parents abandoned them at practices. I did not observe this behavior at practices or games once the children reached age six.

Chapter 9

1. Indoor soccer seasons ran 4-6 weeks in length and consisted of eight matches. The cost for each player was generally $50 per season. There were no practices.
2. Larry Bird made these comments during an interview broadcast during the NBC coverage of the 2000 NBA Championships.

Chapter 10

1. There was one season when the Force did not attend the Thanksgiving tournament. The team did not meet parental expectations for performance, and the parents voted not to go as a form of motivation/punishment to do better in their next out of town tournament.
2. I spent $1,800 on the trip to Minnesota.

REFERENCES

Adler, P. & Adler, P.A. (1985). From idealism to pragmatic detachment: The academic performance of college athletes. *Sociology of Education*, 58, 241-250.

Aicinena. S. (1992). Readiness for youth sport: A predictive model for success. *The Physical Educator*, 49, 58-66.

Bain, L.L. & Wendt, J.C. (1983). Differences in values implicit in teaching and coaching behaviors. *Research Quarterly*, 49, 5-11v.

Barron, R. & Byrne, D. (1981). *Social Psychology*. New York: McGraw-Hill.

Berlage, G.I. (1982). Children's sport and the family. *Arena Review*, 6, 43-47.

Bissinger, H.G. (1990). *Friday Night Lights: A Town, a Team, and a Dream.* Reading, MA: Wesley.

Bredemeir, B. & Shields, D. (1985). Values and violence in sports today. *Psychology Today*, 19, 22-32.

Brower, J. (1979). The professionalization of organized youth sport: Social psychological impacts and outcomes. *Annals of the American Academy of Political and Social Science*, 445, 39-46.

Burton, R. & Martens, R. (1986). Pinned by their own goals: An exploratory investigation into why kids drop out of wrestling. *Journal of Sport Psychology*, 8, 183-197.

Cain, D.J. & Broekhoff, J. (1987). Maturity assessment: A viable measure against physical and psychological insult to the young athlete? *The Physician and Sportsmedicine*, 15, 67-70, 73-80.

Chandler, T.J. L. & Goldberg, A.D. (1990). The academic all-American as vaunted adolescent role-identity. *Sociology of Sport Journal*, 7, 287-293.

Chu, D. (1984). Teacher/coach orientation and role socialization: A description and explanation. *Journal of Teaching in Physical Education*, 3, 3-8.

Coakley, J.J. (2001). *Sport in Society: Issues and Controversies* (7th ed.). New York: McGraw-Hill.

Coakley, J.J. (1994). *Sport in Society: Issues and Controversies* (5th ed). St Louis, MO: Mosby.

Devereux, E. (1987). Backyard versus little league baseball: Some observations on the impoverishment of children's games in America. In A. Yiannakis, T. McIntyre, M. Melnick & D. Hart (Eds.). *Sport Sociology Contemporary Themes,* 3rd edition (pp. 80-86). Dubuque, IA: Kendall/Hunt Publishers.

Dubois, P. (1980). Competition in youth sport: Process or product? *The Physical Educator,* 37, 151-154.

Edwards, H. (1984). The collegiate arms race: Origins and implications of the rule 48 controversy. *Journal of Sport and Social Issues,* 8, 4-22.

Edwards, H. (1973). *Sociology of Sport.* Homewood, IL: The Dorsey Press.

Eitzen, D.S. (1993). Ethical dilemmas in sport. In D.S. Eitzen, *Sport in Contemporary Society,* 4th edition (109-122). New York: St. Martin's Press.

Eitzen, D.S. (1992). Sport and ideological contradictions: Learning from the cultural framing of Soviet values. *Journal of Sport and Social Issues,* 16, 144-149.

Eitzen, S. & Sage, G. (1997). *Sociology of North American Sport* (5th ed). Boston, MA: McGraw-Hill.

Elkind, D. (1981). *The Hurried Child: Growing up too Fast, too soon.* Reading, MA: Addison-Wesley.

Ewing, M. & Feltz, D. (1991). Motivating young athletes. In V. Seefeldt & E. Brown (Eds.), *Program for Athletic Coaches' Education* (pp. 21-1–21-21). Carmel, IN: Benchmark Press.

Ewing, M. & Seefeldt, V. (1996). Patterns of participation and attrition in American agency-sponsored youth sports. In F. Smoll & R. Smith (Eds). *Children and Youth in Sport: A Biopsychosocial Perspective* (pp.31-45). Madison, WI: Brown and Benchmark.

Fact Sheet. (1993). National youth sports foundation for the prevention of athletic injuries, Inc., p.1.

Festinger, L. (1954). A theory of social comparison processes. *Human relations,* 7, 17-140.

Foley, D.E. (1990). The great American football ritual: reproducing race, class and gender inequality. *Sociology of Sport Journal,* 7, 111-135.

Friedrichs, J. & Ludtke, H. (1975). *Participant Observation: Theory and Practices.* Lexington, MA: Lexington Books.

Ferguson, G.A. & Takane, Y. (1989). *Statistical Analysis in Education and Psychology* (6th ed). NY: McGraw-Hill.

Gallagher, J., French, K., Thomas, K. & Thomas, J., (1996). Expertise in youth sport: relations between knowledge and skill. In F. Smoll & R. Smith (Eds). *Children and Youth in Sport: A Biopsychosocial Perspective* (pp. 330-337). Madison, WI: Brown and Benchmark.

Getzels, J.W. & Guba, E.G. (1954). Role, role conflict and effectiveness. *American Sociological Review*, 19, 164-175.

Good, T & Brophy, J. (1990). *Educational Psychology: A Realistic Approach* (4th ed.). New York: Longman.

Gould, D. (1996). Sport psychology: future directions in youth sport research. In F. Smoll & R. Smith (Eds). *Children and Youth in Sport: A Biopsychosocial Perspective* (pp.405-422). Madison, WI: Brown and Benchmark.

Gould, D.; Feltz, D.; Horn, T. & Weiss, M.R. (1982). Reasons for discontinuing involvement in competitive youth swimming. *Journal of Sport Behavior*, 5, 155-165.

Gould, D. & Horn, T. (1984). Participation motivation in young athletes. In J.M. Silva, III & R.S. Weinberg (Eds.), *Psychological Foundations of Sport* (pp. 359-370). Champaign, IL: Human Kinetics.

Gray, M.A. (1992). Sport and immigrant, minority, and Anglo relations in Garden City (Kansas) high school. *Sociology of Sport Journal*, 9, 255-270.

Harris, J. (1983). Interpreting youth baseball: Players' understandings of attention, winning and playing the game. *Research Quarterly for Exercise and Sport*, 54, 330-339.

Hasbrook, C. (1982). The theoretical notion of reciprocity and childhood socialization into sport. In A.D. Dunleavy, A.W. Miracle & C.R. Reese (Eds.), *Studies in the Sociology of Sport* (pp. 139-151). Ft. Worth, TX: Texas Christian University Press.

Haubenstricker, J.C. & Seefeldt, V. (1986). Acquisition of motor skills during childhood. In V. Seefeldt (Ed.), *Physical Activity and Well-Being*. Reston, VA: American Alliance for Health Physical Education, Recreation and Dance, 41-104.

Hill, G. (1993). Youth sport participation of professional baseball players. *Sociology of Sport Journal*, 10, 107-114.

Hill, G. & Hansen, G. (1988). Specialization in high school sports: The pros and cons. *Journal of Physical Education Recreation and Dance*, 59, 76-79.

Hill, G. & Simons, J. (1989). A study of the sport specialization on high school athletics. *Journal of Sport and Social Issues*, 13, 1-13.

Holland, A. & Andre, T. (1994). Athletic participation and the social status of adolescent males and females. *Youth and Society*, 25, 388-407.

Jorgensen, D.L. (1989). *Participation Observation: A Method for Human Studies.* Newberry Park, CA: Sage Publications.

Kane, J.E. (1986). Giftedness in competitive sport. In G. Gleeson (ed.), *The Growing Child in Competitive Sport,* London: Hodder and Stoughton.

Kenyon, G.S. & McPherson, B.D. (1987). An Approach to the study of sport socialization. In A. Yiannakis, T. McIntyre, M. Melnick and D. Hart (Eds.), *Sport Sociology: Contemporary Themes,* 3rd Edition, (pp. 40-46). Dubuque, IA: Kendall/Hunt Publishers.

Kleiber, D & Roberts, G. (1981). The effects of sport experience in the development of social character: An exploratory investigation. *Journal of Sport Psychology,* 3, 114-122.

Koppett, L. (1981). *Sport Illusion, Sports Reality.* Boston: Houghton Mifflin.

Leonard, W.M. (1998). *A Sociological Perspective of Sport* (5th ed.). Boston, MA: Allyn and Bacon.

Lipsyte, R. (1979). Varsity syndrome: The unkindest cut. *Annals of the American Academy of Political and Social Science,* 445, 15-23.

Lofland, J. (1971). *Analyzing Social Settings.* Bellmont, CA: Wadsworth.

Lord, R. & Kozar, B. (1996). Overuse injuries in young athletes. In F. Smoll & R. Smith (Eds). *Children and Youth in Sport: A Biopsychosocial Perspective* (281-293). Madison, WI: Brown and Benchmark.

Magill, R. & Anderson, D. (1996). Critical periods as optimal readiness for learning sports skills. In F. Smoll & R. Smith (Eds). *Children and Youth in Sport: A Biopsychosocial Perspective* (pp.57-72). Madison, WI: Brown and Benchmark.

Malina, R. (1996). The young athlete: biological growth and maturation in a biocultural context. In F. Smoll & R. Smith (Eds). *Children and Youth in Sport: A Biopsychosocial Perspective* (161-186). Madison, WI: Brown and Benchmark.

Malone, T. & Petrie, B. (1972). Professionalization of attitude toward play among school pupils as a function of sex, grade and athletic participation. *Journal of Leisure Research,* 4, 184-195.

Martens, R. (1978). *Joy and Sadness in Youth Sport.* Champaign, IL: Human Kinetics.

Martin, G. & Lumsden, J. (1987). *Coaching: An Effective Behavioral Approach.* St. Louis, MO: Times Mirror/Mosby.

Massengale, J. (1980). Role conflict and the occupational milieu of the teacher/coach: Some real working world perspectives. In V. Crafts (Ed.), *NAPAHE Proceedings,* Vol. II (pp. 47-52), Champaign, IL: Human Kinetics.

Miller, A. (1992). Systematic observation behavior similarities of various youth sport soccer coaches. *The Physical Educator,* 49, 136-143.

Naatz, D. (1990). *College Football Players' Beliefs about Winning and Losing.* Unpublished Master's Thesis, University of North Dakota.

NAIA (2000). 2000 NAIA Men's Soccer All Americans. http://www.naia. org/msoccer/honors/aa/msaa.html

National Federation of State High School Associations (2001). Participation sets record for third straight year. http://www.nfhs.org/press/participation%20survey01.htm

National Youth Sport Safety Foundation (2002). What you should know. http://www.nyssf.org/wframeset.html

Orlick, T. (1974). The athletic dropout: A high price of inefficiency. *CAHPER Journal,* 41, 21-27.

Orlick, T. & Botterill, C. (1975). *Every Kid Can Win.* Chicago: Nelson Hall.

Pascoe, E. (1978). How sports can hurt your child. *McCalls,* May, 1978, 49-50.

Passer, M. (1996). Psychological issues in determining childrens' age-readiness for competition. In F. Smoll & R. Smith (Eds). *Children and Youth in Sport: A Biopsychosocial Perspective* (pp. 73-86). Madison, WI: Brown and Benchmark.

Petlichkoff, L. (1992). Youth sport participation and withdrawal: Is it simply a matter of fun? *Pediatric Exercise Science,* 4, 105-110.

Popke, M. (2000). Family matters: A new program aims to balance family life with youth sports. *Athletic Business,* 24, 36-38.

Ralbovsky, M. (1987). Destiny's forgotten darlings. In A. Yiannakis, T. McIntyre, M. Melnick and D. Hart (Eds.), *Sport Sociology: Contemporary Themes,* 3rd Edition (pp. 90-96). Dubuque, IA: Kendall/Hunt Publishers Ruff, H. A. & Lawson, K.R. (1990). Development of sustained focused attention in young children during play. *Developmental Psychology,* 26, 85-93.

Sage, G. H. (1987). The social world of high school coaches: Multiple role demands and their consequences. *Sociology of Sport Journal,* 4, 213-228.

Sapp, N & Haubenstricker, J. (1978). Motivation for joining and reasons for not continuing in youth programs in Michigan. In A.D. Levens & J.R. Nathon (Eds.), *Sport Psychology: An Introduction,* Chicago: Nelson-Hall.

Scanlan, T. (1996). Social evaluation and the competitive process: a developmental perspective. In F. Smoll & R. Smith (Eds). *Children and*

Youth in Sport: A Biopsychosocial Perspective (pp. 298-308). Madison, WI: Brown and Benchmark.

Seefeldt, V. (1988). The concept of readiness applied to motor skill acquisition. In F.L. Smoll, R.A. Magill & M.J. Ash (Eds.) *Children in Sport*, 3rd edition (pp 45-52). Champaign IL: Human Kinetics.

Seefeldt, V. (1996). The concept of readiness applied to the acquisition of motor skills. In F. Smoll & R. Smith (Eds). *Children and Youth in Sport: A Biopsychosocial Perspective* (49-56). Madison, WI: Brown and Benchmark.

Seefeldt, V. & Gould, D. (1980). Psychological effects of athletic competition on children and youth. Washington, DC: *Eric Clearinghouse on Teacher Education.*

Shaffer, D. R. (1993). *Developmental Psychology: Childhood and Adolescence* (3rd Ed). Pacific Grove, CA: Brooks/Cole.

Shields, A. (1986). Too much too young? *Sport and Leisure,* 27, 34-35.

Shields, D., Bredemeier, B., Gardner, D. & Bostrom, A. (1995). Leadership, cohesion, and team norms regarding cheating and aggression. *Sociology of Sport Journal,* 12, 124-136.

Smith, R. & Smoll, F. (1990). Self-Esteem and children's reactions to youth sport coaching behaviors: A field study of self-enhancement processes. *Developmental Psychology,* 26, 987-993.

Sperber, M. (2000). *Beer and Circus: How Big-Time College Sport is Crippling Undergraduate education.* New York: Owl Books.

Stevenson, C. & Nixon, J. (1972). A conceptual scheme of the social functions of sport. *Sportwissenschaft,* 2, 119-132.

Stier, W.F.(1998). *Coaching Concepts and Strategies.* Boston: American Press.

Strean, W. (1995). Youth sport contexts: Coaches' perceptions and implications for intervention. *Journal of Applied Sport Psychology,* 7, 23-37.

Stover, D. (1993). What to do when grown-ups want to spoil the fun of school sports. In D. Eitzen (ed.), *Sport in Contemporary Society: An Anthology,* 4th Edition (pp. 58-65). New York: St. Martin's Press.

Wankle, L. & Sefton, J. (1989). A season-long investigation of fun in youth sports. *Journal of Sport and Exercise Psychology,* 11, 355-366.

Webb, H. (1969). Professionalization of attitudes toward play among adolescents. In G. Kenyon (Ed.), *Aspects of Contemporary Sport Sociology* (pp. 161-188). Chicago: Athletic Institute.

Weiss, M. & Sisley, B. (1984). Where have all the coaches gone? *Sociology of Sport Journal,* 1, 332-347.

ABOUT THE AUTHOR

Dr. Steven Aicinena is a Professor of Kinesiology at the University of Texas of the Permian Basin. He teaches in the Kinesiology Department, serves as the University's Athletic Director and also as the Head Women's Volleyball Coach. His research interests have ranged from sport pedagogy to youth sport and he has had refereed publications in both areas.